A Politics of All

POLITICAL THEORY FOR TODAY

Series Editor: Richard Avramenko, University of Wisconsin, Madison

Political Theory for Today seeks to bring the history of political thought out of the jargon-filled world of the academy into the everyday world of social and political life. The series brings the wisdom of texts and the tradition of political philosophy to bear on salient issues of our time, especially issues pertaining to human freedom and responsibility, the relationship between individuals and the state, the moral implications of public policy, health and human flourishing, public and private virtues, and more. Great thinkers of the past have thought deeply about the human condition and their situations—books in Political Theory for Today build on that insight.

Titles Published

A Politics of All

Thomas Jefferson and Radical Democracy

Dean Caivano

LEXINGTON BOOKS
Lanham • Boulder • New York • London

Published by Lexington Books
An imprint of The Rowman & Littlefield Publishing Group, Inc.
4501 Forbes Boulevard, Suite 200, Lanham, Maryland 20706
www.rowman.com

86-90 Paul Street, London EC2A 4NE

British Library Cataloguing in Publication Information Available

Library of Congress Cataloging-in-Publication Data Available

ISBN 978-1-7936-5257-7 (cloth)
ISBN 978-1-7936-5259-1 (paper)
ISBN 978-1-7936-5258-4 (electronic)

For Sarah, Florence Lillian, Tye, and Morgan.

Contents

Acknowledgments

This project is the culmination of many years of research, writing, and sacrifices. Its completion was made possible by the support of countless individuals and organizations, for which an acknowledgment is a bare expression of my gratitude. I am particularly thankful for the financial and intellectual support provided by the Robert H. Smith International Center for Jefferson Studies, APSA's Centennial Center for Political Science and Public Affairs, faculty and friends during my graduate studies at York University in Toronto, and my colleagues and amazing students at California State University, Stanislaus, and Merced College.

Beyond these supportive networks, I have received two brilliant scholars' generosity and direction: Martin Breaugh and Richard Matthews. Both have been sources of unparallel encouragement, guidance, and autonomy, and my academic pursuits have mainly been possible because of the two of you. I am forever grateful for your friendships.

Finally, to my partner, Sarah Naumes, everything good in my life has come through, with, and alongside you. You have built our ever-changing, amorphous *maison du bonheur*.

Introduction

In the coming years, as the United States moves closer to its 250th celebration, studies and explorations of the life and mind of Thomas Jefferson are likely to surge. The public and intellectual fascination with Jefferson not only illustrates the political consciousness of an infant and maturing republic but also, in a very nuanced and telling fashion, speaks to the social realities of twenty-first-century America. The irresistible impulse to look back to Jefferson's visionary words that "all men are created equal" challenges our contemporary understanding of political life. Jefferson was, as Kurt Vonnegut fittingly remarked, "a slave owner who was also one of the world's greatest theoreticians on the subject of human liberty."[1]

A renewed interest in Jefferson is timely, but it also invites new approaches to rethink the status of American democracy. Strikingly, the retelling of Jefferson's radical decrees during the American Revolution and throughout his political and private life, inflammatory assertions that incited and legitimized revolutionary action against the British Empire, have endured as national artifacts—mythologized, cherished, yet intensely debated over the necessity to erase Jefferson's influence from the national character.

What is *missing* in a current understanding of American political life—an omission that finds us with a decaying republic defined by the death of healthy civic engagement—is *already* contained within the historical struggles of individuals and collectives. This alternative vision demarcated by attaining political freedom and equality for all members is not codified in constitutional or societal norms. Instead, it survives as an underdeveloped tendency within the writings of Jefferson. A departure point conceives politics as the instantiation of all that challenge efforts to relocate political authority outside the immediate proximity of the local community.

It is certainly appropriate to ask: *Why Jefferson?* How, in an era of American de-democratization, characterized by unsustainable levels of economic inequality, a Trump-led violent mob attack on the Capitol, and the infringement of civil liberties at home and abroad, to name just a few of the critical issues, could an invitation to the thought of Jefferson illuminate a path toward a democratic political project? Undoubtedly, myriad attempts have been made to isolate the driving ethos of his political philosophy, ranging from the influence of Lockean individualism to the Scottish Enlightenment to classical republican thought. These approaches offer varied interpretations and perspectives into the life and mind of Jefferson, often focusing on him in the *singular* as the principal author of the Declaration of Independence; proprietor of Monticello; diplomat to revolutionary France; and, most notably, third president of the United States. Moreover, the lack of a political *magnum opus* has challenged scholars to wade through the countless sources of Jefferson's letters, speeches, and personal notes to present the intrinsic facets of his thought. These endeavors have often set their sights on discovering the "real" Jefferson as a congruent thinker to a particular register of study.

However, a new, pedantic "real" illustration of Jefferson is not the present task; instead, the objective is to uncover an *unknown* Jefferson. A dimension of Jefferson's thought that conceives of democratic politics as the full and active participation of all members of a community sustained by a praxis of action against intruding challenges to erode individual autonomy and communal sovereignty. Such a configuration of politics helps illuminate Jefferson's theory of democracy, which is strikingly more radical, emancipatory, and carefully indeterminate than liberal manifestations.

Jefferson's placement in the pantheon of eighteenth- and nineteenth-century radical democratic thinkers has been lukewarm. Etched into the Western political canon, Jean-Jacques Rousseau, Thomas Paine, Mary Wollstonecraft, and Karl Marx endure as essential contributors to the idea of a society governed by the people. Repudiating a political order demarcated by hierarchical seats of authority in the form of rule by *One* or the *Few*, the promise of democracy offered nothing short of a total reconfiguration and transformation of the limits of political power and, correspondingly, the suitable location for its actualization found in the hands of the *Many*.

In comparison, the democratic theory of the late Enlightenment stood, in many ways, in direct contrast to the highly participatory practices that underscored the ancient Greek *polis* or the Roman *res publica*. A turn toward a representative democratic polity—where the people do not speak directly—emerged as a remedy to overcome the dilemma of finite space and the perils of social and economic alienation that accompanied the emergence of a fledgling market society.[2]

Key events of this period only helped to reaffirm the primacy of popular sovereignty and the possibility of a rule by the Many. From the adoption of the *Declaration des Droits de l'Homme et du Citoyen* to the insurrection and ultimate victory of slave liberation in Saint-Domingue to an establishment of a dictatorship of the proletariat found in the Paris Commune, *the people* were winning back battles for authorship of *the political*. These transformative centuries of revolutionary thought and action evinced by the ongoing struggles of the people signify the difficult terrain that emancipatory politics must maneuver for the ideals of political freedom and equality to be realized. The advances and successes won at the hands of the people to achieve political liberation remain in tension with the forces that seek the suppression, if not assured obliteration, of *vox populi, vox Dei*.[3] Joseph de Maistre famously remarked, "The counter-revolution will not be a revolution in reverse, but the opposite of revolution."[4] In this light, the achievements and failures of prior democratic experiments have much to offer to the contemporary observer, informing us of the limits of emancipatory politics—if we can consider there to be any limitation at all? Moreover, the institutional, social, and cognitive barriers impede a political experience defined by the collective exercise of power.

It is here from this space that an intervention is warranted. An alternative theory of democracy established along the lines of transforming the ossified categories of political rule will be offered in the following pages. A break with the dominant One/Few/Many modeling[5] emerges from a somewhat unexpected place, scattered across nearly seven decades of personal writings from the principal author of the Declaration of Independence. While Jefferson is often cited as a critical figure in the development of American democracy, his placement in the larger project of emancipatory politics is woefully absent.

Instead, an unrecognized dimension of Jefferson's thought remains uncharted and strikingly undertheorized. Theorizing from within and beyond Jefferson's discursive assertions offers a vision of a political community expressed by a *politics of all* that is sustained by perpetual political action situated in a localized setting. A presentation of this type of political configuration aims at not simply destabilizing Jefferson's place in the early American register but situating his thought as an influential voice in the cosmos of radical democratic theory.

However, what is a politics of all? And, crucially, does it represent a theoretical moment unique to the Jeffersonian imagination? Vitally, the idea of a politics of all is not strictly a Jeffersonian meditation. Remarkably, it was Thomas Hobbes that merged democracy, as a form of government, with a politics of all, as the primary activity of the people. For Hobbes, however, democracy was woefully deficient and ineffective, particularly in comparison to a monarchy, because it required the involvement of an "assembly of *all*," as he argued in the *Leviathan* (1651).[6] In expanding the circle of political decision-makers—a shift from One or Few to All—Hobbes was fearful that it would lead to internal divisions, disagreements, and disorder. Hobbes's fears represent common historical—and contemporary—diagnoses that seek to delegitimatize democratic processes and energies. The trepidations held by Hobbes toward democracy are undoubtedly important. On the one hand, it signals the theoretical and practical abandonment of the "All" in favor of the "Many." While on the other hand, it invites a reappraisal of the historical and conceptual possibilities of a politics of all as a constitutive feature of the democratic imagination.

The twentieth century witnessed a return to the promissory and grand mapping of a politics of all. However, these striking articulations emerged within totalitarian regimes, particularly Nazi Germany, Mussolini-led Italy, and Soviet Russia. In these cases, the promise of a politics of all sought to erase the very divisions that come to define all societies.[7] By concealing the precise divisions that permit plurality to appear publicly, totalitarian regimes promoted, by manipulation and force, the idea of a unified and coherent body that would bring an end to internal conflict and dissent. While this spiritual conversion of the people proceeded along the contours of strict obedience to a national leader, it imbued at the very base the pledge that all would be counted as members of the larger community. Crucially, it also inscribed the idea that all would be deemed essential to the vitality and growth of the body politic. To sustain this configuration of a politics of all, articulated by the rhetoric and command of one superior leader or party, and then return to all, totalitarian regimes obliterated the grounding for politics, ostensibly expunging the *publicness* of the human condition.[8]

Jefferson's politics of all, however, is of a different ordering. Through a reorientation of processes of politics back to the people, Jefferson's conceptual horizon strives to expand the political for all yet prevents divisions, specifically those of an artificial distinction and calibration, from dominating public affairs. Instead, natural divisions along the lines of political virtue play a prominent role by bringing to the surface the sociological underpinnings of a political community. Exposure to the origins and permutations of power is always understood in a collective orientation,[9] which reveals the central core of Jefferson's politics and affirms an erasure not of primary societal divisions but of the artificial impediments that prevent all from attaining the complete status of political citizenship. Democratic politics understood in this manner becomes less about winning the right to be counted and more narrowly centered on challenging the very idea of vesting authority outside the proximity of the people to a non-place, a setting absent of individuals exercising their capacities as citizens. Then, a democratic politics of all is disposed to create new relations rendered visible through a series of spaces between all those already counted as citizens announced in the immediate.

Released in 1963, Hannah Arendt's *On Revolution* showcases Jefferson's impulse for a politics of all. Arendt accentuates the concern on Jefferson's part to always maintain a revolutionary spirit throughout the United States. In so doing, Arendt links Jefferson's axiom of active sharers and participators in political power with his theorization of ward republics as the optimal scene for politics to commence. Concerned with the availability of space for the performance of action, Arendt suggests that Jefferson's ward system was designed as a vehicle capable of institutionalizing revolutionary action.[10]

Fearful that the spirit of 1776 would dissipate in the hearts and minds of the citizens of the young republic, Arendt reflects on Jefferson's quest for endless recreation. "It may seem strange," Arendt asserts, "that only Jefferson among the men of the American Revolution ever asked himself the obvious question of how to preserve the revolutionary spirit once the revolution had come to an end."[11] To erect spaces of political creation—those intimately capable of producing and reproducing order of fraternity—Arendt draws attention to Jefferson's ward system as a forgotten proposal in the early republic. Instead of designing a republic demarcated by a division of space for citizens to engage in public affairs properly, the Framers of the Constitution opted to ensure a particular form of political space for entry. However, the safeguarding and assurance of political space designed at the 1787 Constitutional Convention were solely restricted to the activities of representatives rather than the people. For Arendt, the Framers were keenly aware of the necessity for creating a reservoir of space; yet the crafting of the Constitution rendered an institutionalized patrician setting *contra* horizontal structures of communal deliberation and action.[12] For Arendt, the very lifeblood of the revolution—the intimate public moments between individuals—that spurred the transformative restructuring of the colonies had given way to a negation of public space and malaise of civic stasis.

The denial of space and, in turn, the destruction of the means for self-expression, which accompanied the ratification of the Constitution, endowed the people with sources of power. However, power of this order was relegated to the private realm, antithetical and untranslatable into the public sphere. The result was a distortion of citizenship. On the one hand, the Constitution provided a basic framing and understanding of citizenship with a keen eye toward civil liberties. On the other hand, it had failed to provide a space for citizens to *act* as citizens, effectively abating a sense of belonging.

According to Jefferson, the panacea for this substitution of a spirit of complicity, rather than revolutionary zeal, centered on a much-needed division. Of course, the division of space (and subsequent subdivision) was primary to the design of his ward system, reopening sites of engagement for citizens across the nation in a horizontally networked manner. However, the idea of division ran much more profound in Jefferson's thought.

Arendt brings to the surface a percolating infection within Jefferson's thought that points toward a politics of all. According to Arendt, creating the wards brought a devastating division of the category of rule by the Many, widening the circle of political action for all to enter.[13] Briefly, yet powerfully, Arendt refers to this double-tiered application of division, writing, "The ward system was not meant to strengthen the power of the many but the power of 'every one' within the limits of his competence; and only by *breaking up* 'the many' into assemblies where every one could count and be counted upon 'shall we be as republican as a large society can be.'"[14] Jefferson's plan, then, sought the restoration of a revolutionary spirit and a total reconfiguration of the limits of political action fashioned by the coupling of an expansion of public space with a widening of the scope of citizenship.

A configuration of politics in this form requires a specific type of maintenance. Centrally, the requisite space and time for articulating a politics of all necessitate a constant action against external sources of control and authority. The full implication of Jefferson's understanding of political action represents a caesura offering the scope of the expressive activity beyond the terms of agonism, agitation, or even revolutionary action.

Jefferson's radical politics signify an active involvement of all members in matters directly concerning the local community. To challenge threats that seek to undermine this localized fraternal process means to perpetually reopen the space between external forms of authority and the constitutive parts of the political. In turn, the instituting capabilities of the people enable the creation of a kind of society that resists absolute decrees of obedience and conformity to achieve self-sufficiency while, crucially, remaining committed to the immediate community. Therefore, the aim of Jefferson's politics is a reproduction of the conditions necessary for the continuation and intensification of politics.

From this perspective, the remedy for an ailing strain of politics—marked by apathy, disenchantment, or corruption—or conversely, a decaying body politic, is, for Jefferson, integration of *more processes* of politics: an expansion of decision-making opportunities that extend to a minor level of interaction between individuals. To achieve such an outcome, Jefferson's political vision evinces an active vigilance by the people to resist the transplantation of the political to a withdrawn stage. A relocation that results in a distancing—a nearly insurmountable chasm—that banishes the people from the realm of political authorship and citizenship.

What is unique about Jefferson's vision of politics is that it contains five characteristics that form a radical theory of democracy. An examination of historical and conceptual spaces of localized politics will be explored in the following pages. Specifically, attention will be paid to Jefferson's perspectives on the ancient Greek *polis*, the spatial configuration of the Anglo-Saxons pre-Norman invasion, Indigenous societies in North America, the town hall meetings of New England, and finally, as Arendt noted, his system of ward republics. Interrogation of these sites reveals Jefferson's preference for small, highly participatory politics at the local level *contra* national or federal channels as the optimal setting for political training, discussion, and action.

For Jefferson, the high degree and style of political participation found in these historical sites exhibit dynamic energy of radical action that pushes up against the parameters of codified contours of institutional power. These associations, in turn, exist as spaces of democratic politics, according to Jefferson, serving as valuable models of the potentiality that underscores processes of local politics to challenge and, at times, subvert encroaching forms of non-local governmental power. In an important sense, these spaces exist as fully coherent social and political totalities that resist assimilation into regimes defined by arbitrary rule, a hierarchical scaling of power, and oppressive political and economic control mechanisms. Crucially, Jefferson's perspective on the transformative capabilities of local politics—situated in a non-market/non-capital property relation orientation—to cultivate civic engagement through horizontal decision-making practices through a proliferation of opportunities for political participation points toward a horizon of emancipatory politics.

Of course, Jefferson's politics of all is a phantom. It was an unattainable offering terminally negated by the contradictory actions of its architect that failed to escape the settler colonial framework of its conception. Jefferson was undoubtedly a thinker of his time and, at moments, a voice that, in cursory, chaotic notes, transcends the problematic nature of the early republic to the very plane of political ideas. However, the panacea for an emancipatory project *for our times* is not found through or within his thought. Jefferson's compelling rhetoric often seeps in emancipatory inflections, yet crucially remains a system of domination and dehumanization, which he played an active part in legitimizing and reinforcing. Jefferson, the thinker, scientist, politician, and slaveholder, haunts the American psyche in compelling and problematic ways.

Jefferson's political project is marked with limitations: the exclusion of women, Black, and Indigenous peoples from politics.[15] Nevertheless, by exploring the contours of his thought and then transcending beyond its limitations, essential lessons for our present period of political unrest and disenchantment may emerge. Perhaps, the landing point may place us at an impasse, a difficult juncture that helps drag important facets of America's contentious historical legacy into the public sphere. And then, after scrutiny, the people of the present moment may resolve that the figure of Jefferson no longer occupies a place of prominence in our collective memory. In Jeffersonian fashion, subsequently, the present generation might break free from the past and begin anew, reopening the horizons ahead for future generations to an idea of a political community of all, by all, and for all.

NOTES

1. Kurt Vonnegut, Jr., *Breakfast of Champions* (New York: A Delta Book, 1973), 34.

2. In this way, "simple democracy" could be overcome, as Thomas Paine suggests, by grafting representation upon democracy. The result would produce a "system of government capable of embracing and confederating all the various interests and every extent of territory and population." See Thomas Paine, *The Rights of Man, Part the Second* in *The Complete Writings of Thomas Paine*, vol. 1, ed. Philip S. Foner (New York: Citadel Press, 1945), 371.

3. See Sheldon S. Wolin, "Transgression, Equality, and Voice," in *Fugitive Democracy: And Other Essays*, ed. Nicholas Xenos (Princeton, NJ: Princeton University Press, 2016), 76.

4. Joseph de Maistre, *Considerations on France*, ed. Richard A. Lebrun (Cambridge, UK: Cambridge University Press, 1994), 83.

5. See Aristotle, *Politics*, trans. T. A. Sinclair (London: Penguin Books, 1981), BK III, Part VII, 189–90.

6. Thomas Hobbes, *Leviathan* (Indianapolis, IN: Hackett Publishing, 1994), 119. Emphasis added.

7. Claude Lefort, *The Political Forms of Modern Society: Bureaucracy, Democracy, Totalitarianism*, ed. John B. Thompson (Cambridge, MA: The MIT Press, 1986), 286.

8. Hannah Arendt, *The Origins of Totalitarianism* (New York: Harcourt, Brace & Co., 1973), 474.

9. Hannah Arendt, "On Violence," in *Crises of the Republic* (New York: Harcourt, Brace & Co., 1972), 151.

10. The main thrust of Arendt's views on Jefferson and his theorization of the wards can be found in chapter 6, "The Revolutionary Tradition and Its Lost Treasure." See Hannah Arendt, *On Revolution* (New York: Penguin Books, 1990), 215–82.

11. Arendt, *On Revolution*, 238–39.

12. For an engaging look at how the council system in Arendt's thought, including Jefferson's ward system, provided the space for perpetual creation and the conditions for freedom, see Christopher Holman, *Politics as Radical Creation: Herbert Marcuse and Hannah Arendt on Political Performativity* (Toronto: University of Toronto Press, 2013), 115–26.

13. While Sheldon S. Wolin agrees that Arendt's reading of the ward system contains "genuinely democratic features," he suggests that it fails—parallel to the ancient Greek *polis*—to make space for the inclusion of "women, slaves, and aliens." See Sheldon S. Wolin, "Hannah Arendt: Democracy and The Political," *Salmagundi* no. 60 (Spring–Summer 1983): 13.

14. Arendt, *On Revolution*, 254. Emphasis added.

15. On two occasions, Jefferson expressed the belief that a denial of women's suffrage was needed to "prevent depravation of morals." See Thomas Jefferson (hereafter TJ) to Samuel Kercheval, September 5, 1816, *The Papers of Thomas Jefferson* (hereafter cited as *PTJ*), Retirement Series, vol. 10, 367–69; TJ to John Hambden

Pleasants, April 19, 1824, *The Thomas Jefferson Papers* (hereafter cited at *TJP*) at the Library of Congress, Series 1: General Correspondence, 1651–1827, microfilm reel: 054, images 1–3.

Chapter 1

The Ancient Greek *Polis*

Civic Education, Questioning, and the Staging of the Political

Jefferson's ideal vision of politics—a politics of all—rejects the conventional political classification of rule by One, rule by Few, and rule by Many. Beyond these ossified sociological categories, which strive to isolate agents of political action extracted from civil society, the effects of exploring a politics of all (historically and conceptually) are devastatingly far-reaching in our appraisal of the foundations of the American republic as well as for contemporary politics. Standard terms, such as the "demos" or "Multitude," or even "proletariat," idealized figures that inscribe political energy and potential, simply did not suffice for the third president of the United States.

Instead, Jefferson, deeply unsatisfied with these idyllic agents of change, envisioned a political arrangement that would encourage a widening of the legalistic framing of citizenship to extend far beyond patrician limits of property-holding. The erection of such a monolithic political agent is not produced through the recreation of a prior historical moment defined by the active engagement against the totality of governmental power. Instead, Jefferson's categorization of the "all" focuses on how previous regimes saw their members engage in the task of sharing political power as a force as opposed to centralized government authority. The subjectification of all members of a community reverses myopic embodiments of political representation that are authorized to speak, act, and govern on behalf of the people. To theorize a politics of all means to bring into political existence those previously deemed illegible or as figures of non-appearance, constituted in varying forms as property, aliens, enslaved *inter alia*. Alain Badou identified a similar line of thinking held by Jacques Derrida in his discussion on the "non-existent characteristic of political multiplicities."[1] Badiou saw an analogous impulse in Derrida's work that is immanent in Jefferson's politics of all, when he

1

writes, in this context in direct reference to the proletariat, "[f]rom the point of view of their political appearance they are nothing. And becoming 'all' presupposes a change of world, or other words a change of transcendental."[2] Jefferson's politics of all seeks a "change of world," to borrow Badiou *qua* Derrida's phraseology, through a primacy of visibility over nothingness; a political resurrection of sorts that brings to the public stage those prohibited from political existence.

The attraction of the ancient Greek *polis* to Jefferson rested in emphasizing how the ancients constantly contested the enclosure of the political within a singular realm of control, whether it be the State, History, or Reason. The ability of the ancient Greeks to perpetually engage in the affairs of the *polis* naturally relied upon the citizenry's ability to escape the physically and intellectually taxing process of the labor cycle, amplifying the appearance of citizens.

Affinities between Jefferson's radical democratic project and his understanding of the ancient Greeks is an odd textual alignment, for sure. A somewhat contested and unexplored path is warranted to tease out how the ancient *polis* fits within a theoretical lens of a politics of all. Here in this chapter, Jefferson's thought is placed in dialogue with the work of twentieth-century Greek-French philosopher Cornelius Castoriadis. At first glance, the juxtaposition of Jefferson and Castoriadis may appear puzzling. However, Jefferson's theory of politics impinges upon creating a physical space for the maturation of human faculties, the playing out of politics, and centrally, the safeguarding of power away from local hands to distant, centralized forms of authority. Castoriadis's reading of the ancient Greek *polis* reveals how the whole source of explicit power—the articulation of the society's *nomos*, *dike*, and *telos*—was in the hands of the citizenry. This point runs to the heart of Jefferson's political vision.

While the route may be controversial, essential commonalities between these two distant planes of thought are more compatible than expected. Jefferson *does* espouse a deep level of affection for the ancient Greek world, notably concerning their cultural and social forces exhibited in their curious approach to language, literature, and history. Jefferson's view of the ancient Greeks produces an opening in which the affirming praise of the cultural superfluities of the *polis* releases a space that relocates Jefferson's thought inward toward the ontology of the *polis*, centered directly on the question of the political. The geographic choreography of Jefferson's politics of all and Castoriadis's understanding of the *polis* is not mirrored images but articulations of a political vision that rely on a collective sharing of power and perpetual interrogation of the political. For both Jefferson and Castoriadis, this type of political activity is antithetical to a unitary ontology that relocates political power to a transcendental terrain away from the actualized space of the political community.

The first characteristic of radical democracy, typified in the ancient Greek *polis*, appears by approaching this conceptual relationship carefully. The first characteristic of radical democracy is an impulse to create a public space accessible through the supplementation of available time, sustained by perpetual questioning and refusal to enclose the political within the realm of a centralized framework.

First, let us explore how the Jefferson-ancient Greek *polis* interplay can be considered by examining the actualization of this characteristic within the ancient city-state and its subsequent rejection by key American Constitutional Framers before turning to Jefferson's understanding of the ancient world and relation to democratic politics.

THE PHYSICAL, TEMPORAL, AND HISTORICAL DIMENSIONS OF THE *POLIS*

The ancient Greek *polis* has experienced an enduring legacy in the Western political canon. Understood as an inherently political community endowed with the tasks and responsibilities of self/collective rule, the Aristotelian maxim of "ruling and being ruled"[3] continues to provide a concise aphorism of the idea of collective power exercised within the narrow confines of the city-state. The parochial nature of the *polis*, a point that simultaneously demonstrates its strength *in* active political participation and its dark underside characterized by racial homogeneity and exclusion, has continued to raise issues over the necessary conditions for the flourishing of a democratic community. Limited in size, yet not in its unrelenting quest to discover the best political regime through a cosmological lens,[4] the ancient Greek *polis* has become a site of contestation within the canon.[5] Assailed for its restricted spatial dimension, the tectonic design and architecture of the *polis* seem increasingly anachronistic in our current world of politics defined by a transnational, globalized order.

However, the legacy of the ancient *polis* persists because of its ability to overcome the problems of political time-space. To be sure, the *polis* was a physical space, a demarcated partition of land inhabited by a social lifeworld of citizens and non-political subjects. The *polis* was a vibrant city, a living, breathing cornucopia of desires and sensibilities enmeshed in a network of relations between individuals in the *oikos*, the *ekklēsia*, and the *agora*. It was a *public city* defined by sharing and exercising political power collectively in a very profound way. The affairs of the city-state were not subterranean. Instead, they were thrust onto the political, aesthetic, and spiritual scenes of the *agora* and *ekklēsia*, brought into the visible,[6] and deliberated by the words of civically minded individuals. Participation by the citizens and the city's affairs were, thus, inseparable. Life in the city was innately a political experience—a type of existence always shared, celebrated, and sacrificed with others. As Benjamin Constant, the nineteenth-century liberal French thinker suggested in his essay, *De la liberté des Anciens comparée à celle des Modernes*, concerning the importance of participation in the *polis*, "The will of each individual had real influence, and the exercise of this will was a lively pleasure each time it was employed . . . the aim of the ancients was to share social power among the citizens of a single country; that is what they called 'liberty.'"[7]

However, this sharing of social power took on a double meaning in the context of space for the ancient Greek *polis*. Engagement in the city's affairs was undoubtedly a communal endeavor as deliberations were conducted in the open *ekklēsia* rather than in a sequestered, cloistered fashion. The scene of political engagement transpired within the boundaries of the *polis*, as the *agora* served as the social, commercial center-core of the city-state.[8] Beyond the core of the *agora*, the territory of the *polis* had demarcated lines enclosing the physical space of its occupancy. In this manner, the political dimension of the *polis* was fixed with a clear passageway for entry or exit into an association defined by public life. Physical walls wrapped around the ancient community served as protection against foreign invaders and as the ultimate physical marker of the end of political life.[9] To be cast outside of the city through the practice of ostracism was a near-death sentence, an effective termination of the joys and sacrifices publicly carried through the status of citizenship. However, for those inside of the sprawling, monolithic walls, the citizen's life was devoutly oriented to the affairs of the *polis*.

This narrow understanding of how space functioned within the ancient Greek *polis* has rendered the Greek experience unfeasible and incompatible with contemporary life. However, this indictment is not exclusive to the *polis*, for it is the very same criticism vehemently leveled against the Italian city-states of the Renaissance and Rousseau's idealized Genevan city-state.[10] Complaints of a locally erected space fail to consider how communal bonds transcend physical limitations by forging a political community that exists beyond a fixed temporal dimension.

In his *Politics*, Aristotle points to this civic fraternity, posing the question, "When a population lives in the same place, what is the criterion for regarding the state as a unity?" His response problematizes a linkage between citizenship and defined territorial boundaries. He answers, "It cannot be the walls, for it would be possible to put one wall around the whole of Peloponnese."[11] In her work, *The Human Condition*, Hannah Arendt keenly identified this alternate, non-physical dimension of political space that Aristotle briefly alluded to and that was central to classical Attica thought. For Arendt, plurality is a significant element in the public realm as "action is the political activity par excellence."[12] Yet, plurality and freedom presuppose a boundary, a particular space for action. According to Arendt, it is in the public realm, as seen in the Greek *polis*, that action merges with freedom, reflecting the human condition's highest expression. The public domain is a creation—a human construct par excellence—of accessible space in daily life to capture the worldly action phenomenon. However, Arendt's conception of space, drawing directly from Pericles and Aristotle, extends beyond a physical dimension. Influenced considerably by Pericles's famous proclamation to the Athenians, "Wherever you go, you will be a *polis*," Arendt writes, "The *polis*, properly speaking, is not the city-state in its physical location; it is the organization of the people as it arises out of acting and speaking together, and its true space lies between people living together for this purpose."[13] For Arendt, then, the public realm, or the political space necessary to realize freedom, appears "no matter where they happen to be."[14]

The double function of political space—on the one hand, a physically sanctioned space and, on the other hand, a civic, fraternal identity that transcends the geographic limits of the *polis*—was intimately intertwined with the creation and conquering of public time. For the ancient Greeks, a sense of perpetual questioning, not only of the immediacy of the present institutions but also their history and past, pervaded the *polis*. In a rejection of the supremacy of tradition, the ancient Greeks reopened and constantly interrogated the deeds of past generations while at the same time looking toward the future of the *polis*. Herodotus in his foundational work, *Histories*, questions the validity and credibility of sources for historical accounts, establishing a critical methodology that seeks to probe the historical depth of the ancient Greeks.[15] Following Herodotus, this historiographical approach was taken up in the context of the histories of the *poleis* as seen in the works of Hippias, Hellanicus of Lesbos, and Dionysius of Halicarnassus.[16] The civic nature of Attic historiography reaches its most crucial illustration in Pericles' Funeral Oration contained in Thucydides's *History of the Peloponnesian War*. In the rousing speech, Pericles carefully traces the activities of past Athenians from an understanding of subsequent generations while impregnating his words with a future-oriented direction for the sake of Athens.[17]

The ability of the ancient Greeks to pensively, as well as critically, reflect upon the transgressions and accomplishments of their collective past speaks to an understanding of time that is inherently an accessible, public time. Cornelius Castoriadis claims that public space within the *polis* also created shared time. According to Castoriadis, the questioning of time facilitated an "emergence of a dimension where the collectivity can inspect its past as the result of its actions, and where an indeterminate future opens up as domain for its activities."[18] The collective endeavor of creating public time that Castoriadis notes is key to our understanding of how precisely the notion of time functioned within the *polis*, yet it is not complete.

To properly illuminate the creative, instituting force of the *polis*, it is helpful to apply the questioning aspect of the public time to the conquering of the rigidity and necessities of time, a vital defeat that enabled the full participation of the citizens within the *ekklēsia*. The citizens of the *polis* to engage in the city's administration required an escape from the material constraints of the household. This unencumbered entry into civic life was made possible from a system of exclusion that placed women, children, enslaved people, and foreigners outside of the collective power-sharing nexus of the *polis*. The exile of much of the population from citizenship, and in effect, a voice in the discussions of the city, was justified by the ancient Greeks, as Sheldon Wolin suggests, along the lines of size, cultural homogeneity, and political *techne*. According to Wolin, the ancient city-states contained an artificial grating of elitism upon their social structures and institutions, which necessitated the exclusion of those outcasts of the community devoid of invaluable political skills and virtue. This powerful system of exclusion was an intentional chasm between *equality for all* and the *preservation of the political*. The impact of such a configuration of the *polis* was, thus, to erect a political space with exclusive access by those freed from the compulsions of the labor process yet oriented to the concerns of the entire *polis*. "The responsibility for the care of civic life rested with the few," Wolin writes, "although all should support it."[19]

While the design of the *polis* itself was predicated upon the rejection of the Many from the tasks of ruling in favor of a limited, restricted classification of citizenship to permit entry into the political realm—an architectural flaw that resists the impulse for a more inclusive and diverse political community—the design of the ancient Greek *polis* nevertheless reveals an attempt to resolve the pinnacle question that has challenged all body politics: how can a subject overcome the impermanence and complexities of necessary labor, yet, at the same time, develop the essential skills—afforded by availability of time—required to engage in the affairs of the political community actively? For the ancient Greeks, while the solution to the quintessential tension of an existence-with-others and, in turn, the entire structure of the *polis*, was built upon a system of exploited labor and chattel slavery,[20] there was a vital awareness that man's political nature required an escape from the severity of the labor cycle to possess the necessary time to enter a publicly created space designed for the tasks of communal existence.

THE FRAMERS' REPUDIATION OF THE *POLIS*

For the Framers of the American Constitution, the ancient Greek *polis* was anathema to their modern understanding of self-government. The ancient Greek solution to overcome the problems of political time-space was fraught with shortcomings and incompatible with the vicissitudes of eighteenth-century political and economic challenges. James Madison's scheme of government put forward in the Constitution of 1787 offered a repudiation and an inversion of the ancient Greek system. Madison's plan, one profoundly influenced and later shaped by Alexander Hamilton, held steadfast to the intercessions of commerce and empire, devising the American republic through a reversal of the structural design of the *polis* rather than emulation.

As seen in the *polis*, the idea of a restricted space for political engagement by an active citizenry was substituted for a public market space that would destabilize political activity through the depoliticizing effects of constant consumption and production. Space was envisioned with a conquering mentality.[21] It was equipped with a material force to seize untapped and underutilized terrains as a means for the enlargement of the republic. The drive for an expansion of space provided the necessary playing field for the development of a commercial republic while at the same time eliminating localized spaces for political involvement. The *zoon politikon* of the ancient *polis* was, in effect, being relocated directly away from the *ekklēsia* into a newly transformed American *agora* that was decisively market-centric.

Available time for political engagement would now be consumed, literally and figuratively, by the dictates of a fledgling capitalistic marketplace casting the citizenry as market actors rather than power-sharers in the political process.[22] In turn, available political time was exchanged for market-time scheduling and ordering logic. Public time, understood by the ancient Greeks in a political and historical sense, became transplanted upon schedules of production processes. An especially striking illumination of this substitution is the relative lack of American historiographical studies post-founding and throughout the nineteenth century compared to the plethora of analyses emerging from Great Britain and Europe.[23] The historiographical interpretations that did materialize, particularly within Loyalist, Whig, and Imperial traditions, framed the grievances of the American colonists in economic terms, particularly regarding issues concerning taxation and trade, as well as the economic potentiality that the newly formed republic possessed post-revolution.[24] The "time" of the American republic was, thus, absent of inquiry and specifically conceived in a starkly administrative manner as public space became both expansive in market form and politically retracted.

While the Framers were convinced that the American republic represented a new experiment in self-government situated as the design of the newly erected republic was indeed reminiscent of the past. Rather than emulate the scheme of the ancient Greek city-states, the Founders directed their sights toward the image of the vast, sprawling Roman Empire as a source of inspiration. Avid readers of Cicero, the Framers believed that adopting Greek principles would lead to riot and potentially mob rule in the infant American republic, as demonstrated in the wild and eruptive fever brought forth by enacting direct democracy in the *polies*.[25] Madison's distrust of the Many as co-sharers in a collective and direct style of governance elevated the importance of state sovereignty over public control, essentially positioning popular sovereignty as a theoretical construct devoid of practical realization. Directly condemning the active participation and direct supervision of the *ekklēsia*, Madison opines, "Had every Athenian citizen been a Socrates, every Athenian assembly would still have been a mob."[26] Instead, Madison, Hamilton, and Jay saw the Middle Republican era of Rome, spanning from roughly 287 BCE to 133 BCE, as the optimal form of governance for the American scene. Seeking to replicate the mixed polity erected in constitutional form within the Middle Republic as detailed by Polybius, as well as the idea of a division of departmental powers (*trias politica*) found in Montesquieu's *The Spirit of the Laws*,[27] the Framers wanted order, rather than the indeterminacy of public sway, procured through a dilution and scattering of power across governmental branches. The result of such a design is not simply a separation of management for accountability, among other things. Still, it functions as a mechanism to dismantle and disintegrate democratic control *en masse*. The Framers' desire to keep the people away from political power thus found its historical inspiration in the Roman Republic *de jure* as seen in the institutional and symbolical design of the American republic: a Senate rather than *boulai*; Capitol Hill in the nation's capital over a network of *acropolises*; and the affirming utilization of the pseudonym "Publius" throughout the *Federalist Papers*, instead of Cleisthenes.

The Framers' rejection of the *polis* as a potential replication site has been well documented in scholarship, leading some to suggest that the leading American political architects were unfamiliar with ancient Greek history and political culture.[28] What they were able to gather regarding the ancient Greek experience notably emerged in the writings of Plutarch and Thomas Hobbes's translation of Thucydides's *History of the Peloponnesian War*.[29] These sources confirmed the Framers' fears of the Many, based mainly on a presumed lack of civic proficiency. Placing the Many at the center of the American political system threatened the viability and durability of the political process precisely by direct engagement of the commoners. According to

Madison and Hamilton, the result would be disastrous: political and economic tumult and riots rather than stability and order.

JEFFERSON AND CLASSICAL THOUGHT

Jefferson, much like his American contemporaries, was opposed to the adoption of ancient Greek principles and frequently criticized the philosophical projects of Plato and Aristotle. Jefferson's distaste for Plato was undoubtedly genuine and ongoing, writing, "no writer ancient [sic] or modern has bewildered the world with more *ignes fatui* than this renowned philosopher, in Ethics, in Politics & Physics."[30] Jefferson believed that implementing a form of governance within the American republic led by philosopher-kings would destroy individual liberty and stunt scientific progress leaving all "men, women and children [living] pell mell together, like the beasts of the field or forest."[31] A striking fact, however, is that while Jefferson maintained a strong distaste for Plato's *Republic*, significant commonalities exist between the two thinkers. Centrally, civic education and the full active participation of citizens underscore both Jefferson's and Plato's political philosophies, respectively.

Plato's Theory of Forms drew the most ire from Jefferson, who condemned it as "the great delusion of Western history,"[32] existing as the most unambiguous indication of a distorted understanding of materiality and, as a result, reality. Jefferson's disdain for ancient Greek metaphysics revolved around his rejection of a bifurcation of material objects from a foreign, external complete understanding of an object. Instead, Jefferson viewed material conditions not as a deterrent for comprehension or a mere copy or incomplete representation in a spiritual realm but as the only way to approach and experience reality.

The anti-Platonic leanings of Jefferson played a vital part in his denunciation of spiritualism and its subsequent adoption within Christian theology. According to Jefferson, the merging of Platonism and early Christian thought resulted in the contamination and bastardization of the actual teachings and practices of Jesus Christ. This led Jefferson to produce a chronological telling of the life of the messiah devoid of spiritual speculations. The edited gospel rendition helps to reveal his refutation of Platonic Christianity and accentuates his strong materialist leanings. Jefferson's philosophical maxim can sharply capture this assault on Platonic thought, both in its original formation and co-option within the early Christian registers, "I am a Materialist."[33]

However, Jefferson's criticisms were confined to ancient Greek metaphysics and extended to Aristotelian politics. Condemning the presence of unnecessary "jargon,"[34] Aristotle's *Politics* offered few, if any, insights into the structure and problems of modern government. In a letter to Isaac H. Tiffany, dated August 26, 1816, Jefferson provides a scathing commentary after reading John Gillies's English translation of Aristotle's *Politics*.[35] Familiar with the text in Greek, Jefferson praises the latest translation, yet the complimentary tone ceases when discussing the major flaw of Aristotle's account.[36] According to Jefferson, the ancient Greeks were caught between the poles of freedom and tyranny. While knowledgeable of the value and necessity of personal liberty, the ancient Greeks failed to create the proper institutions to safeguard and preserve freedom. A structural flaw—the lack of popular control capable of recalling rulers—enabled the aristocratic class, or tyrants, to rise to power in dangerous times, effectively leaving the people outside the political process. The failure to maintain public control as a force against usurpation and corruption of political power represented the grave defect of the ancient system of government in Jefferson's mind.

The identification of the emergence of tyrants within the ancient Greek system is indicative of Jefferson's somber concern with political structures that legitimize the recognition of a singular ruler for *any period*. The lack of constant vigilance on the part of the citizenry within the ancient Greek case, coupled with the impulse for the authorization of dictators in times of critical need, as seen in the Roman Empire, led to the destruction of personal freedom. Jefferson cautions against the approval of a dictator in times of crisis in his proposed modifications to the Constitution of the Commonwealth of Virginia in 1776 and then again in 1781.[37] Any constitutional arrangement or regime that *permits* the authorization of a dictator, even if only temporary, or *negates* the force of the people as a safeguard against encroachments does not exist as a model for emulation. In the same letter to Tiffany, Jefferson offers a solution to the tendency of relocating power away from local control, pointing directly to a politics of all rooted in a network of local political theaters. He writes, "my most earnest wish is to see the republican element of popular control *pushed to the maximum* of it's practicable exercise. I shall then believe that our government may be pure & perpetual."[38]

For all his condemnation of Platonic metaphysics and Aristotelian politics, Jefferson did believe that the study of ancient Greek thought and culture possessed an intrinsic educational value. His introduction into the ancient world began at the age of nine from his schooling under the tutelage of Reverend Mr. Douglass, a Scottish clergyman with a devout penchant for teaching the French language.[39] Enamored with the ethical values explored within classical thought, as well as the promissory fulfillment of a death wish on his father's part, young Thomas continued his exploration of the classics throughout his adolescence under the watchful eye of Reverend Mr. Maury and throughout periods of formal schooling at the College of William and Mary.

As a timid and uncomfortable orator due to a speech handicap, even throughout his two terms as president, the young Jefferson was known to memorize and recite eloquent speeches of Demosthenes, Livy, and Cicero.[40] His fascination with the classics rested heavily on the importance of honor and friendship as first principles within the Homeric and Stoic systems of ethics. This central theme would strongly resonate with Cicero's thoughts.[41] Even at a young age, Jefferson denounced the spiritual mysticism of the Christian ethic, opting instead for a moral code based upon the material conditions of the present to "join actuality with philosophy."[42]

During his first term in the White House, Jefferson spent late evenings and, at times, long nights studying, writing, and commenting on the teachings of the Christian faith. Jefferson committed countless hours interpreting and reorganizing the Christian Bible during this period. However, Jefferson's scrutiny and revisionist approach were not confined to the teachings of Jesus Christ alone; additionally, he explored the affinities between the words and deeds of Christ and other registers of thought, particularly classical sources. In a document titled "Doctrines of Jesus Compared with Others," written on April 21, 1803, Jefferson carefully crafted a syllabus examining the commonalities between Jesus and classical thinkers, including Pythagoras, Socrates, Epicurus, Cicero, Epictetus, Seneca, and Antoninus.[43] In the section labeled "Philosophers," Jefferson affirms a strong emphasis of duty and fraternity in the ancient world. He writes, "they embraced indeed the circles of kindred & friends; and inculcated patriotism, or the love of our country in the aggregate, as a primary obligation."

Further, Jefferson underscores a communitarian bent to classical ethics believing that justice was taught to "neighbors & countrymen."[44] However, Jefferson was hesitant to fully embrace the duty-based system of ethics due to one fatal flaw: an inability to situate this system of thought and action within a "circle of benevolence" toward the "whole family of mankind."[45] Here, the arch of Jefferson's worldview freely permits inquiry along the lines of political, economic, and ethical grounds for creating a *kind of society* that is defined by the actions of all, not just the One, Few, or Many.

Classical languages and literature were also invaluable areas of scholarly pursuit because they were expressly concerned with the act of questioning. What Jefferson located in ancient Greek and Roman thought as well as the Epicurean and Stoic traditions was an explicit interrogation and pursuit of the good life—Jefferson's *summum bonum* of happiness as well as Epicurus' "aim of life"[46]—through the development of a method to achieve a flourishing existence. The fluidity and inherently scientific nature of these schools of thought existed as a negation of theological dogmas. This error gravely tarnished traditional Christian doctrines by promoting miracles and spiritual fanaticism. Jefferson's frustration with Christianity's extension of the idea of messianic omnipresence, a move that operates beyond the spatial and temporal dimension of Christ's earthly dwelling, can be seen in his document,

The Life and Morals of Jesus of Nazareth. Jefferson redacted biblical events that were incompatible with verifiable scientific examination and knowledge. Instead, the supernatural powers of Christ became nullified in Jefferson's account, reducing the *historical figure* of Jesus to a teaching capacity presented as a sagacious sage endowed with indispensable acumens into how best to lead a virtuous life. The stripping down of the fantastical spiritual elements of the Synoptic Gospels is telling, as it stresses Jefferson's reliance on classical thought as an entry point into an ongoing, cumulative questioning of ethical and political considerations while still orienting the quest for happiness within the mysterious interplays of the cosmos.

The perpetual act of questioning by the ancients regarding the proper development of the individual and, centrally, the intertwined association between the individual and the political community attracted Jefferson as an excellent foundational point for *all types* of scientific inquiry. Writing to his nephew, Peter Carr, concerning the suitable path for acquiring a rich and thought-provoking education, Jefferson lays out a schedule of readings and subjects necessary for cultivating all other fields of knowledge. Cautioning Carr, Jefferson believes that before his scholarly novice nephew can genuinely examine the areas of mathematics, natural history, physics, and astronomy, he must begin with the ancient world, most notably ancient Greek history.[47] In addition, a thirst for poetry is also helpful, promoted by a careful reading of Virgil, Theocritus, and Homer. Questions concerning morality can be found by exploring the works of "Epictetus, Xenophontis memorabilia, Plato's Socratic dialogues, Cicero's philosophies."[48] Through an examination of canonical texts, Jefferson is steadfast in his belief that these sources will provide the necessary groundwork for further studies because of the explicit act of questioning characterized by a scientific cosmological ethos. Only after firmly acquiring the scientific process skills *qua* the methodological attractions of the ancient style of inquiry can his eager and inquisitive nephew expand his educational pursuits, particularly in the field of languages. According to Jefferson, this regimen of texts is not simply designed for his nephew's own sake and benefit. Still, it is necessary for the development and maturation of young Carr into a "public man."[49]

Jefferson's scholarly prescriptions all point toward a suitable level of maturity for his nephew, a point of development where he decisively acquires a sense of *publicness*. The concern here expressed by Jefferson is undoubtedly based on his belief that Carr would one day enter the arena of politics, thereby providing him with an invaluable worldview sustained through an inquisitive scientific approach. However, Jefferson's prudential advice runs much deeper than merely elucidating practical career development counsels. It helps to tease out his understanding of how the act of questioning itself is constitutive of an autonomous public sphere. In the same letter, Jefferson presses his nephew to be diligent and steadfast, carefully avoiding a lackluster immersion in his academic pursuits. Fearful that avoidance would lead to an atrophy of intellectual and civic virtues, Jefferson frames a well-developed curriculum as a necessary condition for the "entrance" onto the "public stage."[50] This passage—a shift from the private to the public realm—thus signifies an announcement of appearance, a declaration of one's existence in service of *the political.*

Jefferson returns to the image of society as a stage in a letter to the inhabitants of Albemarle County dated April 3, 1809. Shortly after retiring from political office, Jefferson returned to Monticello in Albemarle County, Virginia. Neighbors and friends alike sent the former president a formal letter welcoming him home and congratulating him on his life of civic service. Jefferson speaks to the various stations he served throughout his political tenure in his reply. These positions, Jefferson writes, have taken place "on the theatre of public life" through an offering and submission in fulfillment of "duties."[51] Aware that his occupancy of prestigious government titles bestowed upon him a level of national esteem and respect, Jefferson offers an invitation of scrutiny to be placed on him by his friends and neighbors. Jefferson asks, imploring "observers . . . from triers of the vicinage" to render a verdict on his performance while active on the public stage, lifting directly from 1 Samuel of the Old Testament, "'whose ox have I taken, or whom have I defrauded? whom have I oppressed? or of whose hand have I received [sic] a bribe to blind mine eyes therewith?'"[52]

This plane of Jefferson's thought carefully balances the force that a perpetual sense of questioning—a method of inquiry drawn along epistemological and political lines—epitomized the ancients' methodological approach and framing of *the political* in terms of an accessible and inherently public creation. What these letters help to illuminate is how Jefferson's scientific worldview was generated not in opposition but ran congruently with the act of interrogation found within the ancient Greek *polis.*

The proximity between Jefferson's thought and the ancient Greek *polis* thus runs deeper than anticipated. The main roads of the Jefferson-ancient Greek *polis* interplay have been thoroughly explored through the republican paradigm, which, according to J. G. A. Pocock and Bernard Bailyn, existed as the ideological inspiration for creating the American republic.[53] Tenets of classical republicanism, namely the innately political nature of man, the strong emphasis on civic participation, and the establishment of a political space defined by freedom through the nexus of non-domination, were quickly detected in Jefferson's thought and, as a result, serve as a central lens for understanding his speculative ward system, which I will detail in chapter 5. Jefferson's devotion to sustaining the wards through active participation has been seen in Michael Knox Bean's words as a direct attempt to "resurrect the Athenian ideal in America."⁵⁴ Bean rightly picks up that the ancient Greek *polis* was designed as a pattern of a political community that challenged political subjects to minimize their *idios* or self-interest in pursuit of becoming citizens.⁵⁵ It was becoming full members of the political community that brought with it an imperative level of responsibility that challenged citizens to resist usurpations by tyrants, both in their domestic and foreign manifestations, of the collectively shared political power. In *The Philosophy of Thomas Jefferson*, Adrienne Koch carefully points out this concern for Jefferson. To Koch, Jefferson's vision of the localized ward republics contained a pivotal internal *power-checking* mechanism that challenged the ascendance of "petty tyrants at home in the immediate community."⁵⁶ Koch's reading of Jefferson, particularly her identification of Jefferson's desire for a constant level of vigilance against the corruption of political power, therefore, necessitates those members of the wards to remain *active* in the tasks and sacrifices of the community through an ongoing politics of all.

The full import of such a strong emphasis on civic engagement by Jefferson—a central feature of the classical republican paradigm spanning from Aristotle's *Politics* to Polybius's *Histories* to Machiavelli's *Discourses on Livy*—is that the task of ruling extends beyond a cadre of political elites to an accessible plane open to everyday citizens. It is here that, according to Suzanne W. Morse, Jefferson's emphasis on civic participation runs parallel with the ancient Greek *polis*, primarily with the thought of Pericles and Aristotle. Morse contends that Jefferson relied heavily on Aristotle's notion that citizenship meant active involvement in matters concerning the public. Morse additionally suggests that Jefferson envisioned the wards as a public space consistent with Pericles's idea of everyday citizens "executing the life of the community."⁵⁷

In *Thomas Jefferson and American Nationhood*, historian Brian Steele continues with this common theme by locating the influential sway that the commitment to civic engagement within the *polis* played on Jefferson's theorization of the wards. Steele writes, "[. . .] Jefferson saw the wards as the ground where ordinary people could practice the reasoned discourse and cooperative action that would sustain the American spirit he valued by affording those citizens at least a hint of the meaningful participation that characterized the ideal ancient Greek polis."⁵⁸ Steele further elaborates, pushing the actions of the wards to their potential limits, writing, "The national state itself could be affected, shaped, and turned, in fact, by the voice of the people as expressed in and through the wards."⁵⁹ Steele maintains, "This was a relationship between government and its citizens unprecedented in human history, since at least the Greek city-states, and on a scale that the Greeks could never have imagined."⁶⁰

What is so compelling about Steele's understanding of the synergy between the ward system and the ancient city-states is how there contains an emphasis on Jefferson's desire to see the wards ignite and proliferate an "American spirit" that could potentially transform the entire mechanism of the federal government. Jefferson's understanding of democratic politics and the ancient *polis* rests on similar ground, although it necessitates a theoretical pivotal toward the position that at the core of Jefferson's thought there exists an elevation of a politics of all over a thin application of political engagement. The in-roads between Jefferson's reliance on civic participation and that of the ancient Greek *polis* are nevertheless central; however, the difference between the dominant scholarly reading of Jefferson and the *polis* and a radical democratic reading of Jefferson is that the former approach grounds his understanding of politics as an exchange of mediation, negotiation, and compromise. In contrast, a heterodox interpretation opens the space to envision politics as a contested terrain defined by the actions of all members of a political community concomitant with an unrelenting questioning of the political. Politics from this position shifts from activity confined to regulated, institutionalized spaces, understood as everyday procedural politics, to eruptions of extraordinary politics enacted in amorphous and rhizomatic areas. Breaugh and Caivano have suggested that the distinction between "ordinary and extraordinary politics" is a primary aspect of radical democracy.[61] It ignites collective action against the status quo of representation, renewing the reservoir of democratic imagination and energies.

The exposition of the Jefferson-ancient Greek *polis* device has, up until this point, followed a strictly textual route. In this sense, the contribution of classical thought to the Jeffersonian imagination has rested on a realignment of crucial letters and commentaries that affirm a deep level of emulation on the part of Jefferson. Following Jefferson's affirmative reception of ancient sources, the anticipation of revision is expected. Because Jefferson owes much of his political, moral, and scientific thinking to Enlightenment thought—especially between the matrix of Newton, Bacon, and Locke[62]—an impulse is quickly produced to purge, or in a minimal sense, to relegate the *publicness* of inquiry within a political community that defined the *polis* as an anachronistic artifact, devoid of any substantive content. Undoubtedly, this plateau of thought produces clean lines of demarcation, an ability to situate the American Framers, and ostensibly the American republic itself, as transcendence beyond the problems that plagued the ancient world. It, in turn, legitimizes an escape in thought and praxis: a reversal of public scrutiny amongst co-equals to a passage of stasis between market actors.

However, this way of engaging with the Jefferson-*polis* interplay—as a fundamental antagonism between ancient and Enlightenment thought—expresses an interpretation that is situated within a totality of thought, namely a settling and intensification of the architectonic structure of centralized governmental power. By redirecting the philosophical pathways of Jefferson's thought in alignment with the role that autonomy, political interrogation, and civic education played within the ancient *polis*, an arrival commences that reveals a subordination of the logic of centralized power in favor of the importance of politics scattered across a network of decentralized geographic locales. Understanding this shift requires a speculative foray into Jefferson's thought's potentiality with the ancient city-state. By entering a dialogue between Jefferson and Castoriadis, a critical stance against a unitary ontology of centralized power from within the Jeffersonian imaginary emerges, helping to identify the first characteristic of radical democracy.

PERPETUAL QUESTIONING AND AN
OPENING OF EXPLICIT POWER

Jefferson's reception of the ancient world maintains somewhat unexpected compatibility rather than a strict refutation. Such a path opens to explore how his vision of politics is complimented when read alongside the structure of the ancient Greek *polis*, mainly through the sharing of power and an ethos of questioning. From this entry point, the work of Cornelius Castoriadis elucidates a central impulse shared by the ancient Greeks and Jefferson to institute a physical and public space open for the questions concerning communal life.

To sufficiently approach this speculative dialogue to sketch out the first characteristic of Jefferson's theory of radical democracy, it is necessary to examine Castoriadis's vision of the ancient *polis* embedded within the project of autonomy. From there, a conceptual and historical position exposes a central core of Jefferson's political thought: the ability of everyday people to gain political status to institute anything through a renunciation of *monos phronein*, while at the same time, fully aware of the necessity for self-limitation.

For Cornelius Castoriadis, philosophy was born within the ancient Greek *polis*. In this movement of reflectivity and creativity, philosophy emerged in ancient Greek society, bringing forth a perpetual questioning of the representations of the world and an interrogation of the governing institutions of Greek life *qua* the birth of democracy. As fundamental aspects of autonomy, philosophy and democracy represent a radical break with the prevailing and antecedent state of affairs, not as tendencies of the social-historical but rather as *creations*. In this sense, philosophy and democracy move along the same current as an ongoing reflective and questioning activity rapturing the social-historical by creating individual and social autonomy.

The creation of philosophy and democracy—occurring through human activity at a specific spatiotemporal nodal point of recorded human history—owes its heritage to the ancient Greek *polis* and the Athenian citizens. It is at the scene of the ancient Greek *polis* where the real source of explicit power was placed within the hands of the *demos* in the articulation of the society's *nomos*, *dike*, and *telos*. For the ancient Greek *polis* was *a particular* scene that saw the natural source of explicit power belonged to the citizenry and constantly remained open for participation.[63] In all forms of explicit power, the effective involvement of Athenian citizens facilitated individual and social autonomy by bringing to the scene—the physical, material theater of the democratic intellectual *agora*—society's instituting power and "rendering it explicit in reflection."[64] The ancient Greek *polis* and the Athenian citizens thus remain for our contemporary imaginary as a germ of the first instantiation of the project of autonomy that witnessed the resorbing of the political *via* explicit power into politics directed at the "*common ends* and the *public endeavors* the society deliberately proposes to itself."[65] For Castoriadis, the ancient Greek *polis* serves as the locus for the creation of philosophy and democracy; however, the social-historical specificities of the ancient *polis* remain petrified within the totality of a socially constructed time, unable and unavailable for replication. In this manner, the ancient *polis* is not a model or a political corpus that can or even ought to be reproduced. Still, it is a sign of individual and social autonomy functioning merely as a theoretical germ within our present society.

According to Castoriadis, the democratic Greek city-state was the creation *ex nihilo* of a world of meaning and the institution of its governing social significations. The destruction of Athens was equivalent to the dissolution of a world of symbols, values, and institutions—the complete disintegration of the governing social imaginary significations. By this thought, there is no return to the ancient Greek *polis* for Castoriadis; there is no replication of the *nomos* of the Greek *polis*, but only a germ immanent within the totality of social thought that breaks the rigidity of the totality by the appearance of autonomy. In his essay, "The Greek *Polis* and the Creation of Democracy," Castoriadis clarifies this point, "Greece is for us a germ, neither a 'model,' nor one specimen among others, but a germ. History is creation: the creation of total forms of human life. Social-historical forms are not 'determined' by natural or historical laws. Society is self-creation."[66] In this sense, the advancement of the ancient Greek *polis* as the paradigmatic beacon of human flourishing through an imitation of laws and institutions must be abandoned. Instead, what is helpful to extrapolate from that scene of autonomy is how the creation of the ancient *polis* provided a radical break with the then-existing structures of power and in what ways this germ of autonomy can be located across a time-space continuum.

Since returning to the ancient Greek *polis* is not tenable, a project of autonomy can only recognize, contextualize, and question the inherent manifestations of freedom within ancient Greek society. The material and conceptual
parameters of the *polis* must be constantly interrogated not from the Athenian
imaginary but from our social-historical vantage point. To question the Greek
polis while simultaneously questioning the social imaginary significations
and institutions of our present world means to break with the rigidity of a
unitary ontology of postmodernity by reinstituting the project of autonomy.
This movement toward independence, then, is not an actualization of Martin
Heidegger's proclamation of the "end of philosophy"[67] nor an emblem of
a postmodern malaise that announces the death of democracy but offers a
resuscitation and reconstitution of the democratic intellectual *agora*.

For Castoriadis, philosophy and democracy are born together within the
same movement at the same time and place.[68] From this movement—the
refusal of heteronomy and external authority—individual and social autonomy is reflected by questioning existing institutions' foundational underpinnings and the world's hegemonic representations. The creation of philosophy
does not render a foundational ontological point for political activity, as it
is a continuous process of questioning situated within the "horizon of an
unlimited interrogation."[69] Philosophy does not facilitate a foundational point
that generates any schematic materialization of external objects or systems of
thought. Philosophy itself is a social-historical creation that is entirely contingent upon the world in which it is created and instituted.

Although philosophy is deficient as the locus of ontological genesis, the
act or activity of philosophizing means to think. Thinking means entering the
paradoxical enterprise of philosophy, which creates new forms of thought
through its creation and utilization of its systematic structure of thought.
The design of democratic philosophic thought escapes the oscillating aporia
of the metaphysical and transcendental scheme endowed with the essentialist conception of the atomized subject by emerging as a creative, renewing,
uncontainable system of thought that thinks beyond that which lays beyond
belief. For Castoriadis, this datum point of thought cuts across the democratic
philosophic plane culminating at the critical issue of arrival for philosophy:
to the scene of what is.

The unrelenting interrogative nature of philosophy originates in the ancient
Greek *polis.* The Athenian citizen embarked upon a mode of living committed to beauty, wisdom, and the common good.[70] Haunted by questions concerning the nature of justice and the proper ordering and *telos* of the *polis*,
the Athenian citizen carried forth these inquiries to the *agora* to engage in
acts of perpetual questioning and interrogation. The intellectual activity of
the Athenian citizen—through a direct challenge to the very object of the
political institutions of society—led to an *expansion of space* where effective

freedom was realized.[71] Philosophy, in this sense, enlarges the physical theater for questioning, not only in the present moment but across an inter-temporal dimension facilitating a critical interrogation of present and past representations and institutions.[72]

Concurrent with the same movement in ancient Greece that brought forth philosophy, Castoriadis contends that democracy was also created in the *polis*. Greek democracy was undoubtedly a lucid collective activity aimed directly at the institutions of society.[73] Through an explicit putting into question the established institutions of society, the democratic experience aims to break closure at the collective level, whereas a project of philosophy challenges the closure of thought through self-reflective subjectivity.[74] The constant challenging and refusal of closure—collective on the one hand and at the individual subjective level on the other—by democracy and philosophy are not only two sides of the same coin but twin expressions of a *creative co-partnership* that exists as a social-historical rupture creating a new form: a new space splintered across the social totality of historical time that generates an alternative type of relation that is situated between the instituting and the instituted at the singular and collective level.[75]

Democracy then, for Castoriadis, is the theater—the geographic scene of a political choreography—for the actualization of effective freedom for *a new type of being* that reflectively gives itself the laws of its being. It is the regime of self-reflectiveness constantly in pursuit and faced with the struggle to articulate self-government.[76] The democratic movement challenges the overall institution of society by positing a *reinstitution of a community* that is inherently materialized through the utilization of democratic philosophy.[77] There rests an implicit understanding from this position that all citizens can attain a properly ordered *doxa*, which can, and must, be staged on the demo-cratic philosophic *agora*.[78] Collective decisions are not susceptible to a par-ticular political *episteme* but are explicitly founded upon the "confrontations of opinions, the formation of a common opinion."[79] Viewing democracy as a regime of *doxa*—or more aptly considered, *doxae*—politics is not reduced to a determinist orientation but an open terrain for permanent expression, disagreement, and tragedy.[80]

From this vantage point, a turn back toward Jefferson is necessary. Although Jefferson's theory of radical democracy comes to light by inter-rogating the actions of specific historical subjects—inscribed on specific geographic terrains—that demonstrated challenges against unitary bodies of authority and political power, there also rests a crucial concern with the *nec-essary form* of self-government that would permit a politics of all to material-ize. Jefferson's politics of all can be seen as an attempt to re-saturate an ailing form of democratic republicanism in the early republic through persistent challenges against centralized seats of political authority.

The perpetual sway of agitation coupled with civic engagement, central to Jefferson's theory of radical democracy, draws close parallels to Castoriadis's theorization of worker councils and self-management. For Castoriadis, worker councils exist beyond an economic function: they are created to enact equality and effective freedom central to the autonomy project. Castoriadis contends that equality infers an obligation—a responsibility for forming collective life as a *co-equal* in power participation in an autonomous society. Freedom, in this way, cannot be founded on an extra-social basis, as it would lead to enslavement by decree. Instead, the autonomous individual participates equally, shares in the power of the community, and lives entirely under its laws, knowing that it cannot live without rules. Here, the limits of freedom and law coincide.

Worker councils that operate along a horizontal plane of cooperation among other councils,[81] similar to the destabilization of centralized state power offered by Jefferson's ward system, facilitating a coherent presentation of possibilities to the people and the authority and capacity to articulate its position.[82] Indeed, this has economic implications for the production and consumption of goods, but for Castoriadis, the councils take on a vital social and political dimension.[83] Essentially, the function of councils is to provide the setting for forming political opinions and political confrontations.[84] In this sense, Castoriadis's worker councils exist as the training site of a political education by positing new modes of *being-with-others* through the institution of a public space driven by a *nomos* of isonomy.

Tracing the lines of Jefferson's thought, from his praise of ancient studies to a vision of the political sketched out in the Carr and Albemarle letters, set against the backdrop of Castoriadis's interrogative and instituting *polis* rearticulates the *vita activa* imbued within democratic republicanism: a regime of autonomy, equality, and self-limitation.[85] Jefferson's democratic politics and Castoriadis's worker councils reaffirm the *vita activa* by socio-historical subjects, seen in the image of the farmer and the industrial worker, aim to transform the real while remaining mindful of the "real conditions and inspiring an activity."[86] Radical democracy is inherently a revolutionary politics that impinges upon a praxis that takes its object as the reorganization of society and orientates its focus toward a new vision of society: one only possible and sustained "through people's autonomous activity."[87] Castoriadis captures the transformative experience of a democratic praxis, writing,

> The revolutionary movement will be able to fulfill these tasks only if it ceases to appear as a traditional revolutionary movement—traditional politics are dead—and becomes a total movement concerned with everything people do in society

and, above all, with their *actual daily lives*. Likewise, it, therefore, should cease being an organization of specialists and become instead a place for positive socialization where individuals *relearn* how to live a *genuinely collective life* by managing their affairs and by developing themselves through their work in a joint endeavor.[88]

The passage cuts to the very heart of Jefferson's theory of radical democracy: an anti-conformist form of political activity that opens *new spaces* for the daily participation of socio-historical subjects against centralized seats of authority. Political energies are thus directed locally within the accessibly created spaces for political activity but also outward against larger structures of political authority. Jefferson's vision and subsequent defense of federalism, which was "never entirely consistent,"[89] as Thomas Kidd makes excellent note of, should thereby be seen less as a homogenizing, neutralizing, overarching political structure and more of a system designed to amplify political conflict across all levels of the American federal government.

Jefferson's understanding of American federalism helps draw out his promotion for localized spaces of democratic activity and, generally, the potential impact on the nation. Jefferson saw American federalism as a vehicle for unity against foreign adversaries at the base level, ensuring a coordinated approach and response to international affairs. Nevertheless, what a federal system would create at home was even more critical than a stabilizing geopolitical strategy. On this point, Jefferson saw federalism as a productive instrument giving visible outlines to the "proper division of powers between the general and particular governments."[90] The division here served as a safeguard against any singular governmental department—at any geographic level—from usurping too much authority in a despotic manner. Put differently, federalism for Jefferson ensured the creation of boundaries for politics to commence across the nation, with the very distinct possibility that the people could transform national laws and policies from the bottom up.

While much attention has been placed on Jefferson's criticism of the lack of a Bill of Rights following the 1788 ratification and his contentious relation with Alexander Hamilton's fiscal policy under Washington's administration, these framings are woefully fraught. These narrow interpretations miss the mark crucially as they eschew the inherent necessity Jefferson places on establishing a federal system precisely because it would enable more political energy to flow through all government channels. Jefferson's frustration and criticism of Hamilton and other leading Federalists were less about the specificities of their economic agenda and more about how these policies would ultimately divorce the people from government affairs. As John Lauritz Larson points out, Jefferson's scorn of the Federalists centered on the belief that the assumption of debt and establishment of a national bank, among other plans, would lead to corruption. Larson writes, "[i]t was not the honest exercise of federal power, but the apparent usurpation of that power for counterrevolutionary purposes [. . .]."[91] From this standpoint, Jefferson's belief in federalism was a belief in a permanent division of powers permitting action, engagement, and dialogue to always occur.

A robust, dynamic vision of American society emerges when Jefferson's perspectives of the ancient Greek polis and American federalism are enjoined. Centrally, under federalism, democratic control of the American state, including the economy, judiciary, and bureaucratic apparatuses, has remained limited. In contemporary politics, the scope of state power has assumed an even more significant role, erecting barriers to mitigate democratic energy while prioritizing economic interests and technocratic rule. The result is that the economy and offices of political authority are insulated from the public, preventing dialogue and decision-making across varying levels of government.

In a hyper form of patrician politics, a technocratic approach to government has ascended to a dominant plane in American politics, strikingly undermining the possibility of democratic decision-making across local and state levels, stifling input pressure from the people.

As a result, activists, community organizers, and citizens have sought new spaces for inclusive decision-making and an expansion of democratic relations. Primarily, democratic experiments designed at the local level have successfully erected decision-making bodies constituted by citizens that are autonomous from state control yet still maintain a crucial dialogical connection with state and federal level governmental agencies.

The most notable example of cultivating civic engagement and coordination with state officials is participatory budgeting practices in Porto Alegre, Brazil. As an offshoot of participatory democracy, participatory budgeting enables citizens to actively determine the allocation of resources within their local community while remaining autonomous. Since 1989, the success of Porto Alegre, designed to create effective strategies to enact more expansive institutional changes, has spurred new participatory budgeting projects across the globe. Cities across the United States and Canada have followed suit in recent years. In New York City, thousands of residents—eligibility begins at age eleven—have democratically engaged in allocating over $200 million in public funds relating to new educational, transit, and environmental projects. The Neighborhood Support Coalition, established in Guelph, Ontario, has followed Porto Alegre's route, empowering citizens with the task of allocating resources for local support groups, clinics for tax assistance, and language classes.

These examples maintain an essential affinity with Jefferson's vision of local political activity within a federal system as they strive to create and preserve spaces for individuals to exercise their capacities as citizens. While the relationship between these local spaces of democratic action and the central state is not structured along antagonistic lines, they do contain a potential for rupture: an explicit scene of training and action that produces a qualitatively different set of human relations antithetical to forms of disciplinary state power.

This chapter delineated the first characteristic of Jefferson's theory of radical democracy. The first characteristic is an impulse to create a public space accessible through the supplementation of available time, sustained by perpetual questioning and refusal to enclose the political within the realm of a centralized framework. To draw this central feature of Jefferson's program out, I suggested that his thought contains points of commonality with the ancient Greek *polis*. These affinities rested along several planes of textual and conceptual engagement.

Firstly, Jefferson's concern for the necessity of civic education draws heavily from ancient sources as a foundational point to cultivate the act of interrogation in a political sense. The educative capacity of such a historically rich curriculum pointed directly to the very question of the creation of the political and necessity for action in the theater of public life.

Secondly, a turn to the treatment of Jefferson within the republic tradition helped to import the main thrust of the political nature of the Jeffersonian actor within his political worldview. Turning to the commonalities between Jefferson and classical republican thought, an entry point emerged into the ancient world that confirmed, rather than negated, the positive content of both Jefferson and the ancient Greeks' vision of a political community. From this position, politics for both Jefferson and the ancients meant action *against* settled forms of institutionalized power and authority, a fraternal engagement *between* and *with* others directed toward the community's public affairs. Here, political action aims to repeal the erasure of space and time that circumscribes the abstract, unitary politics of heteronomy by creating new sites for engagement to pursue a transient opening of the political accessible by all.

Thirdly, exploring Jefferson's thought *through* Cornelius Castoriadis's understanding of the ancient Greek *polis* illuminated the issue of perpetual questioning by citizens. Fundamental to this ethos of unrelenting interrogation exhibited by the ancient Greeks was public scrutiny directed against the polis's social, political, and economic institutions. The ancients' depth of such a recalcitrant temperament was sustained by a rejection of singular authority deposits favoring a collective sharing of explicit power. By taking up this conceptual framing of the *polis* by Castoriadis, the Jeffersonian imaginary acquires a deeper, more theoretically rich dimension than a flat, statist reading of his thought would afford. Instead, Jefferson's radical democratic politics, seen in this manner, function as an assembly of singular composites of political contestation embedded within a national, protracted republic sustained through civic education, perpetual questioning, and the ongoing struggle against centralized power for the staging of the political. These three approaches (textual/republican/speculative) introduce a crucial feature of Jefferson's theory of radical democracy, suggesting a further separation between himself and other prominent thinkers of the early American republic.

NOTES

1. Alain Badiou, *Pocket Pantheon*, trans. David Macey (London: Verso, 2016), 130.
2. Badiou, *Pocket Pantheon*, 131.
3. Aristotle, *Politics*, trans. T. A. Sinclair (London: Penguin, 1981), 181.
4. For a discussion on the importance of how man is situated within the cosmos and, in turn, how it directly relates to a search for political philosophy, see Leo Strauss, "What is Political Philosophy?" in *The Journal of Politics*, vol. 19, no. 3 (Aug. 1957), 367.
5. To see how the very idea of the *polis* has emerged as a contested terrain in contemporary political philosophy, see *Athenian Political Thought and the Reconstruction of American Democracy*, eds. J. Peter Euben, Josiah Ober, and John R. Wallach (Ithaca, NY: Cornell University Press, 1994).
6. Here I am making a clear distinction between the face-to-face, intimate nature of politics epitomized in a city-state setting compared to the abstract politics of the imperial republic found not only in the Roman Empire but also in James Madison and Alexander Hamilton's vision of the American republic. See Sheldon S. Wolin, *Politics and Vision* (Princeton, NJ: Princeton University Press, 2004), 65–70.
7. Benjamin Constant, *De la liberté des Anciens comparée à celle des Modernes* in *Oeuvres politiques de Benjamin Constant*, ed. Charles Loundre (Paris, 1874), 260–62.
8. The configuration of the *polis* indeed contained an economic dimension to its design. Access to trade routes via land and sea routes was central to the economy of the *poleis*. The positioning of the *agora* existed as the core hub for commercial activity, with resources from merchants and farmers flowing directly into the heart of the city-state. For the critical factors on the economic health of the *polis*, see Aristotle, *Politics*, 405–11.
9. There is much debate over when the Athenian walls were constructed among historians and archeologists. There is, however, a tepid consensus that indicates construction occurred as early as the mid-sixth century BCE under the tyranny of the Peisistratos family. Additionally, new walls were constructed during the democratic turn of 508/507 BCE of Cleisthenes and the crating of the Constitution of the Athenians, far prior to the Peloponnesian War. See Noel Robertson, "From Popular Sovereignty to the Sovereignty of Law: Law, Society, and Politics in Fifth-Century Athens by Martin Ostwald," (Review) *Phoenix*, vol. 43, no. 4 (Winter 1989), 365–75; Robert G. A. Weir, "The Lost Archaic Wall around Athens," *Phoenix*, vol. 49, no. 3 (Autumn, 1995), 247–58. Also see Anna Maria Theocharaki, "The Ancient Circuit Wall of Athens: Its Changing Course and the Phases of Construction," *Hesperia:*

The Journal of the American School of Classical Studies at Athens, vol. 80, no. 1 (January–March 2011), 71–156.

10. For a critical stance on Rousseau's localized understanding of participatory politics, see Joseph de Maistre, *Against Rousseau: On the State of Nature and On the Sovereignty of the People*, trans. and ed. Richard A. Lebrun (Montreal: McGill-Queen's University Press, 1996).

11. Aristotle, *Politics*, 175.

12. Hannah Arendt, *The Human Condition* (Chicago: The University of Chicago Press, 1998), 9.

13. Arendt, *The Human Condition*, 198.

14. Ibid., 198. While Arendt's presentation of the ancient Greek *polis* and the Roman *res publica* thickly applies an import of *publicness* and heroic deeds as constitutive features of political action, Sheldon Wolin carefully stresses how the anti-democratic practices of the ancient world are vitally neglected in Arendt's thought. In turn, Wolin suggests that the exclusionary structure of ancient Greece and Rome are not adequately resolved in Arendt's account, producing a theorization of a restricted inequitable political realm. See Sheldon S. Wolin, "Hannah Arendt: Democracy and The Political," *Salmagundi*, no. 60, On Hannah Arendt (Spring–Summer 1983), 3–19. Like Wolin, Jacques Rancière laments Arendt for theorizing a political stage defined by the magnificent displays of words and deeds from a limited pool of citizens. According to Rancière, Arendt can sketch out such an image of the political sphere by narrowly focusing on the particularities of Pericles's speech while ignoring the fundamental tensions between Athenian freedom and the militarism of Spartan life that underscored discourse. See Jacques Rancière, *On the Shores of Politics*, trans. Liz Heron (London: Verso, 2007), 67–68.

15. See Herodotus, *The History of Herodotus*, vol. 1, trans. Isaac Littlebury (London: Printed for D. Midwinter, A. Bettesworth and C. Hitch, J. and J. Pemberton, R. Ware, C. Rivington, J. Batley, and J. Wood, F. Clay, A. Ward, J. and P. Knapton, T. Longman, and R. Hett, 1737), Bks. I–IV.

16. For comprehensive studies of these historiographical works, see Felix Jacoby, *Atthis, The Local Chronicles of Ancient Athens* (Oxford, UK: Clarendon Press, 1949); Thomas F. Scanlon, *Greek Historiography* (Chichester, UK: Wiley Blackwell, 2015); Gordon S. Shrimpton, *History and Memory in Ancient Greece* (Montreal: McGill-Queen's University Press, 1997); Christopher Pelling, *Literary Texts and the Greek Historian* (London: Routledge, 2000); J. B. Bury, *The Ancient Greek Historians* (New York: Dover Publications, 1958); Charles William Fornara, *The Nature of History in Ancient Greece and Rome* (Berkeley, CA: University of California Press, 1983).

17. Thucydides, *History of the Peloponnesian War: The Complete Hobbes Translation*, notes by David Green (Chicago: The University of Chicago Press, 1989), 111–25.

18. Cornelius Castoriadis, "The Greek *Polis* and the Creation of Democracy," in *Philosophy, Politics, Autonomy: Essays in Political Philosophy*, ed. David Ames Curtis (New York: Oxford University Press, 1991), 113–14.

19. Wolin, *Politics and Vision*, 598–99.

20. To analyze the economic structure and the rampant institution of chattel slavery in ancient Greece and Rome, see Ellen Meiksins Wood, *Democracy Against Capitalism: Renewing Historical Materialism* (Cambridge, UK: Cambridge University Press, 1995), 181–96.

21. Tocqueville carefully identifies this mentality for the conquering of space with America's westward expansion and its prospects for global maritime control likening it to the pursuits of the Roman Empire. See Alexis de Tocqueville, *Democracy in America*, Harvey C. Mansfield and Delba Winthrop, eds. and trans. (Chicago: The University of Chicago Press, 2000), 390.

22. For how the northern states rapidly transformed following the revolution from agricultural growth to internal development and the subsequent production of capital goods leading to the advance of capitalism and an accompanying change in social-property relations, see Charles Post, *The American Road to Capitalism: Studies in Class-Structure, Economic Development, and Political Conflict, 1620–1877* (Leiden, Netherlands: Brill Press, 2011), 155–94.

23. This does not suggest that historiographical studies were absent in the early republic. However, the general focus was strikingly concerned with economic matters, except resting on republican historiographical material, as J. G. A. Pocock and Bernard Bailyn have stressed. For an appreciation of these economic-centric analyses in a contemporary lens and how they pay particular attention to how physical space can be understood in the logic of capitalism, see Herbert G. Gutman, "Work, Culture, and Society in Industrializing America, 1815–1919," *The American Historical Review*, vol. 78, no. 3 (June 1973), 531–88; Kingston Wm Heath, *The Patina of Place: The Cultural Weathering of a New England Industrial Landscape* (Knoxville, TN: The University of Tennessee Press, 2001); Janet Greenlees, *Female Labour Power: Women Workers' Influence on Business Practices in the British and American Cotton Industries, 1780–1860* (Hampshire, UK: Ashgate Publishing Limited, 2007); Margaret Crawford, *Building the Workingman's Paradise: The Design of American Company Towns* (London: Verso, 1995), 11–28.

24. For Loyalist studies, see Joseph Galloway, *The Claim of the American Loyalists, Reviewed and Maintained upon Incontrovertible Principles of Law and Justice* (Boston: Gregg Press, 1972); Jonathan Boucher, *Reminiscences of an American Loyalist, 1738–1789* (Boston: Houghton Mifflin, 1925); Peter Oliver, *Origin & Progress of the American Rebellion: a Tory View*, eds. Douglass Adair and John A. Schultz (Stanford, CA: Stanford University Press, 1961); For Whig analyses, see George Bancroft, *History of the Formation of the Constitution of the United States of America* (New York: D. Appleton, 1882); George Bancroft, *A History of the United States, From the Discovery of the American Continent* (Boston: Little, Brown and Company, 1834); Finally, for Imperial historians, see George L. Beer, *The Commercial Policy of England toward the American Colonies* (New York: Columbia College, 1893); Lawrence Gibson, *The British Empire Before the American Revolution* (New York: Knopf, 1958); Lawrence Gibson, *The British Empire in the Eighteenth Century: Its Strength and its Weakness, an inaugural lecture delivered before the University of Oxford on 13 November 1951* (Oxford, UK: Clarendon Press, 1952).

25. For the influence of classical political thought on the Founders, see Carl J. Richard, *Greeks and Romans Bearing Gifts: How the Ancients Inspired the Founding Fathers* (Lanham, MD: Rowman & Littlefield Publishers, 2008); Eric Nelson, *The Greek Tradition in Republican Thought* (Cambridge: Cambridge University Press, 2004), 195–233; Zera S.Fink, *The Classical Republicans: An Essay in the Recovery of a Pattern of Thought in Seventeenth-Century England* (Chicago: Northwestern University Press, 1945); Howard Mumford Jones, *O Strange New World* (New York: Viking Press, 1964); H. Trevor Colbourn, *The Lamp of Experience: Whig History and the Intellectual Origins of the American Revolution* (Chapel Hill: University of North Carolina Press, 1965); Carl J. Richard, *The Founders and the Classics: Greece, Rome, and the American Enlightenment* (Cambridge, MA: Harvard University Press, 1994); Gilbert Chinard, "Polybius and the American Constitution," *Journal of the History of Ideas*, vol. 1, no. 1 (Jan. 1940), 38–58.

26. *The Federalist* No. 55, February 13, 1788, *The Papers of James Madison*, vol. 10, 27 May 27, 1787–March 3, 1788, eds. Robert A. Rutland, Charles F. Hobson, William M. E. Rachal, and Frederika J. Teute (Chicago: The University of Chicago Press, 1977), 504–8.

27. See Charles de Secondat, Baron de Montesquieu, *The Spirit of the Laws*, trans. Thomas Nugent (New York: Hafner Publishing Co., 1949). See Books IV, VI, and XI.

28. Paul Cartledge, *Democracy: A Life* (Oxford, UK: Oxford University Press, 2016), 293.

29. For Madison's scorn of the Many and Thucydides's thoughts on oligarchy, see James Madison, "For the *National Gazette*, 31 December 1791," *The Papers of James Madison*, vol. 14, April 6, 1791–March 16, 1793, ed. Robert A. Rutland and Thomas A. Mason (Charlottesville: University Press of Virginia, 1983), 178–79; the influence of the thought of Plutarch can be seen in *Federalist* Nos. 18 and 38, both written by Madison.

30. TJ to William Short, August 4, 1820. *Founders Online* (hereafter cited as *FO)*, National Archives, http://founders.archives.gov/documents/Jefferson/98-01-02 -1438.

31. TJ to John Adams, July 5, 1814, in Looney, *PTJ*, Retirement Series, 7: 451–55.

32. Garry Wills, *Inventing America: Jefferson's Declaration of Independence* (New York: Vintage Books, 1979), xxii.

33. TJ to William Short, April 13, 1820, *FO,* National Archives, http://founders .archives.gov/documents/Jefferson/98-01-02-1218.

34. TJ to Benjamin Waterhouse, October 13, 1815, in Looney, *PTJ*, Retirement Series, 9: 78–79.

35. TJ to Isaac H. Tiffany, August 26, 1816, in Looney, *PTJ*, Retirement Series, 10: 349.

36. Jefferson preferred the Gillies translation to the more dominant English version of the time, William Ellis's *A Treatise on Government, Translated from the Greek of Aristotle* (London: Sowerby, 1778).

37. Jefferson's fear of a dictator emerging in America should not be understated. His concerns are drawn heavily from Roman history and are discussed in his *Notes on the State of Virginia* (hereafter cited as *Notes*). See TJ, *Notes* (Boston: Wells and

Lilly, 1829), Queries XIII and XXIII. Also see Andreas Kalyvas, "The Tyranny of Dictatorship: When the Greek Tyrant Met the Roman Dictator," in *Political Theory,* vol. 35, no. 4 (Aug. 2007), 429–31.

38. TJ to Isaac H. Tiffany, 349. Emphasis added.

39. Winfield E. Nagley, *Foundations of Thomas Jefferson's Philosophy* (University of Hawaii: Hawaii Bicentennial Commission, 1976), 8.

40. Gilbert Chinard, *Thomas Jefferson: The Apostle of Americanism* (Ann Arbor: The University of Michigan Press, 1957), 63.

41. On countless occasions, Jefferson stressed his strong praise and respect for Cicero. See TJ to John Adams, December 10, 1819; TJ to Francis Eppes, January 19, 1821; TJ to Francis Walker Gilmer, November 25, 1823.

42. Nagley, *Foundations of Thomas Jefferson's Philosophy*, 12.

43. TJ, "Doctrines of Jesus Compared with Others," April 21, 1803, in Oberg, *PTJ,* 40: 253–55.

44. Ibid., 254.

45. Ibid., 254.

46. For a thorough detailing of Jefferson's understanding of the fundamental principles of Epicureanism, including how happiness is situated as the axiomatic core, see TJ to William Short, October 31, 1819, *FO,* National Archives, http://founders.archives.gov/documents/Jefferson/98-01-02-0850.

47. TJ to Peter Carr, August 19, 1785, in Boyd, *PTJ*, 8: 405–8.

48. Ibid.

49. Ibid.

50. Ibid.

51. TJ to the Inhabitants of Albemarle County, April 3, 1809, in Looney, *PTJ*, Retirement Series, 1: 102–3.

52. Ibid.

53. See J. G. A. Pocock, *The Machiavellian Moment: Florentine Political Thought and the Atlantic Republican Tradition* (Princeton, NJ: Princeton University Press, 2003), 506–52; J. G. A. Pocock, "Virtue and Commerce in the Eighteenth Century," *Journal of Interdisciplinary History*, vol. 3, no. 1 (1972), 119–34; for the influence of civic humanism and the republic tradition on the American Republic and Anglo-American political thought more broadly, see J. G. A. Pocock, *Politics, Language and Time: Essays on Political Thought and History* (Chicago: The University of Chicago Press, 1989), 80–103. Also see Bernard Bailyn, *The Ideological Origins of the American Revolution* (Cambridge, MA: Belknap Press of Harvard University Press, 1967), 62–101. Finally, the import of traditional republican features of government was deeply ingrained in the drafting of the Constitution of 1787, particularly under the guidance of James Madison as a transformative moment in the history of American political thought conceptualized as the "Madisonian Moment," see Jack N. Rakove, *Original Meanings: Politics and Ideas in the Making of the Constitution* (New York: Vintage Books, 1997), 35–56.

54. Michael Knox Bean, *Jefferson's Demons: Portrait of a Restless Mind* (New York: Free Press, 2003), 196.

55. Ibid.

56. Adrienne Koch, *The Philosophy of Thomas Jefferson* (Gloucester, MA: P. Smith, 1957), 162.

57. Suzanne W. Morse, "Ward Republics: The Wisest Invention for Self-Government" in *Thomas Jefferson and the Education of a Citizen*, ed. James Gilreath (Washington, D.C.: Library of Congress), 266. Also, see Werner Jaeger, *Paideia: The Ideals of Greek Culture: Volume III: The Conflict of Cultural Ideals in the Age of Plato*, trans. Gilbert Highet (Oxford: Oxford University Press, 1986), 111–12.

58. Brian Steele, *Thomas Jefferson and American Nationhood* (Cambridge, UK: Cambridge University Press, 2012), 153.

59. Steele, *Thomas Jefferson and American Nationhood*, 154.

60. Ibid.

61. Martin Breaugh and Dean Caivano, "A Living Critique of Domination: Exemplars of Radical Democracy from Black Lives Matter to #MeToo," *Philosophy and Social Criticism* (May 2022). doi:10.1177/01914537221093726.

62. Jefferson recalls a meeting during his tenure as Secretary of State with Alexander Hamilton in a letter to Benjamin Rush. Hamilton noticed three portraits hanging on the wall during their discussions and inquired who these men were. Jefferson replied, "I told him they were my trinity of the three greatest men the world had ever produced, naming them." The portraits were, of course, Newton, Bacon, and Locke. Jefferson continued, presenting Hamilton's unsurprising retort: "he paused for some time: 'the greatest man, said he, that ever lived was Julius Caesar.'" See TJ to Benjamin Rush, January 16, 1811, in Looney, *PTJ*, Retirement Series, 3: 304–8.

63. Castoriadis, "Power, Politics, Autonomy," in *Philosophy, Politics, Autonomy*, 168.

64. Ibid., 174.

65. Ibid. Castoriadis's emphasis.

66. Castoriadis, "The Greek *Polis* and the Creation of Democracy," 84.

67. Castoriadis, "The 'End of Philosophy'?" in *Philosophy, Politics, Autonomy*, 13.

68. Ibid., 20.

69. Castoriadis, "The Nature and Value of Equality," in *Philosophy, Politics, Autonomy*, 124–25.

70. Castoriadis, "The Greek *Polis* and the Creation of Democracy," 123.

71. Castoriadis, "The 'End of Philosophy'?" 17.

72. Ibid., 15.

73. Castoriadis, "Power, Politics, Autonomy," 160.

74. Castoriadis, "The 'End of Philosophy'?" 21.

75. Ibid., 31.

76. Ibid., 19.

77. Castoriadis, "Power, Politics, Autonomy," 159.

78. Castoriadis, "The Greek *Polis* and the Creation of Democracy," 104.

79. Castoriadis, "Intellectuals and History," in *Philosophy, Politics, Autonomy*, 7.

80. Castoriadis, "The 'End of Philosophy'?" 17.

81. Cornelius Castoriadis, "On the Content of Socialism," in *The Castoriadis Reader*, trans. And ed. David Ames Curtis (Oxford, UK: Blackwell Publishers, 1997), 71.

82. Ibid., 84.

83. Ibid., 66.

84. Ibid., 101. Emphasis added.

85. Castoriadis, "The Greek *Polis* and the Creation of Democracy," 115.

86. Castoriadis, "Marxism and Revolutionary Theory," in *The Castoriadis Reader*, 152.

87. Ibid.

88. Cornelius Castoriadis, *Political and Social Writings, Volume 2*, trans. David Ames Curtis (Minneapolis, MN: University of Minnesota Press, 1988), 230. Emphasis added.

89. Thomas Kidd, *Thomas Jefferson: A Biography of Spirit and Flesh* (New Haven, CT: Yale University Press, 2022), 232.

90. TJ to James Madison, December 16, 1786, in Boyd, *TJP*, 10: 602–6.

91. John Lauritz Larson, "Jefferson's Union and the Problem of Internal Improvements," in *Jeffersonian Legacies*, ed. Peter Onuf (Charlottesville: The University of Virginia Press, 1993), 351.

Chapter 2

The Unwritten Law

Perpetual Reconstitution
in Saxon Britain

Jefferson maintained a strong dislike for perpetuity. Institutions, laws, and even debts constrain a present generation's natural right to create, experiment, and succeed or fail on its terms. "No society can make a perpetual constitution or even a perpetual law," Jefferson offered in a letter to James Madison in 1789, affirming that "the earth belongs always to the living generation."[1] While a radical element to Jefferson's generational claim *sans* an infusion of prior institutions is present, there is also, importantly, a dimension of his thought that showcases an embrace of historical precedent. This chapter explores this side of Jefferson's vision of radical democracy.

Within his political philosophy, there is an emphasis on generational renewal greatly influenced by his historical appraisal of the Anglo-Saxons. As Merrill Peterson claimed in *Thomas Jefferson and the New Nation*, "the shadow of the English heritage hovered over Jefferson's mind."[2] While Jefferson's Whig interpretation of the Saxons has been well documented, especially concerning common law, constitutional engineering, and orthography, it is helpful to return to these topics in an explicitly political context. Specifically, an impulse remains through a strictly liberal or republican account, which morphs Jefferson's reading of the Saxons *always concerning the past*, as a quasi-artifact of historical interpretation or even as a complete fabrication.[3]

Jefferson's assessment of the Anglo-Saxons reveals his preference for small, localized spaces of politics populated by active, duty-bound citizens.[4] By exploring this aspect of his thought, the second characteristic of radical democracy will be offered: a rejection of codified, entrenched laws that place authorship outside of self-government in favor of the constant renewal of guiding principles determined by the community itself.

Jefferson's reading of Anglo-Saxon history is structured around four central positions, which ultimately inform his political vision: unencumbered mobility for the establishment of self-government; a future-oriented theory of freedom; an allodial claim to property *contra* feudal titles; and finally, a reliance on custom and revision over fixed conventions. To showcase how these themes operate within Jefferson's thought and, in turn, help underscore the terrain or to stage the scene *for* politics, it is necessary to examine several key texts, namely: Jefferson's Legal Commonplace Books (1762–1767), "A Summary View of the Rights of British America" (1774), "The Declaration of the Causes and Necessity of Taking Up Arms" (1775), co-written by John Dickinson, and an assortment of personal letters penned later in his life after leaving political office. These central themes (mobility, freedom, property, and law), the breath of which spans over six decades, animate Jefferson's radical politics beyond mere "theoretical justification for American independence"[5] offerings, instead, a rich and fruitful commentary on the potential for democratic politics in the United States.

THE NATURAL RIGHT OF EXPATRIATION

A central feature of the history of the Anglo-Saxons for Jefferson centered on the occurrence of mobility. Key was the movement of the Saxon tribes from the Germanic forests across Western Europe to the island of Britain in the fifth century. The migration and ultimate settlement by the Saxons symbolized to Jefferson an experiment in self-government, not dissimilar to the American cause. What Jefferson identified in the history of the Anglo-Saxons was *proof* of an experiment in pursuit of freedom, founded upon the natural right rather than tradition.

The legacy of the history of the Anglo-Saxons often described as the "Saxon myth" by historians, particularly of the legal orientation, has imported a full slate of civil liberties and protections.[6] A portrayal of this "primitive democracy" found as early as Tacitus's *Germania* presented the crowning achievements of the Saxon heritage in the areas of the formation of common law, the institution of an elective monarchy, a tribal assembly, and the legal protection of trial by jury, to name just a few.[7] Jon Meacham details the impact of Tacitus's account on Jefferson's writing: "He read Tacitus's *Germania* and became an adherent of the theory that England was initially populated by freedom-loving Saxons who were subjugated by the monarchical and feudal forces of William the Conqueror."[8] An interruption of these democratic ideals and practices came about with the Norman Conquest in the eleventh century of England and the subsequent imposition of a feudal social structure. The Saxon myth suggests that the corruption of these rights lasted until *the people* were able to thwart "usurpations of the crown on the people"[9] through a direct challenge of the supremacy of Norman tyranny, it reflected in the drafting of the Magna Carta of 1215 ("the Great Charter of the Liberties") and, ultimately, in the Glorious Revolution of 1688.[10] Restoration of these rights denoted, somewhat anachronistically, a quixotic return to the principles of the Anglo-Saxons prior to the Norman Conquest and displayed a defining feature of English history in a recurring struggle against centralized political power.[11]

Jefferson encountered this portrait of the golden era of English liberty— embedded within the Saxon myth—during his formal education and train- ing as a lawyer. Primarily, an idyllic vision of the Saxons was presented to Jefferson, one that described a pre-feudal polity inhabited by "simple inde- pendent farmers free of rents, entails, and other burdens."[12] Such a picture was drawn by historians, political philosophers, and legal commentators, the likes of which Jefferson scrupulously read, including Lord Kames's *Historical Law Tracts*, John Dalrymple's *Feudal Property*, John Trenchard and Thomas Gordon's *Cato Letters*, and Algernon Sidney's *Discourses on Government*.[13] While these writings helped to shape Jefferson's perspective on the Saxons, in addition to its development in eighteenth-century Whig historical interpre- tations,[14] he broke with the more formal Whig apologists by suggesting that the Conquest introduced corrosive elements *still present* within the English regime. In line with other radical thinkers, such as Trenchard and Gordon, James Burgh, and Obadiah Hulme, Jefferson maintained that an infectious substance blighted the English body politic and that purification was neces- sary to purge the malignant ailments.[15] The history of the Anglo-Saxons is key in this regard, not as a model for confirmation of the present regime but as a reflection of the possibility of a freer, less flawed system of government in the present and future.

Central to the narrative of the Saxon myth and quintessential for Jefferson's understanding and, in turn, his counterbalancing angle of comparison to the plight of the Americans was the idea of movement. As the Anglo-Saxons left their native lands, embarking upon a journey to erect a new society, Jefferson saw parallels between their continental trek and the transatlantic voyage of the colonists as crucial moments in the progression of humankind. An endeavor to leave behind a former way of life defined by the past to create a new com- munity in the present while remaining open to revision processes for future generations. Andrew Burstein and Nancy Isenberg stress this point, writing,

For Jefferson, the legal philosopher, British Americans had created a parallel country to their distant motherland. England's offspring were, in effect, a new race of people—a new lineage, a new bloodline—possessing a real but some- what thinned blood connection to their transatlantic relatives. In reasoning thus,

Jefferson transformed the entire continent into a frontier nation formed by a righteous, independent, conquering people.[16]

Founding movements, in this light, thereby commence, not at points of institutional design and implementation, nor through public visibility of governing laws by sanction or force, but rather via an exerted physical departure away from the territoriality of the past, marking a decisive break with a conservative ordering and enclosure of political time-space.

Jefferson brings the role of mobility to the forefront of his argument in "A Summary View of the Rights of British America," written in 1774 and heavily debated during the First Continental Congress. In this rousing and widely read address, Jefferson appeals to King George III to support the colonists' rights inhabiting British America. Objecting to the pattern of abuses upon the colonists, Jefferson believed that Parliament possessed an illegitimate arrogation of power over the colonies.[17] According to Jefferson, all power is directly derived from the people, rather than Parliament made visible in a fractious relationship between the colonists and Westminster. Jefferson stresses that rights are derived from nature as a precursor to a more explicit articulation in the Declaration two years later. In this tract, he carefully presents only two examples found in the category of natural rights, which directly relate to the necessity of mobility: the right of expatriation and free trade.

To establish the natural right of expatriation, Jefferson turns to historical precedent, specifically the migration of the Saxons. Describing the movement of the Saxons from the "native wilds and woods in the north of Europe" to the island of Britain, Jefferson highlights the action as an enactment of "universal law."[18] Crucially, he points out that the migration, which resulted in establishing a new society and an enduring "system of laws," mirrors the formation of settlements in America "at the expence of individuals, and not of the British public."[19] Jefferson follows, suggesting that "blood was split" and "fortunes expended" by the true founders of America in their efforts to create a new society.[20] The outcome of this profoundly monumental act has, according to Jefferson, resulted in a conquering of America and, consequently, an absolute right on the part of those that have made the "settlement effectual" to retain such desserts.[21]

The actions undertaken by both the Saxons and the American colonists on the erection of a new society—impressed as visual invocations of democratic self-evidence—functioned as two notable instances of the natural right of expatriation at play.[22] Jefferson believes that the colonists exercised the natural right to determine their configuration of society and all accompanying aspects of the newly established association by leaving England.[23] Clarifying the full scope of this natural right, Jefferson stakes his claims of expatriation on the concerted move away from land *not of one's choosing* to engage in an expedition of freedom defined by an expenditure of sacrifice, energy, and risk. Referring to the rights of British subjects *before* they migrated to America, he takes up the depth of this right, writing that they "possessed a right which nature has given to all men, of departing from the country in which chance, not choice, has placed them, of going in quest of new habitations, and of there establishing new societies, under such laws and regulations as to them shall seem most likely to promote public happiness."[24] Therefore, the departure from Britain and the subsequent cultivation and conquering of America confers upon the colonists a substantial key holding—both in natural and legal terms—over the authorship of law and land, precisely because it is an exercise of natural right.[25] From this position, Jefferson is clear: neither King George III nor Westminster Parliament retains sovereign power in this regard. As he draws careful attention, any interference is a direct violation of natural rights.

The importance of mobility features significantly in Jefferson's discussion of trade. Affirming that free trade is a natural right, Jefferson claims that the right of the colonists to engage in unfettered commerce fell "victim to arbitrary power."[26] Restrictions were imposed as early as the Navigation Act of 1651 under King Charles I. As recent as the passage of the Hat Act in 1732 and the Iron Act in 1750 by Parliament under King George II's reign severely limited economic opportunities for the colonists.[27] These acts strongly drew the ire of Jefferson, as he vehemently denounced the Hat Act, suggesting that its effects mark "an instance of despotism to which no parallel can be produced in the most arbitrary ages of British history."[28] While the main objective of these acts, along with the broader platform of the Navigation Acts, was to limit trade routes enabling an exclusive exchange between the colonies and mainland England, it was precisely this inability of the colonists to engage in an economic enterprise that so distraught Jefferson freely. As an advocate for free trade, Jefferson here reveals his more classical liberal leanings, holding a resolute belief that it will stimulate the prosperity of humankind. Nevertheless, its justification is firmly based on natural rights.[29] For Jefferson, the right to free trade requires the removal of impediments, thereby permitting free movement for individuals and, of course, material goods. Highlighting Jefferson's frustrations, Alf J. Mapp writes, "He detailed the deleterious effects of Parliament's restrictions on American trade and manufactures and pointed out that London's legislators could subject Americans to many hardships not imposed on the people of Great Britain."[30]

Jefferson's assessment of mobility and its corresponding relationship to the natural rights of expatriation and free trade presented in his "Summary View" relies heavily on the history of the Saxons. Methodically making his case reminiscent of a legal brief, Jefferson utilizes the migration of the Saxons as historical precedent to challenge encroachments by Parliament and the Crown

upon the colonists. The physical pilgrimage of the Saxons maintains a valuable place in Jefferson's exploratory historical search for moments of political
freedom by signifying a collective relocation to new domains.

THE POLITICAL STRUGGLE TO REOPEN FREEDOM

A year after his "Summary View," Jefferson would again turn to the history of
the Anglo-Saxons to help make a case for American independence. Adopted
by Congress on July 6, 1775, "The Declaration of the Causes and Necessity
for Taking Up Arms" represents a synthesis of Jefferson's radicalism and
John Dickinson's conservatism. As a co-written piece, one that labored
through several drafts, evident in Jefferson's "Composition Draft" and "Fair
Copy for the Committee,"[31] the outcome would present a justification for
separation in a more severe and pressing manner than his earlier "Summary
View." A more determined and revolutionary-focused Jefferson vastly over-
matched Dickinson's apparent willingness to remain open to reconciliation
with Great Britain.[32] Dickinson's convoluted and excessively wordy stylistic
approach detracted from Jefferson's concise legalistic writing. Nonetheless,
the development of the document, and notably, its dissemination, played a
crucial role in building a valid case on the world's stage for the rights of the
American colonists.

Not surprisingly, the style and substance of the document were a source
of contestation between authors. Most notably, evaluations of the drafting
process indicate numerous revisions on the part of Dickinson, both rejecting
and altering the phraseology employed by Jefferson. While Jefferson's influence is apparent throughout the text, historians generally accept that crucial
passages of the document are overwhelmingly, if not verbatim, the words of
Jefferson.[33] However persnickety Dickinson's objections may have been to
modify Jefferson's earlier drafts, what is clear is that the overall structure
and outline of Jefferson's drafts were followed. John P. Kaminski details the
influence of Jefferson's pen on the document, suggesting, "Unable to improve
upon Jefferson's closing four paragraphs, Dickinson incorporated them into
his draft, which Congress accepted. The rhetoric of these paragraphs was
characteristically Jefferson's—powerful, eloquent, stirring. It surely angered
the king and probably made reconciliation impossible."[34] The form of the
document, not unlike Jefferson's "Summary View," a technical device that
he would return to his 1776 drafting of the Declaration of Independence,
contains familiar themes: an origin story of the formation of the colonies; an
exposition of grievances typified in a pattern of abuses; a challenge to the
King and Parliament to prove their legitimacy; a direct appeal to reason as the

viable path to mediation; and a necessary shift from reason to direct violent action, a taking up of arms as the final option in combating tyranny.

For both Jefferson and Dickinson, the question of freedom is a central thread that connects each of the primary textual themes and claims. Dickinson opens the text in a tone perfectly illustrative of the scientific methods of the Enlightenment through a direct challenge to Parliament to prove their legitimate powers over the colonies. Since Parliament has consistently failed on this front, Dickinson, lifting direct text from Jefferson's two drafts, describes the situation of the colonists as dire, one that has commenced a change to a crucial plateau. "Enslaving these Colonies by Violence," Dickinson claims on the current condition of the colonists, legitimizes a particular type of action that, here, copying Jefferson's words again, renders it "necessary for us to close with their last Appeal from Reason to Arms."[35] The effects of this enslavement by violence help to shape Dickinson's understanding of freedom, a proposed perspective in classical republican terms. Since Parliament has shown an "intemperate rage for unlimited Domination,"[36] Dickinson is fearful that British America will persist as a colony defined by quasi-slavery indefinitely, manifest in their paternalistic approach. Dickinson cites a strong mandate of the Declaratory Act, which provided Parliament with a right to "make Laws to bind us in all Cases whatsoever," as evidence of their apparent desire to enslave the colonists.[37]

The depiction of this lack of freedom provided by Dickinson in the earlier passages finds further articulation in the closing sections by Jefferson. The continuing pattern of tyrannical behavior from Parliament and King George III had presented the colonists with a straightforward option. Both Jefferson and Dickinson indicate only two paths forward to remedy the colonists' plight: a "conditional submission" to tyranny as a further continuation of the status quo or a *"resistance by force"* to gain political freedom.[38] Such a dilemma positioned the colonists between the poles of tyranny and freedom. Although the conceptual framing of freedom by Jefferson and Dickinson, among other leading voices of dissent in the revolutionary period, conceived of an interplay between freedom and reason, a presentation that reveals more than it conceals an influence of liberal thought, there contains a recognition of the arduous struggle for freedom. A struggle of great importance that is strikingly devoid of a promise of attainment, as the battle for the winning of political freedom is always indeterminate, only narrowly left open on the horizons of history by perpetual contestation to resist its permanent enclosure. Importantly, Jefferson stakes the attainment of freedom for the colonists as a matter of life or death. "Servitude or death" remains the colonists' fate, inciting a necessary call to arms, a course of action that *may* or *may not* result in a reclaiming of freedom. Perseverance of this magnitude on the part of the colonists was undoubtedly influential. According to Jefferson and Dickinson, there was a resolute acceptance to "Die freeman rather than to live as slaves" in the struggle for independence.[39]

Central to the exposition of freedom by Jefferson is the place of history, specifically the heritage of the Anglo-Saxons. For Jefferson, the struggle for liberty serves as a defense, an attempt to reclaim what had been endowed upon them as a birthright from their ancestors.[40] Opposing the "voluntary Slavery" that awaits a continued relationship with Great Britain enlists a tribute to the "gallant Ancestors" of the colonists from whom and where they had received freedom.[41] In turn, a call to take up arms proceeds as a necessary route to avoid a surrendering of freedom, an ancestral blessing that was already fought and gained for by the Saxons.

Jefferson's hereditary claim of independence, first suggested in his assertion of continental acquisition via blood split in his "Summary View" and then again in "Declaration on Taking Up Arms" as a transmissible birthright, stirred objections by British loyalists and even the King himself. In the October 1775 convening of Parliament, King George III dismissed the colonists' claim of independence based on the rights and efforts of prior settlers. "The object is too important, the spirit of the British nation too high, the resources with which God hath blessed too numerous," he announced, pointing to the legitimacy of British rule, "to give up so many colonies which she has planted with great industry, nursed with great tenderness, encouraged with many commercial advantages, and protected and defended at much expence and treasure."[42] A few months following King George III's speech concerning British legitimacy, Jefferson would pen a response in January 1776, titled "A Refutation of the Argument that the Colonies Were Established at the Expense of the British Nation." In this text, Jefferson dismantles and attacks a prominent figure in the history of British colonization in North America by suggesting that Sir Walter Raleigh had received "no assistance from the crown."[43] Instead, drawing heavily from Hakluty's *Voyages*, Jefferson provides a chronological telling of colonial development largely absent of British influence and support. Since Raleigh's corporation was crucially separate and independent from the Crown, King George III's October 1775 speech emphasized that the American colonies owed Great Britain both a "natural or legal debt of gratitude" was untenable.[44] The actions by Raleigh and his companions were committed by free agents helping to erect a new society founded in a state of freedom through the enactment of a natural right of expatriation, yet consistent with a Whig perspective, as demonstrated in the mobility of the Saxons.[45]

Jefferson, would, once again, return to the idea of ancestral freedom to help make a case for American independence in his drafting of the Declaration of Independence. In his "Original Rough Draught," written between June 11–July 4, 1776, Jefferson directly references his recurring refutation of British entitlement over the colonies. "We have reminded them of the circumstances of our emigration & settlement here," Jefferson writes in the penultimate paragraph, "no one of which could warrant so strange a pretension: that these were effected at the expence of our blood & treasure, unassisted by the wealth or the strength of Great Britain."[46]

While Jefferson's claim of colonial freedom *qua* ancestral birthright in "Summary View" and "Declaration on Taking Up Arms" contains a certain dimensionality of conservative thinking, it escapes a static and fixed nodal point of thought by pointing to the possibility of an open future.[47] Central to Jefferson's promotion for colonial separation is continued domination's impact on future generations. To free "succeeding Generations" from the "wretchedness which inevitably awaits them" by the continuation of British tyranny, action by the colonists aims to destroy not only present-day oppression but, importantly, obliterate the yoke of "hereditary Bondage."[48] This is key to understanding Jefferson's political vision. It reveals that the people possess constituent power *always in the present* rather than the structural apparatuses of a *people-less* government. Jefferson's future-oriented claim suggests that the past and present can jointly enslave future generations in explicit and covert ways. It is not surprising that Jefferson would maintain a devout ecological concern for the land and a resolute insistence on abolishing laws, debts, and even constitutions every eighteen years and eight months to trigger a renewal and regeneration of political time-space.

Moreover, Jefferson's writing exposes the interconnection between freedom and civic action. Since the colonists are the constitutive force of an erected society within British America, rather than the parliamentary organs of the archaic Monarch, the autonomy of the colonies is derived from intra-society. The primacy of constituent political power thus rests in the hands of the colonists. At the same time, institutional barriers, such as the vice-admiralty courts, quartered troops, and appointed magistrates, had been improperly imposed upon the colonies. In this way, the powers of the Monarch and Parliament are necessarily secondary to the sovereign primacy of the colonists. Jefferson's steadfast call for separation as a path to independence illuminates a political relationship between *the people* (the colonists, in this case) and *the government* (represented here in King George III and Westminster Parliament). Challenges against this secondary tier of the political-power relation serve as a physical, often violent, reminder that society is derived and sustained by the people, not the culminating government force. To resist governmental power, then, exceedingly when it has erred in a continuingly destructive manner, is to reassert the primacy of the people to reclaim freedom. For Jefferson, this is the vital task of the colonists. A battle waged in opposition to an illegitimate sovereign force that has violently infringed upon the autonomy of a new society to reacquire a prior inheritance of freedom disrupted from a history of tyranny and reopens a possibility of space for all.

The concern for future-held-freedom expressed by Jefferson in "Declaration on Taking Up Arms" acquires a greater appreciation when situated alongside his understanding of property relations in the development of British America. For Jefferson, property holding was a necessary requisite for freedom. Access to property existed as a safeguard against forced entry into wage slavery by providing citizens with an ability to provide for their subsistence. It also, importantly, meant the absence of obedience to a force beyond one's authorship and control. Profoundly, it ensured freedom *from* tyranny. Jefferson's understanding of property, and its corresponding connection to economic equality, is intimately tied to political liberty as a deficiency in one realm directly detracts from the other. To Jefferson, politics and economics are inseparable, symbiotically related to the holistic development of an individual.

ALLODIAL HOLDINGS IN COLONIAL AMERICA, FIFTY ACRES FOR ALL, AND A RETURN TO THE HUNDREDS

The substantial thrust of his property worldview is sketched out in his "Summary View." Jefferson appeals to Anglo-Saxon practices of allodial property to show how it has been severely misunderstood in the American colonies, turning to the historical treatises of John Dalrymple, Henry Spelman, and William Somner, as he carefully notes in his Commonplace Books.[49] Rejecting the claim that property holdings in the colonies were instituted by the legitimacy of the Monarch's transfer, Jefferson traces the introduction of feudal property relations in Anglo-Saxon England. "Our Saxon ancestors held their lands, as they did their personal property, in absolute domination, disencumbered with any superior, answering nearly to the nature of those possessions which the feudalists term allodial," Jefferson attests.[50] While the Saxons were free from any superior force over their land, Jefferson suggests that William's conquest halted this practice following the Battle of Hastings. From this crucial moment, Jefferson notes that freedom experienced anterior to the disastrous Norman invasion became *interrupted*—including property holdings—by monarchical-feudal laws of possession. However, Jefferson contends that the Norman Conquest, and the subsequent insurrections that procured an enlargement of the kingdom, failed to bring about a total consolidation of property relations for *all members* of Saxon Britain.

Specifically, the Saxons' refusal to engage in a non-consensual transfer of allodial holdings to the Crown counteracted the scope of feudal conditions. In the practice of "persuasions or threats,"[51] Royal officials sought to force surrender from a withholding enclave of non-conformists. However, according to Jefferson's understanding of history as a "weapon in a perpetual struggle between liberty and tyranny,"[52] his reading of the Saxons offered substantial challenges against the Crown, refusing to capitulate and relinquish their property to a superior entity, even in the face of legal punishments inflicted by "Norman lawyers" to break their spirit.[53] The lands held by the Saxons, specifically those who refused to swear feudal fiat to the Crown, had crucially, therefore, "not been surrendered to the king" and, consequently, were not beholden to him.[54] In this way, an understanding of a hierarchical feudal system in England was a misnomer to Jefferson; instead, "Feudal holdings were therefore but exceptions out of the Saxon laws of possessions," rather than the rule.[55]

In Jefferson's view, the colonists' struggle was similar yet ripe with a possibility to transcend the imperfections of the Anglo-Saxons. Accordingly, Saxon's reliance on allodial holdings and, importantly, a challenge against an entry of superior power over one's property, continued to form the basis of common law *even* in the colonies.[56] Land grants bequeathed by the Crown in British America, often at the expense of small fees and rents, perpetuated a myth in the eyes of the colonists that all lands settled and vacant were held under the jurisdictional realm of sovereign monarchical authority *in perpetuity*. As a result, deception took root in the colonies as the first settlers were convinced that newly discovered lands were under the command of a foreign, transatlantic power upheld by feudal encumbrances.[57] For Jefferson, the Crown—operating behind a veil of duplicity—had violated the historical lineage of allodial property and a fundamental right of a new society to establish civil laws concerning property relations on their terms.[58] In Jefferson's view, this right—vitally denied to the colonists—forms civil institutions' basis and entire purpose within a specific society. A right that importantly showcases Jefferson's democratic leanings through his belief that a legislature or even an entire society assembled collectively can determine the governing principles of property.[59]

The fraudulent nature of the Crown's claim of title over British America signifies a grave transgression committed against the colonists, severely destroying the underlying foundational "art of government" predicated upon a necessary reciprocal exchange of honesty between the sovereign and the people.[60] For Jefferson, the Crown was guilty of severing such a vital bond between these two distinct bodies. The colonists must contest persuasion by word and force committed by the Crown to regain their right of absolute possession in British America.

The actions of the Anglo-Saxons toward the encroaching and pervasive usurpations at the hands of the Normans serve as historical proof of the validity of the American colonists' right to allodial property holding and justification for challenges—diplomatically and violently, if necessary—against the Crown. Again, Jefferson turns to the history of the Anglo-Saxons prior to the Norman Conquest to make his case. "America was not conquered by William the Norman," Jefferson holds, "nor its lands surrendered to him, or any of his successors." He continues, bringing history into the present moment into the colonists' pulsating need for action, "Possessions there are undoubtedly of the allodial nature. Our ancestors, however, who migrated hither, were laborers, not lawyers."[61] Jefferson's claim that the ancestors of America were not trained lawyers but rather laborers of the earth is crucial. It is important to recall that Jefferson views "Norman lawyers" at fault for their shrewd and scheming conduct that led to allodial landholdings being given up to the victorious, conquering Normans. In this light, lawyers were responsible for ending the lineage of rightful ownership of property in England and help-ing to institute a feudal system that left the people at the mercy of superior power. To Jefferson, these power-hungry minions of the Crown were not the true founders of the new American society. America, according to Jefferson, was discovered and cultivated by those committed to toiling the soil and establishing a system of self-government reminiscent of basic principles of the Anglo-Saxon tradition.

While Jefferson only tentatively alludes to a symbiotic relationship between property and politics in his "Summary View," just a year later, it would play a prominent role in his thought. In June 1776, Jefferson took up the task of drafting a new constitution for his home state, hopeful for its adoption at the Fifth Virginia Convention. Written during the same summer months, Jefferson's constitution drafts lack the sweeping, grandiose language expressed in the Declaration of Independence. However, its originality and radical vision are no less apparent and actual.

In his view of Virginia's new proposed government scheme, Jefferson would utilize institutional mechanisms to marry together idealistic promises of economic/political freedom and equality. Specifically, Jefferson sought to extend the vote to all free, male inhabitants of the commonwealth to pre-serve individual liberty, promote civic virtue, and obliterate patrician politics ordered by artificial titles of wealth and status. The economic dimension of Jefferson's position here is amplified when one situates his enlargement of the idea of the political, a shift from a politics of the few to the many to all, to his instrumentalist view of property that sees its real value as a means to protect individual freedom against a growing exploitive economic system in America.[62] In a letter addressed to Edmund Pendleton, written one month after his constitutional proposals were defeated in convention, Jefferson reveals the primary objective of his efforts.[63] He offers,

I was for extending the right of suffrage (or, in other words, the rights of a citizen) to all who had a permanent intention of living in the country. Take what circumstances you please as evidence of this, either the having resided a certain time, or having a family, or having property, any or all of them. Whoever intends to live in a country must wish that country well, and has a natural right of assisting in the preservation of it. I think you cannot distinguish between such a person residing in the country and having no fixed property, and one residing in a township whom you say you would admit to a vote.[64]

While Jefferson was keenly aware that his romantic proposal of a dynamic extension of suffrage would agitate his fellow Virginians, he opted to placate the sharp criticisms by implementing a property requirement for the vote. However, Jefferson's appeasement efforts were underscored by pragmatics and a sleight-of-hand mastery of logic to produce his intended conclusions. Establishing a property requirement for suffrage, Jefferson fixes the threshold at either one-fourth of an acre within the boundaries of a town or possession of at least twenty-five acres in the country. Importantly, this requisite merges property ownership with an individual's right to vote; however, in the final section of the draft, titled "Rights Private and Public," Jefferson effectively invalidates the condition. He writes, "Every person of full age neither owning nor having owned 50 acres of land, shall be entitled to an appropriation of 50 acres or to so much as shall make up what he owns or has owned 50 acres in full and absolute dominion."[65] From these premises, Jefferson, at once, implements a property requirement by barring those with less than twenty-five acres from voting, only to quickly reverse the claim by guaranteeing fifty acres to all those without the stated plot of acreage. The result is a syllogism *par excellence* effectively permitting all free men to vote precisely because of an assured holding in a property. It is crucial to note that Jefferson's efforts to extend the vote did not include women or racialized Americans.

Jefferson neatly concludes his egalitarian property plea with indirect homage to the allodial nature of the Anglo-Saxons. He urges, "Lands heretofore holden of the crown in fee simple, and those hereafter to be appropriated shall be holden in full and absolute dominion, of *no superior whatever.*"[66] What Jefferson is advocating for here is a return to a type of society that is not necessarily absent of divisions but is defined by the continuous action of citizens against an entry of superior power over the people. Jefferson's advocacy for land equality directly transforms into political equality enabling individuals to experience freedom on their terms rather than at the mercy of hierarchical and often arbitrary forms of governmental power. His identification with Anglo-Saxon commitment to allodial property-holdings *contra* feudal conditions permeates his constitutional modeling. The Anglo-Saxons of the pre-Norman invasion configuration thus became superimposed upon his bucolic, pastoral vision of the Virginian countryside as the optimal setting for enacting a politics of all.

Jefferson's understanding of how property functioned as a positive right for the Anglo-Saxons helped shape his condemnation of feudal and colonial *qua* monarchical-authority holdings of property in the American colonies. Jefferson's scorn for hierarchical, inequitable property divisions remained constant throughout his life-long writings, forming the nucleus for a permeating critique of liberal justifications of property outlined in Chapter V of John Locke's *Second Treatise of Government*.

Almost a decade after he attempted to grant fifty acres of land to all white males in Virginia, Jefferson expressed severe hesitation and concern over property inequality. Shortly after arriving in France to begin his duties as Minister Plenipotentiary, he penned an illuminating letter to Reverend James Madison on October 28, 1785. In the letter, Jefferson recounts an encounter with a "poor woman" forty miles outside of Paris in Fontainebleau. Eager to acquire insights into the conditions of the "labouring poor," Jefferson converses with her at length. He chronicles her daily struggles,

> She told me she was a day labourer, at 8. sous or 4 d. sterling the day; that she had two children to maintain, and to pay a rent of 30 livres for her house (which would consume the hire of 75 days), that often she could get no emploiment, and of course was without bread. As we had walked together near a mile and she had so far served me as a guide, I gave her, on parting 24 sous. She burst into tears of a gratitude which I could perceive was unfeigned, because she was unable to utter a word. She had probably never before received so great an aid. This little attendrissement, with the solitude of my walk led me into a train of reflections on that unequal division of property which occasions the numberless instances of wretchedness which I had observed in this country and is to be observed all over Europe. The property of this country is absolutely concentered in a very few hands, having revenues of from half a million of guineas a year downwards.[67]

Pondering the plight of the grateful Frenchwoman and the laboring class writ large, Jefferson asks a probing, potentially threatening question, "I asked myself what could be the reason that so many should be permitted to beg who are willing to work, in a country where there is a very considerable proportion of uncultivated lands?"[68] Echoing his proposed solution found in the 1776 Virginia Constitution draft, he admits that the "consequences of this enormous inequality" have tremendous "misery to the bulk of mankind," necessitating a much-needed political remedy.[69] "Legislators cannot invent too many devices for subdividing property," he proclaims, in an attempt to alleviate an "inequality of property."[70]

Jefferson continues his remarks on property inequality by summoning a Lockean position, albeit cautiously. Jefferson writes in a line of text that would fit seamlessly in the *Second Treatise*, "The earth is given as a common stock for man to labour and live on."[71] Jefferson's Lockean sensibilities of linking property with labor are certainly at play here; however, his argument carefully departs at this point, ultimately terminating a probable Lockean conclusion.[72] While Locke's proviso of "enough, and as good left"[73] would eventually reach its limits on the European continent, prompting a logical invitation to seek out new uncultivated lands in America; Jefferson foresaw the dynamics of a commercial society defined by individualistic liberal subjectivity as problematic for the new republic. Testing the limits of Locke's theory of property, Jefferson turns to a natural rights position to advance his argument. Unlike Locke, though, Jefferson's natural rights language deployed in the letter is not directly linked to a fundamental right of property but rather to his pantheon of natural rights: life, liberty, and the pursuit of happiness.[74] Jefferson makes the point, "Whenever there is in any country, uncultivated lands and unemployed poor, it is clear that the laws of property have been so far extended as to violate natural right."[75] While Jefferson's claim that the unemployed poor could reasonably take up appropriate open plots of land conforms to a Lockean impulse for further exploration of uncultivated vistas, Jefferson dramatically contests such a landing point. Instead, he concludes, *contra* Locke and, crucially, a corresponding acceleration toward Hamiltonian economics, by stressing that "it is not too soon to provide by every possible means" that all should possess, at the very minimum, "a little portion of land."[76]

Jefferson's insistence for a far-reaching redistribution of property, first detailed in his Virginia constitution drafting and then again in the more polemical and biting presentation of his October 1785 letter to Madison, is thus central for unpacking his views on property. On both occasions, a fear of an external, supreme power over the people helps to shape the contours of his urgings and recommendations. Jefferson advocated for the proper implementation of political devices to assuage the dehumanizing effects of property inequality. While his prescriptions to ameliorate the unequal effects of highly concentrated property holdings may be rendered palliative, the real thrust of his property worldview maturates within the conceptual bounds of his ward system.

In chapter 5, careful attention is paid to a June 1824 letter addressed to Major John Cartwright. In that letter, Jefferson sketched out the parameters of the wards, both in terms of territory and logistical operations, to showcase the far-reaching scope of his ideal configuration of a network of self-governments. What is necessary to stress is where Jefferson turns to in that letter to explain his vision of an extensive division of space into the form of the wards.

Jefferson opens the lengthy letter with an affirming tone, quickly situating the Anglo-Saxons as the rightful authors of the English Constitution. He continues, offering a historical telling, similar in substance to his January 1776 statement of refutation, albeit in abbreviated form, of the Normans' violations committed against the Anglo-Saxons. Taking direct aim at Tory interpretations of history, found archetypically in the thought of the "great Apostle of toryism,"[77] David Hume, Jefferson rejected a commonly held Tory position that saw the people as aggressors against the authority of the sovereign. Particularly, Jefferson condemned Hume's *History of England*, accusing the Scottish thinker of historical misinterpretation, which endangered America by its veneration of centralized forms of governmental power.[78] Deeply concerned over the engaging style of Hume's writings, such that it could potentially conceal inaccuracies to an inattentive reader, Jefferson was also alarmed by the content of his reading of history, explaining,

> He gave his history the aspect of an apology, or rather a justification of his countrymen, the Stuarts. Their good deeds were displayed their bad ones disguised or explained away, or altogether suppressed where they admitted no palliation, and a constant vein of fine ridicule was employed to disparage the patriots who opposed their usurpations, and vindicated the freedom and rights of the of their country. The success of this work induced him to go back to the history of the Tudors, and having now taken his side as the apologist of arbitrary power in England, the new work was to be made a support for the old. [. . .] *the powers of the Monarch were everything, and the rights of the people nothing.*[79]

Continuing, Jefferson expresses the dangers of Hume's thoughts on the American mind,[80] describing the detrimental effects, "he will become also the tory of our constitution, disposed to monarchise the government, by strengthening the Executive, and weakening the popular branch, and by drawing the municipal administration of the states into the vortex of the general authority."[81] Instead, Jefferson makes clear—in a point of significant commonality with radical Whig thought—that "all power is inherent in the people,"[82] and can rightfully challenge encroachments advanced upon them. In this way, Jefferson's scorn of Hume's Tory reading mutes the efficacy of Douglass Adair's analysis that relies on the solid compatibility and influence of Humean thought in the American revolutionary period.[83] Instead, Jefferson's tentative Whiggish historical rendition is situated alongside the events that precipitated the American Revolution, effectively linking the colonists' plight with the battle to reclaim the sense of freedom that defined the Anglo-Saxons anterior to the Norman invasion.

As Jefferson further expounds on the Anglo-Saxons/American colonists' ancestral exchange, he abruptly, yet skillfully, takes up the issue of renewal and revision in the realm of public affairs. Citing his efforts to modify the constitution of Virginia, he focuses on a key "improvement" that he is optimistic about adopting. "I hope they will adopt the subdivision of our counties into wards," he stresses, directly shifting the letter's focus toward the idea of the ward system.[84] He continues, first pointing to the physical specifications of each ward and then, importantly, to its historical equivalent, writing, "the former may be estimated at an average of 24. miles square; the latter should be about 6. miles each; and would answer to the *Hundreds of your Saxon Alfred*."[85] This passage helps to pivot the realm of politics away from a macroscopic plane to an intimate, fraternal localized setting. What is most interesting in the Cartwright letter is that Jefferson's coherent and detailed account of the operational capacities of the wards is placed in a historical dialogue with the Hundreds of the Anglo-Saxons.[86] The idea of dividing political space in line with the design of the Hundreds can also be found in David Hume's essay, "Idea of a Perfect Commonwealth." Turning "small-territory republic theory"[87] on its head, Hume contends, "Let Great Britain and Ireland, or any territory of equal extend, be divided into one hundred counties, and each county into one hundred parishes, making it all ten thousand."[88] However, Hume's call for division is offered as a plan to erect an extended body politic *contra* Montesquieu's small-republic theory to provide more *space* for the personal interests of citizens. The effects, according to Hume, will lead to a stable, well-balanced, large republic shielded from the direct sway and influence of the people. Summarizing a distancing between the people and higher seats of government, which "direct all the movements," Hume writes, "the parts are so distant and remote that it is very difficult, either by intrigue, prejudice, or passion, to hurry them into any measures against the public interest."[89] While Hume's use of division is striking—instrumental in shaping Madison's remedy for factions—the intent and implication of his vision and Jefferson terminate in opposite directions. Of course, Jefferson's impulse to position his wards within the same lineage as the Anglo-Saxons is not arbitrary. Instead, it once again circles back upon his reading of history, one that elevates the chronicles of a free people before an entry of domination.[90] Here, Jefferson's reference to Alfred the Great carefully exposes the rupture break in the Anglo-Saxons' experience of freedom, a move that, on the one hand, merges equality and liberty as an inseparable condition accessible only in a particular type of political community and, on the other hand, a necessary call for vigilance—and action—against the arrival of an external, superior force that relocates political authorship away from the people.

The political and economic autonomy of the Anglo-Saxons, carefully arranged in a township configuration that permitted the viable time and space for a life of independent subsistence, yet strikingly rooted through communal bonds, is key to surveying Jefferson's perspective on the interplay between freedom/equality and property. What the Anglo-Saxons demonstrated, according to Jefferson, before the conquest of the Normans, and then exemplified under an era of Alfred's kingship, was a challenge against external forms of power. Primarily, this emerged in a persistent opposition to a *giving-away* of one's right to life, liberty, and the pursuit of happiness through the utilization of property as a mechanism to safeguard against excessive exploitation.

From Jefferson's perspective, it is now necessary to explore the method of political action exercised by the Anglo-Saxons. Jefferson extrapolates from the history of the Anglo-Saxons an understanding of law creation *by the people* and the subsequent institutionalization of laws through governmental bodies as necessary sites for revision. A discussion is thus needed to evaluate Jefferson's understanding of the political challenges by the Anglo-Saxons toward ossified, settled laws and their corresponding impact on the possibility of political freedom and equality.

THE UNWRITTEN NATURAL LAW: CHALLENGING SETTLED FORMS

During his formal legal training at the College of William and Mary, Jefferson invested significant effort in examining the origins of English law. Citing Dalrymple's *An Essay Toward a General History of Feudal Property in Great Britain* and Francis Stoughton Sullivan's *An Historical Treatise of the Feudal Laws and the Constitution of the Laws of England* in his Legal Commonplace Books, Jefferson carefully studied the roots of entails as well as primogeniture.[91] Crucially, he concluded that neither was present in the township configuration of the Anglo-Saxons prior to the Norman Conquest and "were incompatible with liberty."[92] As a result, he saw the origins of these generational and hierarchical institutions as incompatible with nature and in violation of law, produced and ultimately maintained through force and deception.

Jefferson's concerns with the origins of entails and primogeniture—two crucial social institutions that prevent the full realization of political freedom and equality—and its connection with common law were significant. In both his lengthy dissertation on English common law and indicated by copious notes in his Legal Commonplace Books, Jefferson engages in a constitutional historical account through legal sociology to illustrate how a simple, natural system of laws defined the way of life for the Anglo-Saxons. Citing the prevalence of customs as a checking and ordering mechanism and a *commitment to unwritten laws*,[93] Jefferson firmly frames the arrival of the Normans as a critical turning point in legal history. In a February 10, 1814 letter to Thomas

Cooper, Jefferson casts blame on Norman lawyers—as previously asserted in his "Summary View"—but also, in a biting tone, on the "pious disposition of the English judges to connive at the frauds of the clergy."[94]

Jefferson's understanding of natural law in a simplistic coding and its subsequent corruption is featured prominently in his pre-revolution writings. Before the revolution, Jefferson went to great lengths to argue against the Crown's violation of natural law procured through heavy-handed taxation,[95] the suppression and suspension of the colonial legislative powers, and a subverting of allodial landholdings in favor of land tenure. Moreover, Jefferson's explorations into the origins of entails and primogeniture became a central feature of his efforts to help erect a more equitable and accessible Virginia. This commonwealth would be more appropriately aligned as a political community of free men. Specifically, his legal philosophy's natural law structure helped influence his energies to abolish entails and primogeniture. Discussing his proposed 1776 bill to abolish primogeniture and entail, Jefferson summarizes its intent and the effect of societal leveling.[96] He avows,

> The transmission of this property from generation to generation in the same name raised up a distinct set of families who, being privileged by law in the perpetuation of their wealth were thus formed into a Patrician order, distinguished by the splendor and luxury of their establishments. from this order too the king habitually selected his Counsellors of State, the hope of which distinction devoted the whole corps to the interests & will of the Crown. to annul this privilege, and instead of an Aristocracy of wealth, of more harm and danger, than benefit, to society, to make an opening for the aristocracy of virtue and talent, which nature has wisely provided for the direction of the interests of society, & scattered with equal hand thro' all it's conditions, was deemed essential to a well ordered republic.[97]

He links the necessity for abolishment to erase concentrations of wealth and status conferred across generations, cutting directly to his dislike of perpetuity. He writes, "the repeal of the laws of entail would prevent the accumulation and perpetuation of wealth in select families, [. . .] the abolition of primogeniture, and equal partition of inheritances removed the *feudal* and *unnatural distinctions* which made one member of every family rich and all the rest poor."[98] In this light, Jefferson sees the ending of primogeniture and entails in a purifying fashion, absolving future generations of the stain of feudal and unnatural hierarchies initiated by the Norman Conquest.

The repercussion of eradicating social barriers of rank thereby cuts two ways in Jefferson's analysis. Primarily, it demonstrates an impulse for a re-vindication of Anglo-Saxon principles, which imbues the very possibility that a community could be established upon an ethos that strives to erect a particular space in which all inhabitants are considered active participants.

Beyond the solid ancestral implication of Jefferson's efforts, there is also a decisively American strain of thought operating here. Namely, the 1776 bill aims to obliterate artificial distinctions to reopen a new plane of history for the progression of human rights. The purging of archaic titles suspends and then, at once, yet repeatedly through collective action, moves beyond an axis of domination through creating a new kind of society, one that announces its discontinuity with a conservative ordering of time, history, and politics. This position is key to Jefferson's entire progressive worldview and vision for an enlightened American nation-state. For Jefferson, barbarianism in America was a real threat that could potentially undermine and thwart an enlightened society from taking root. Crucially, Jefferson saw the High Federalists, steadfast conservatives, and religious fanatics as "barbarians" capable of initiating despotism at home.[99] The devasting outcome would lead to abolishing a free government and a villainization of science in favor of superstition and dogma.

Although Jefferson's understanding of English law and its treatment of the Anglo-Saxons was not wholly original—a track of thinking that was entirely consistent with English jurists of his time—there was an important distinction. Breaking with the narrative arc of the "Saxon myth" and English thinkers, Jefferson offered a uniquely fresh assessment of the key to the Saxons' creation and maintenance of a free society.

For Jefferson, the Anglo-Saxons were able to develop intellectually and physically and experience happiness precisely because they lived under customs, properly devising a legal system generated by nature. Central to this application of legality, Jefferson noted that it was the Saxons' impulse to resist the codification of law into written form. Instead, the Saxons were governed by controls of innate morality and societal mores that constantly prevented settling law, opting instead for the openness of law creation. In this manner, revision, scrutiny, and change became guiding principles of the legal system, devoid of permanently settled form.

Central to this position is the necessity for the people to challenge forms of tyranny constantly. This affirms both a Whig historical interpretation of politics and Sir William Blackstone's progressive telling of legal development found in the concluding chapter of his *Commentaries on the Laws of England*.[100] However, deploying either a Whig historiographical lens or a strictly sociolegal account suffices to capture the conceptual depth of his writings and what is at stake in his position. Jefferson's vision of the Anglo-Saxons moves beyond the struggles of an abstract image of the people—in a purely English setting—as well as a static reading of legal history by elevating the very idea of political action toward settled law and the exclusive authorship of law creation outside of the hands of the people.

Law, post-Norman invasion, as understood by Jefferson, thereby contains an element of intractable permanency that expresses myriad forms of oppressive power that is always in opposition to the people. The intricate, metaphysical structure of law exhibited by the nefarious behaviors of jurists, judges, and clergy stood not only as a rejection of natural law but, more importantly, as an institutionalized mechanism devised to separate the people from the very source of law creation, commanding obedience to a symbolic image of government power amassed with a total concentration of moral, political, and economic forces. To Jefferson, then, the transferal of law from an unwritten approach to codified form emerged as a weapon of discipline and conformity used by concentrated seats of authority, specifically the Monarch and church.

To salve the tyrannical elements of law found within the current English system and then injected into the colonies, Jefferson sees the idea of revision and custom as demonstrated by the Saxons as a method for emulation in British America. Elevated to the level of politico-historical importance, the plight of the American colonists emerges from a lineage of an interrupted experience of political freedom and equality. However, the American struggle was entirely new, endowed with a promissory offering to subvert governments' pitfalls of natural decay by instituting a politics of all. The Americans' political activities proceeded along the plane of the Anglo-Saxons to reclaim the sole authorship of law creation. This was necessary to obliterate settled forms of power and erect a society defined by self-government. However, the challenges enacted by the colonists signify not simply a continuation of a suspended lineage, but instead, a mutation from an ancient body politic that reaffirms its power against the decaying properties of time by opening new horizons for future generations to become the authors of their fate.

His historical reading greatly informed Jefferson's thoughts on mobility, freedom, property, and the law of the Anglo-Saxons. Central to his historical interpretation was a resuscitation and a reimagining of critical elements of Anglo-Saxon mythology that affirmed the colonists' belief in their "own special role in history."[101] Notably, Jefferson's historical lens acquired an understanding of ancestral right of movement, a resolute commitment to eradicate hierarchies of status for an opening of freedom for future generations, and a rejection of a legal system (which actively manages property relations) structured in opposition to the people. These points elucidated the second characteristic of a theory of radical democracy: a rejection of codified, entrenched laws that place authorship outside of self-government in favor of the constant renewal of guiding principles determined by the community itself. Jefferson's political philosophy thereby obtains a call for constant action against settled forms of power and authority. The desire for perpetual vigilance and challenges is central to the specter of radical democratic politics.

NOTES

1. TJ to James Madison, September 6, 1789, in Boyd, *PTJ*, 15: 392–98.

2. Merrill D. Peterson, *Thomas Jefferson & the New Nation: A Biography* (London: Oxford University Press, 1970), 57.

3. Joseph J. Ellis, *American Sphinx: The Character of Thomas Jefferson* (New York: Alfred A. Knopf, 1997), 34.

4. See TJ to Miles King, September 26, 1814, in Looney, *PTJ*, Retirement Series, 7: 704–6. Also, see TJ to John Adams, October 14, 1816, in Looney, *PTJ*, Retirement Series, 10: 458–61.

5. Garrett Ward Sheldon, *The Political Philosophy of Thomas Jefferson* (Baltimore, MD: The Johns Hopkins University Press, 1991), 25.

6. For a thorough discussion on the role that the Saxon myth played in the American Revolution and early founding, see H. Trevor Colbourn, *The Lamp of Experience: Whig History and the Intellectual Origins of the American Revolution* (Chapel Hill: University of North Carolina, 1965); Reginald Horsman, *Race and Manifest Destiny: The Origins of American Racial Anglo-Saxonism* (Cambridge, MA: Harvard University Press, 1981).

7. On countless occasions, Jefferson recommends Tacitus's *Germania* as an essential historical text when developing reading lists for his friends and colleagues. See TJ, "Course of Reading for William G. Munford," December 5, 1798, in Oberg, *PTJ*, 30: 594–97; "A Course of Reading for Joseph C. Cabell," September 1800, in Oberg, *PTJ*, 32: 176–81; TJ to Mathew Carey, January 12, 1801, in Oberg, *PTJ*, 32: 447.

8. Jon Meacham, *Thomas Jefferson: The Art of Power* (New York: Random House, 2012), 29.

9. TJ to George W. Lewis, October 25, 1825, Photostatic copy examined at the Albert and Shirley Small Special Collections Library, University of Virginia, Charlottesville, VA.

10. These two events mark significant moments in the history of political freedom. To see how they shaped the idea of freedom morally, legally, and politically, both on the continent and in America, see the following studies: A. J. Beitzinger, *A History of American Political Thought* (Eugene, OR: Resource Publications, 1972), Parts I, II, and III; J. G. A. Pocock, *The Ancient Constitution and the Feudal Law: A Study of English Historical Thought in the Seventeenth Century* (London: Cambridge University Press, 1987), Part II, Ch. III; Peter Linebaugh, *The Magna Carta Manifesto: Liberties and Commons for All* (Berkeley: University of California Press, 2008), Ch. VIII; Benjamin Fletcher Wright, *American Interpretations of Natural Law: A Study in the History of Political Thought* (London: Routledge, 2017), Chs. II and III; Max Radin, "The Myth of Magna Carta," *Harvard Law Review* 60, no. 7 (1947): 1060–91; J. C. Holt, *Magna Carta* (Cambridge, UK: Cambridge University Press, 2015), Chs. I, VIII, IX, and XI.

11. Norman K. Risjord, *Thomas Jefferson* (Lanham, MD: Rowman & Littlefield Publishers, 1994), 7–8.

12. Peterson, *Thomas Jefferson & the New Nation*, 57.

13. For the Saxon myth's influence on Jefferson and which texts helped shape this image, see Peterson, *Thomas Jefferson & the New Nation*, 57–61. Also, see Dumas Malone, *Jefferson and His Time: The Sage of Monticello, Vol. VI* (Boston: Little, Brown and Company, 1981), 202.

14. For studies on the presence of a Whig interpretation of history in early American thought, see Gordon S. Wood, *The Creation of the American Republic, 1776–1787* (Chapel Hill: University of North Carolina Press, 1998), Part I, Ch. I; Bernard Bailyn, *The Ideological Origins of the American Revolution* (Cambridge, MA: Belknap Press of Harvard University Press, 1992), Ch. II; Robert E. Shalhope, "Republicanism and Early American Historiography," *The William and Mary Quarterly* 39, no. 2 (1982): 334–56; Pauline Maier, *From Resistance to Revolution: Colonial Radicals and the Development of American Opposition to Britain, 1765–1776* (New York: W. W. Norton & Co., 1972); Alan Rogers, *Empire and Liberty: American Resistance to British Authority, 1755–1763* (Berkeley: University of California Press, 1974).

15. This idea that an infectious matter can linger within a body politic will resurface during the Constitutional Convention of 1787. In his June 18 speech on the plan of government, James Madison went as far as to liken the events surrounding Shays' Rebellion to a permanently noxious substance.

16. Andrew Burstein and Nancy Isenberg, *Madison and Jefferson* (New York: Random House, 2010), 30–31.

17. See Stephen Howard Browne, "Jefferson's First Declaration of Independence: A Summary View of the Rights of British America Revisited," *Quarterly Journal of Speech* 89, no. 3 (2003): 235–52.

18. TJ, "A Summary View of the Rights of British America: Set Forth in Some Resolutions Intended for the Inspection of the Present Delegates of the People of Virginia, Now In Convention," American Imprint Collection, *Thomas Jefferson Library Collection*, Library of Congress, Washington, D.C. (Williamsburg, VA: Printed by Clementina Rind, 1774), 6.

19. TJ, "Summary View," 6.

20. Ibid.

21. Ibid.

22. For the aesthetic dimension of Jefferson's argument, see Jay Fliegelman, *Declaring Independence: Jefferson, Natural Language & the Culture of Performance* (Stanford, CA: Stanford University Press, 1993), 52.

23. Scott Douglas Gerber, *To Secure These Rights: The Declaration of Independence and Constitutional Interpretation* (New York: New York University Press, 1995), 49–50.

24. TJ, "Summary View," 6.

25. Allen Jayne, *Jefferson's Declaration of Independence: Origins, Philosophy, and Theology* (Lexington: The University Press of Kentucky, 1998), 53–55.

26. TJ, "Summary View," 9.

27. See Oliver Morton Dickerson, *The Navigation Acts and the American Revolution* (New York: A. S. Barnes, 1963).

28. TJ, "Summary View," 10.

29. For insights into Jefferson's unwavering commitment to free trade, see Stanley N. Katz, "Thomas Jefferson and the Right to Property in Revolutionary America," *The Journal of Law & Economics* 19, no. 3 (1976): 467–88; Robert W. Tucker and David C. Hendrickson, *Empire of Liberty: The Statecraft of Thomas Jefferson* (Oxford, UK: Oxford University Press, 1990), 17–30, 212; Merrill D. Peterson, "Jefferson and Commercial Policy, 1783–1793," *The William and Mary Quarterly* 22, no. 4 (1965): 584–610.

30. Alf J. Mapp, Jr., *Thomas Jefferson: America's Paradoxical Patriot* (Lanham, MD: Rowman & Littlefield Publishers, 1987), 82.

31. See TJ's earlier drafts, "Composition Draft," June 26–July 6, 1775 in Boyd, *PTJ*, 1: 193–99; "Fair Copy for the Committee," June 26–July 6, 1775, in Boyd, *PTJ*, 1: 199–204.

32. See Natalie S. Bober, *Thomas Jefferson: Draftsman of a Nation* (Charlottesville: The University of Virginia Press, 2007), 89.

33. For an excellent account of the mystery surrounding the text's authorship, see "Editorial Note: Declaration of the Causes and Necessity for Taking Up Arms," *PTJ*, 1: 187–92. A definitive answer is clouded by Jefferson's claim in his *Autobiography* of 1821 that he was the original author. This stood in opposition to Dickinson's 1801 assertion of authorship. Before Boyd's editorial note, historians commonly accepted that Jefferson was primarily responsible for the text's final four and a half paragraphs. However, an analysis of Jefferson's two earlier drafts and Dickinson's "Composition Draft" of late June and early July 1775 suggests that explicit language and phrases written by Jefferson were interspersed throughout the document, not simply in its final passages. For TJ's claim, see *The Writings of Thomas Jefferson*, vol. 1: 1760–1775, ed. Paul Leicester Ford (New York: G. P. Putnam's Sons, 1892), 463. For the 1801 assertion that the document has "always been ascribed to the pen of Mr. Dickinson," see *The Political Writings of John Dickinson, Esquire, Late President of the State of Delaware, and of the Commonwealth of Pennsylvania*, vol. 2, Archives and Special Collections, Dickinson College, Carlisle, PA (Wilmington, DE: Bonsal and Niles, 1801), 2.

34. John P. Kaminski, *Thomas Jefferson: Philosopher and Politician* (Madison, WI: Parallel Press, 2005), 19.

35. "The Declaration as Adopted by Congress," July 6, 1775, in Boyd, *PTJ*, 1: 213–19. In his "Composition Draft," Jefferson writes, "The large strides of late taken by the legislature of Great Britain toward establishing over the colonies their absolute rule, and the hardiness of their present attempt to effect by force of arms what by law or right they could never effect render it necessary for us also to change the ground of opposition and to close with their last appeal from reason to arms" ("Composition Draft," June 26–July 6, 1775, 193). Again, in his "Fair Copy for the Committee," he stresses the need to take up arms, writing that the current conditions "render it necessary for us also to change the ground of opposition, and to close with their last appeal from reason to arms" ("Fair Copy for the Committee," June 26–July 6, 1775, 199–200).

36. "The Declaration," in Boyd, 213–19.

37. Ibid.

38. Ibid. Emphasis added.

39. Ibid.

40. Christopher Hitchens, *Thomas Jefferson* (New York: HarperCollins, 2005), 23.

41. "The Declaration," in Boyd, 213–19.

42. King George III's speech—delivered on October 26, 1775—opened the second session of the 14th Parliament of Great Britain. In it, he focused exclusively on the "present situation of America," referring to the colonists' as an "unhappy and deluded multitude," offering "tenderness and mercy" in return to them once they become aware of their errors. See "The King's Speech on Opening the Session" in *The Parliamentary History of England: From the Earliest Period to the Year 1803*, vol. XVIII, eds. William Cobbett and Thomas Cursor Hansard (London: Printed by T. C. Hansard, 1813), 695–98. Jefferson most likely did not become aware of this speech until January 1776, when reported in the January 19 edition of the *Virginia Gazette*, No. 51.

43. TJ, "Refutation of the Argument that the Colonies were Established at the Expense of the British Nation, after 19 January 1776," in Boyd, *PTJ*, 1: 277–85.

44. Fliegelman, *Declaring Independence*, 145. Also, see Christopher Michael Curtis, *Jefferson's Freeholders and the Politics of Ownership in the Old Dominion* (Cambridge, UK: Cambridge University Press, 2012), 49; Brian Steele, *Thomas Jefferson and American Nationhood* (Cambridge, UK: Cambridge University Press, 2012), 32.

45. Hans L. Eicholz, *Harmonizing Sentiments: The Declaration of Independence and the Jeffersonian Idea of Self-Government* (New York: Peter Lang Publishing, 2001), 80.

46. TJ, "original Rough draught" of the Declaration of Independence," June 11–July 4, 1776, in Boyd, *PTJ*, 1: 423–28.

47. Jefferson clarifies that the American republic must not look back to their ancestors for emulation but rather forward into an open history. Directly separating the American experiment from the Anglo-Saxons and a conservative ordering, he contends, "it suffices for a man to be a philosopher, and to believe that human affairs are susceptible of improvement, & to look forward, rather than back to the Gothic ages." See TJ to Thomas Mann Randolph, May 3, 1798, in Oberg, *PTJ*, 30: 325–27. Also, see TJ to Joseph Priestley, January 27, 1800, in Oberg, *PTJ*, 31: 339–41.

48. "The Declaration," in Boyd, 213–19.

49. Curtis, *Jefferson's Freeholders*, 23.

50. TJ, "Summary View," 20.

51. Ibid., 20.

52. Francis D. Cogliano, *Thomas Jefferson: Reputation and Legacy* (Charlottesville: The University of Virginia Press, 2006), 23.

53. TJ, "Summary View," 20.

54. Ibid.

55. Ibid.

56. Harold Hellenbrand, *The Unfinished Revolution: Education and Politics in the Thought of Thomas Jefferson* (Newark: University of Delaware Press, 1990), 99.

57. James R. Stoner, "Jefferson and the Common Law Tradition," in *Reason and Republicanism: Thomas Jefferson's Legacy of Liberty*, eds. Gary L. McDowell and Sharon L. Noble (Lanham, MD: Rowman & Littlefield Publishers, 1997), 108.

58. See Karl Lehmann, *Thomas Jefferson, American Humanist* (Charlottesville: The University Press of Virginia, 1985), 95–96.

59. TJ, "Summary View," 21. After advancing this position, Jefferson clarifies that if a delegated sovereign authority does not determine property relations, an individual may appropriate only vacant land, conferring title through occupancy. Notably, the individual remains a member of society and is thus not transplanted or inserted into a state of nature devoid of governing customs or habits.

60. Significantly, Jefferson's claim here emerges at the sweeping conclusion of his "Summary View." The line of text preceding his contention that government impinges upon honesty further reveals his inclusive moral philosophy. This point further separates him from other thinkers, notably John Adams and James Madison. Jefferson writes, "The great principles of right and wrong are legible to every reader; to pursue them requires not the aid of many counsellors." Demonstrating a touch of Scottish thought rather than strict English liberalism, Jefferson's position highlights an innate moral code in individuals and their capacity to read, think, scrutinize, and engage in democratic politics. See TJ, "Summary View," 22–23.

61. TJ, "Summary View," 20. In his initial draft, Jefferson wrote "farmers" rather than "laborers." However, Jefferson amended the phrase, first superimposing "laborers," then again in another round of revisions, deleting "farmers" before handing it over to the Virginian delegates headed to the Continental Congress. See TJ, "Draft of Instructions to the Virginia Delegates in the Continental Congress (M.S. Text of *A Summary View*, &c.)," July 1774, in Boyd, *PTJ*, 1: 121–37.

62. Jefferson's view of property as a social/political construct and its importance in preventing excessive poverty levels and its corresponding impact on political freedom is not a far step away from Jean-Jacques Rousseau's republican considerations. Although Rousseau refers to property as a "sacred right" in "Discourse on Political Economy" (128), he, much like Jefferson, denies that it is a *natural right*. For Rousseau, legislation is warranted to prevent the ill effects of unequal property and wealth inequality, as proposed in *On The Social Contract* (BK II, Ch. XI; 170–72). However, Rousseau's theory aims at a specific type of topography, decisively landlocked compared to Jefferson's open terrain of the North American continent. See Jean-Jacques Rousseau, *The Basic Political Writings*, trans. Donald A. Cress (Indianapolis, IN: Hackett Publishing Company, 1987).

63. Jefferson was highly disenchanted by the ratification of the Virginia Constitution of 1776, referring to it in his *Notes* as responsible for producing an "elective despotism." Primarily, Jefferson was frustrated with the passage of a unicameral House of Assembly and the disproportionate legislative representation for the populace. According to Jefferson, the drafting of the Constitution ultimately failed because it was constructed by those "new and unexperienced [sic] in the science of government." Jefferson does admit that he, too, was not immune from this problem. See TJ, *Notes*, 121–23.

64. TJ to Edmund Pendleton, 26 August 1776, in Boyd, *PTJ*, 1: 503–6.

65. TJ, "Third Draft," before June 1776, in Boyd, *PTJ*, 1: 356–65.

66. Ibid. Emphasis added.

67. TJ to James Madison, October 28, 1785, in Boyd, *PTJ*, 8: 681–83.

68. Ibid.

69. Ibid.

70. Ibid.

71. Ibid.

72. Richard K. Matthews and Elric M. Kline argue convincingly that Jefferson's October 28, 1785 letter should be read as an "implicit transcendence of Locke's theory of property," highlighting the intertwined nature of "property, equality, and economic freedom" to Jefferson's political philosophy. See Richard K. Matthews and Elric M. Kline, "Jefferson Un-Locked: The Rousseauan Moment in American Political Thought," in *History, On Proper Principles: Essays in Honor of Forrest McDonald*, eds. Lenore T. Early and Stephen M. Klugewicz (Wilmington, DE: ISI Books, 2010), 133–66.

73. John Locke, *Second Treatise of Government*, ed. C. B. Macpherson (Indianapolis, IN: Hackett Publishing Company, 1980), Ch. V, §33, 21.

74. While these three rights are famously attached to the legacy of Jefferson, he crucially links these rights with the natural right of expatriation, which was explicitly influenced by his historical reading of the Anglo-Saxons. The connection between the tripartite classification of first-order natural rights and the right to free mobility can be in Jefferson's efforts to amend the Virginia Constitution and, later, in epistolary form. See TJ, "A Bill Declaring Who Shall Be Deemed Citizens of This Commonwealth," June 18, 1779, in Boyd, *PTJ*, 2: 476–79; TJ to John Manners, June 12, 1817, in Looney, *PTJ*, Retirement Series, 11: 432–34.

75. TJ to James Madison, October 28, 1785, in Boyd, *PTJ*, 8: 681–83.

76. Ibid.

77. TJ to John Cartwright, June 5, 1824, *TJP* at the Library of Congress, Series 1: General Correspondence, 1651–1827, microfilm reel: 054, image 2.

78. See Douglas L. Wilson, "Jefferson vs. Hume," *The William and Mary Quarterly* 46, no. 1 (1989): 49–70.

79. TJ to Matthew Carey, November 22, 1818, *TJP* at the Library of Congress, Series 1: General Correspondence, 1651–1827, microfilm reel: 051, images 1–4. Emphasis added.

80. Jefferson went as far as to suggest that a corrected version of Hume's *History of England* be released in America. Jefferson unsuccessfully lobbied to have John Baxter's *A New Impartial History of England* published to replace Hume's text in the later years of his life. See TJ to William Duane, August 12, 1810, in Looney, *PTJ*, Retirement Series, 3: 4–7; TJ to George Washington Lewis, October 25, 1825, *TJP* at the Library of Congress, Series 1: General Correspondence, 1651–1827, microfilm reel: 055, images 1–4.

81. TJ to Matthew Carey, November 22, 1818, images 1–4.

82. TJ to John Cartwright, June 5, 1824, image 2.

83. See Douglass Adair, *The Intellectual Origins of Jeffersonian Democracy: Republicanism, the Class Struggle, and the Virtuous Farmer*, ed. Mark E. Yellin (New York: Lexington Books, 2000), Chs. 6 and 7. Mainly, Adair shows the influence of Hume's thought on James Madison and Alexander Hamilton, especially in their conception of man and governmental design. Also, see Douglass Adair, *Fame and the*

Founding Fathers: Essays of Douglass Adair, ed. H. Trevor Colburn (Indianapolis, IN: Liberty Fund, 1998), 132–75.

84. TJ to John Cartwright, June 5, 1824, image 3.

85. Ibid. Emphasis added.

86. See Eric P. Kaufman, *The Rise and Fall of Anglo-America* (Cambridge, MA: Harvard University Press, 2004), 21.

87. Adair, *The Intellectual Origins of Jeffersonian Democracy*, 132.

88. David Hume, *Hume's Moral and Political Philosophy*, ed. Henry D. Aiken (New York: Hafner Publishing Company, 1948), 375.

89. Ibid., 385.

90. The idea of replicating land following the geometric and population patterns of the Hundreds seems to have haunted Jefferson's thoughts for over four decades. Strikingly, his writings concerning the Hundreds were presented as a panacea: a feasible way to construct a more equitable and accessible educational system at the local level. See TJ, "A Bill for the More General Diffusion of Knowledge," June 18, 1779, in Boyd, *PTJ*, 2: 526–35; TJ to Peter Carr, September 7, 1814, in Looney, *PTJ*, Retirement Series, 7: 636–42; TJ, "27 July, 1821, Autobiography Draft Fragment, 6 January through 27 July," *TJP* at the Library of Congress, Series 1: General Correspondence, 1651–1827, microfilm reel: 052, image 25.

91. See TJ, "Legal Commonplace Book," *TJP* at the Library of Congress, Series 5: Commonplace Books, 1758–1772, microfilm reel: 059.

92. Herbert E. Sloan, *Principle and Interest: Thomas Jefferson and the Problem of Debt* (Charlottesville: The University of Virginia Press, 1995), 70.

93. It is important to note that Jefferson's fascination with the Anglo-Saxons centered primarily on their written language. Jefferson was so enamored by the Saxons' development of an alphabet, orthography, linguistic pronunciations, and grammatical structure that he composed a lengthy, detailed account of its influence on the English language. Written a year before his death, Jefferson strongly advocated for his essay on language to be taught at the University of Virginia. See TJ, "An Essay Toward Facilitating Instruction in the Anglo-Saxon and Modern Dialects of the English Language for the Use of the University of Virginia," (New York: J. F. Trow, Printer, 1851). This pamphlet was printed and disseminated under the order of the Board of Trustees at the University of Virginia.

94. TJ to Thomas Cooper, February 10, 1814, in Looney, *PTJ*, Retirement Series, 7: 190–91.

95. Here, Jefferson drew from Paul de Rapin-Thoyras's *History of England*, helping to shape his critique of excessive taxation, mainly when levied by the will of the Crown against the people. See Kevin J. Hayes, *The Road to Monticello: The Life and Mind of Thomas Jefferson* (Oxford, UK: Oxford University Press, 2008), 26–27. Also, see H. Trevor Colburn, "Thomas Jefferson's Use of the Past," *The William and Mary Qua rterly* 15, no. 3 (1958): 60.

96. See TJ, "Bill to Enable Tenants in Fee Tail to Convey Their Lands in Fee Simple," October 14, 1776, in Boyd, *PTJ*, 1: 560–62.

97. TJ, "6 January 1821, Autobiography Draft Fragment," *TJP* at the Library of Congress, Series 1: General Correspondence, 1651–1827, microfilm reel: 052, image 13.

98. Ibid., image 26. Emphasis added.

99. TJ to Joseph Priestly, March 21, 1801, in Oberg, *PTJ*, 33: 395–98.

100. Affirming the role of ancestors in the development of English law, Blackstone writes, "The protection of THE LIBERTY OF BRITAIN is a duty which they owe to themselves, who enjoy it; to their ancestors, who transmitted it down; and to their posterity, who will claim at their hands this, the best birthright, and noblest inheritance of mankind." See William Blackstone, *Commentaries on the Laws of England* (Buffalo, NY: William S. Hein & Co., 1992), 436. This argument is extensively discussed in BK IV, Ch. XXXIII, "Of the rise, progress and gradual improvements of the laws of England."

101. Bailyn, *The Ideological Origins of the American Revolution*, 80–81.

Chapter 3

Politics Without Centralized Government

Political Power and Happiness in Indigenous Societies

In January 1787, Jefferson penned two letters that underscore his political vision. These letters—addressed to Edward Carrington and James Madison—importantly point to his understanding of the social organization and political regimes. In them, he briefly sketches out a political typology that places societies *without* a centralized government as the optimal configuration of society. According to Jefferson, these types of communities—ones notably absent of a coercive governmental apparatus and positive law—are best represented by the indigenous cultures of North America.

Jefferson's regime classification serves as empirical *proof* of man's sociability in a naturalized setting, one that is carefully devoid of tyrannical or corruptive forms of governmental power. This regime typology reveals the ontological source of Jefferson's vision of political power: its radical communal orientation. Politics understood in this manner comes to embody the interplay between individuals as a decision-making process generated through opinion, discussion, and sharing that makes "everything else possible,"[1] reveals a defining feature of Jefferson's political vision: less government, more politics.

This chapter examines Jefferson's view on the moral nature and communal ethos of indigenous societies in North America. In so doing, I engage in a presentation that is both conceptual and historical to draw out his thinking on political power, happiness, and societal forms. As a result, I argue that such a reading elicits the third characteristic of radical democracy: a moral and sociable view of human nature compels political subjects to collaborate with a powerless figurehead, serving as a conciliator for internal peace and harmony.

To demonstrate this side of Jefferson's thought, two primary study deposits will be explored. Firstly, two central sections, Query VI, "Productions, mineral, vegetable, and animal," and Query XI, "Aborigines," from his *Notes on the State of Virginia*, which were first completed in 1781 and later revised in the winter of 1782, are utilized. In this text, Jefferson carefully explores the North American continent's linguistic, cultural, and environmental conditions, offering a strong condemnation of the French naturalist Comte de Buffon's claim of the inferiority of the New World compared to European society. Secondly, drawing upon a careful assortment of letters ranging from 1787 to 1824, Jefferson's limited analysis of indigenous societies provided in *Notes on Virginia* will be supplemented and enhanced. While these letters are brief and fail to construct a systematic theory, they further point to a new plane of Jefferson's thought, one that locates and further envisions communities without centralized government, yet remarkably peaceful, participatory, and harmonious.

Engaging in the act of textual reconstruction is undoubtedly an act of theorizing. It is to interrogate a text's particularities to provide a coherent mapping of the topography of the text itself. Our current reading of Jefferson, and consequently his appraisal of indigenous societies, should be seen as an exercise in political theorizing. However, to ignore Jefferson's quest for an "empire of liberty,"[2] seen in his writings on western development and more concretely discernable in his acquisition of Louisiana, is to forgive America's impulse for expansion and its subsequent erasure of entire populations.[3] Therefore, a critical viewpoint of Jefferson is undoubtedly warranted, and more scholarship is needed on how America's founding is predicated upon an incompatibility with a non-white, non-propertied identity.[4] Even Jefferson's quasi-scientific, anthropological interpretations found in his *Notes on Virginia* are a source of trepidation. Robert A. Williams, Jr. suggests it was an attempt to integrate "Indians into the social evolutionary theories mapped out by the then-fashionable eighteenth-century Scottish school on human civilization's progress."[5] The effect of such a commitment was supported by a plan that sought to establish that the societal organization of Native Americans "had nothing to do with America's potentiality for surpassing Europe."[6]

The point of this chapter is neither to ignore the acts of genocide that were central to Indian policy of the early republic nor the settler-colonial impulse to conquer the western frontier. This chapter rests on a lacuna—mindful and vigilant of historical processes of violence, on the one hand, and cautious, yet open to a revisionist perspective, on the other—that presents Jefferson in a fashion that challenges and expands the norms of his thought.

AMERICAN DEGENERATION AND AN INVITATION

In late 1780, Jefferson received a correspondence containing twenty-two questions about Virginia's historical, geographical, and political development. Marquis François de Barbé-Marbois, Secretary to the French Minister, La Luzerne, sent the query, Jefferson recalls in his *Autobiography*, as he was "instructed by his government to obtain such statistical accounts of the different states of our Union, as might be useful for their information."[7] Marbois's inquiries were exhaustive and far-reaching, ranging from the "particular Customs and manners that may happen to be received in that State" to "a description of the Indians established in the State before the European Settlements and of those who are still remaining."[8]

The questions by Marbois challenged Jefferson, spurring him to set out on a detailed, scientific, and historical reply to the probing inquiry. The result would be enormous—a landmark work of the eighteenth-century thought—producing Jefferson's most popular completed manuscript:[9] *Notes on the State of Virginia*. "I had always made it a practice whenever an opportunity occurred of obtaining any information of our country," Jefferson commented on his desire to entertain the litany of questions from the French delegate, "which might be of use to me in any station public or private, to commit it to writing."[10] Written over two years (1781–1782), the loosely formed manuscript arrived with Jefferson in Paris in 1785. After rounds of revision, both correcting and enlarging the text, Jefferson had two hundred copies printed, gifting them to friends in Europe and back home in America.[11]

While Marbois's invitation offered Jefferson a much-needed return to philosophical and scientific investigations, an avenue of activity that had been sparse in the years preceding his *Notes on Virginia* due to duties as Governor of Virginia, there remained a primary incentive to deliver a thorough analysis. Specifically, Jefferson saw the opportunity as ripe to refute the work of French naturalist Comte de Buffon and his critical opinions of the New World. According to Jefferson, Buffon was the greatest of all naturalists, particularly in the science of animal history. In *Histoire Naturelle: Générale et Particulière*, a comprehensive thirty-six volume study, Buffon provided his theory of the superiority of the Old World compared to the degenerative nature of the New World couched within "a massive review of the entire history of life."[12] The central substantive claims concerning American degeneracy appear in Volumes IX and XIV as Buffon carefully laid out his condemnation of the continent's limited nature.[13] Jefferson was fully aware of Buffon's flimsy assertion on the nature of America, quoting a central line of text in his *Notes on Virginia*: "'*La nature vivante est beaucoup moins agissante, beaucoup moins forte*'; that nature is less active, less energetic on one side of the globe than she is on the other."[14]

Across these two volumes, Buffon accentuates his thesis of degeneration in four essential treatises, "Dissertation on Animals Peculiar to the Old World," "Dissertation on Animals Peculiar to the New World," "Dissertation on Animals Common to Both Continents," and, finally, "Treatise of Degeneration of Animals." According to Buffon, the absence of certain animals in the New World is especially telling. Buffon stresses that the vital deficiency of magnificent creatures in the New World, such as the elephant, lion, and tiger, suggests that a limited and stunted nature is at play on the continent.[15] Consequently, since these animals could not be found in America, *something* had to be problematic within its confines. While Buffon's illustration of a defective sense of nature in the New World provided a contextual background to his analysis, its effect was stirring, grounded on four central claims. Jefferson summarizes these assertions in his *Notes on Virginia* in list form: "1. That the animals common both to the old and new world, are smaller in the latter. 2. That those peculiar to the new are on a smaller scale. 3. That those which have been domesticated in both have degenerated in America; and 4. That on the whole, it exhibits fewer species."[16] The reason behind the degenerative condition of nature in America was apparent to Buffon; the New World was colder and contained more humidity due to moisture.[17] A colder climate inhibited the propagation of particular creatures that required a warmer setting. For this reason, large and stunning animals could only be found in the hot environment of the Old World.

Buffon's climate claim was also more thoroughly connected to his mapping of geographic migration. In Buffon's view, the North American continent was once linked to Eurasia via a land bridge enabling migration into the New World. Due to the poor climate of the continent, in large part because of its infant period of development that had "not had time to heat up or dry out,"[18] Buffon claimed that the inhabitants of the New World were biologically inferior. The key to Buffon's degeneration theory is his problematic view of indigenous peoples. In Volume IX, he provides a disparaging analysis of the biological, psychological, and cultural deficiencies of the "American savage." He writes,

> In the savage, the organs of generation are small and feeble. He has no hair, no beard, no ardour for the female . . . He has no vivacity, no activity of mind . . . He remains in stupid repose, on his limbs or couch, for whole days . . . They have been refused the most precious spark of Nature's fire: They have no ardour for women, and, of course, no love to mankind . . . Their love to parents and children is extremely weak. The bonds of the most intimate of all societies, that of the same family, are feeble; and one family has no attachment to another . . .

Their heart is frozen, their society cold, and their empire cruel. They regard their females as servants destined to labour, or as beasts of burden, whom they load unmercifully with the produce of their hunting, and oblige, without pity or gratitude, to perform labours which often exceed their strength. They have few children, and pay little attention to them. They are indifferent, because they are weak.[19]

While his views are damning, there also contains a claim of responsibility for the degeneration of the New World, one that holds indigenous peoples at fault for the deplorable conditions of the physical terrain and wildlife. In Buffon's assessment, the continent's animals were not culpable for its underdevelopment; however, indigenous peoples failed to *master* nature. By draining the swamps and engaging in a transfer of stagnant bodies of water, Buffon believes that such endeavors would produce an influx in humidity levels, ultimately increasing continental temperature levels and, in turn, mitigating a degree of degeneration. Speaking of the dissociation of indigenous peoples from an attempt to control nature, Buffon writes, "In these melancholy regions, Nature remains concealed under old garments, and never exhibits herself in fresh attire."[20] Continuing in a highly bombastic and metaphoric tone, one that renders a human quality to Nature, he claims, "Being neither cherished nor cultivated by man, she never opens her fruitful and beneficent womb."[21] Buffon's American degenerative thesis is thus tightly fashioned around the inferiority of both animals and indigenous peoples, with the continent's only shred of hope resting in the rapid development and cultivation undertaken by Europeans. In a rousing line, one that nearly forecasts the impending acceleration of territorial conquest and the destruction of indigenous populations, Buffon conjectures, "In several centuries, when the earth has been tilled, the forests cut down, the rivers controlled, and the waters contained, this same land will become the most fruitful, healthy, and rich of all, as it is seen to be already in the parts that man has cultivated."[22]

JEFFERSON'S REPLY

In Query VI of *Notes on the State of Virginia*, Jefferson provides his most detailed and calculated refutation of Buffon's American degeneracy hypothesis. In this chapter, "Productions, mineral, vegetable, and animal"—the most extended section of the work—Jefferson enlists table after table to challenge Buffon. While Jefferson does accept that climate may affect the development of animals, he makes evident that there is no evidence to support the tentative claim.[23] Instead, Jefferson sets out to debunk the theory of New World degeneracy by providing an exhaustive litany of statistical data on the population growth of specific animals in America compared to Europe. William Howard Adams points to Jefferson's efforts to affirm the natural features of America to assimilate nature into the political. Adams writes, "Jefferson had long recognized that the organization of the limitless countryside in his ideal American republic would have to accommodate both primitive nature and human intervention."[24]

The scene of Jefferson's analysis in Query VI is decisively Virginian. The depth of the land's natural resources is breathtaking as he provides a detailed enumeration: copper, coal, lead, marble, limestone, medicinal springs, and even "a single instance of gold."[25] Moreover, Jefferson details the high-volume, natural scope of the vegetative growth found in the state's trees, plants, and fruits. Across numerous pages, Jefferson catalogs native plants, indexing them based on utility categories concerning medicinal, esculent, ornamental, and fabrication.[26] Jefferson distinguishes between those species of plant life naturally found in the region and those cultivated by the productive forces of agriculture. In the latter, Jefferson showcases how farms, gardens, and orchards in Virginia produce plenty, capable of harvesting a diverse cornucopia of pleasures, including figs, apples, pumpkins, and pomegranates.[27] Jefferson then paints the fertile Virginian landscape as an archetype of the New World, a quasi-Eden abundant in resources and riches with a sweeping brush.[28] While Jefferson casts Virginia in the mold of a paradise-like setting, it also contains a dialectical dressing: freedom *and* slavery, growth *and* degeneration, fertility *and* desolation.

The way Jefferson confronts this negative, or dark side, of the state—meaning those elements both naturally occurring and those because of human activities[29]—proceeds along two distinct yet entwined paths: a zoological track and a cultural track. Jefferson's analysis stands *contra* Buffon to reject his thesis of American degeneracy on these fronts.[30] Instead, Jefferson argues that there exists an autochthonous dimension to the continent, both in a particular type of animal and in the societies of indigenous peoples—one that is essential, not inferior to the Old World.[31] Jacques Roger summarizes Jefferson's perspective, writing, "Jefferson made himself the strong advocate not only of the colonists settled in the New World but especially of the Indians of North America; he lauded their courage, moral and family virtues, loyalty in friendship, intelligence, and even eloquence [. . .]. The differences that could be noticed between them and *Homo sapiens Europaeus* came from those of lifestyle but did not imply innate inferiority."[32]

The first hint of Jefferson's zoological argument unfolds in Query VI. Here, Jefferson initiates an exploratory search for an elusive giant, "mammoth"-like animal known and described by the natives of the continent.[33] He hoped to show that an enormous creature—strikingly more prominent than the elephant or hippopotamus of the Old World—still exists, albeit only on the

North American continent.[34] Central to Jefferson's natural philosophy was the idea that all creatures were links in a chain, from the tiniest molecular level to a developed, enlightened human being to the mammoth of North America. By locating this near-mythological type figure, Jefferson stood to gain a successful refutation of Buffon's claim of more minor, inferior animals endemic to the New World. The key to discovering the mammoth was Jefferson's belief in non-extinction, suggesting that only particular specimens but not entire species could become extinct.[35] "It is certain such a one has existed in America," Jefferson comments on this grand *Americana* animal, "it has been the largest of all terrestrial beings."[36]

The haunting figure of Query VI only finds additional support for the larger size of other animals on the continent. Specifically, Jefferson presents numbers that affirm a heavier size of the black bear, otter, and flying squirrel in contradiction to Buffon's tabulation.[37] The zoological track of his analysis would not come full circle until nearly five years after his initial claims in *Notes on Virginia*. Upon arriving in Paris in 1785, Jefferson sent Buffon a copy of the text as a first step in discrediting and disproving his degeneracy theory. However, Jefferson knew that it would take more than detailed size comparison charts to persuade the prolific naturalist. What was needed was actual proof, a physical specimen that would change the Count's thinking on his views of the New World.[38] Jefferson's plan was complicated, but the idea was simple: an American moose must be sent to Paris.[39] After a complex set of arrangements to secure the transfer of the remains of a seven-foot-tall moose between Jefferson and General John Sullivan, the moose finally arrived, at Jefferson's jubilant reception, in late September 1787.[40] Almost immediately, Jefferson wrote to Buffon concerning his newly acquired treasure:

> I had the honour of informing you some time ago that I had written to some of my friends in America, desiring they would send me such of the spoils of the Moose, Caribou, Elk and deer as might throw light on that class of animals; but more particularly to send me the complete skeleton, skin, and horns of the Moose, in such condition as that the skin might be sowed up and stuffed on it's arrival here. I am happy to be able to present to you at this moment the bones and skin of a Moose, the horns of [another] individual of the same species, the horns of the Caribou, the el[k,] the deer, the spiked horned buck, and the Roebuck of America. They all come from New Hampshire and Massachusetts. [. . .] This is the animal which we call elk in the Southern parts of America, and of which I have given some description in the *Notes on Virginia*, of which I had the honour of presenting you a copy. [. . .] I really suspect you will find that the Moose, the Round horned elk, and the American deer are species not existing in Europe. The Moose is perhaps of a new class.[41]

Jefferson's enthusiasm was short-lived, however. Conflicting reports describe the events that followed the arrival of the moose in Paris. While the specimen box did arrive at Buffon's estate, the Count was away, and the shipment contents were "entrusted to his associate, L. J. M. d'Aubenton."[42] Jefferson attests to this delivery in a letter to Sullivan, writing, "He was in the country when I sent the box to the Cabinet so that I have as yet no answer from him. I am persuaded he will find the Moose to be a different animal from any he had described in his work."[43]

In a conversation with Daniel Webster at Monticello in 1824, Jefferson reveals the ending of the story, the outcome of his quest to elevate America's natural wonders in the eyes of the Old World. "After many difficulties, [Sullivan] caught my Moose, boiled his bones in the desert, stuffed his skin, & remitted him to me," Jefferson tells, continuing, "This accounted for my debt, & convinced M. Buffon. He promised in his next volume, to set these things right."[44] There was, of course, no subsequent volume of *Histoire Naturelle*, no denouncement of the theory of American degeneration, and no celebratory praise for Jefferson's judicious investigations. After receiving the moose, six months later, the world-renowned French naturalist, Comte de Buffon, was dead. Jefferson's endeavor to promote the terrain of the New World—including all peoples, animals, and physical elements linked together as a complete *natural* unit[45]—thus fell short.

While Jefferson's zoological track unfolded on two levels, primarily through the display of statistical data in *Notes on Virginia* and secondarily, with a theatrical, human presentation of the moose, it sought to level the playing field between the potentiality of nature within the Old and New Worlds, his cultural thesis of indigenous peoples "illustrated the excellence of nature on the American continent."[46] While Query VI was comprised primarily of Jefferson's natural history *contra* Buffon it also importantly contained his analysis of indigenous societies.[47] By embedding a classification of Native Americans in a framework of nature, a shift occurs from a plane of natural history *to* natural philosophy.[48] This transition enables the categories of morality and societal arrangement to be transposed upon a tableau of an American setting to demonstrate a social, moral reading of man, one capable of prevailing "over the dictates of power."[49] Much like Jefferson challenged Buffon's claims of a deficient nature of the New World, Query VI, in conjunction with Query XI, "Aborigines," functions as a refutation of an apolitical, pre-social telling of the indigenous peoples of the continent. Although these two claims—an inferior continental nature and a "backward," archaic interpretation of indigenous peoples—appear as distinct modes of inquiry, they function in concert as two sides of the same coin for Jefferson as a further instantiation of the potentiality for self-government within America precisely because of its natural and moral capacities.[50]

The first substantial claim that Jefferson accentuates about indigenous peoples, an integral point to the very possibility of a politics of all, is their innate moral sense. Here, Jefferson stresses that this claim of their moral code and their societies writ large are discernable due to the proximity of their associations to not only Jefferson, but to those he intimately trusts.[51] In this manner, Jefferson is staking his assertions on observable facts and interactions with indigenous societies. "I have seen of man, white, red, and black,"[52] Jefferson alleges. Of indigenous peoples in North America, "I can speak of him somewhat from my own knowledge, but more from the information of others better acquainted with him, and on whose truth and judgment I can rely."[53] A speculative account will not suffice; Jefferson, the scientist, needs verifiable data.

Jefferson begins by quickly disputing the mantle of the European narrative toward indigenous peoples. "I am able to say, in contradiction to this representation," Jefferson declares, "that he is neither more defective in ardour, nor more impotent with his female, than the white reduced to the same diet and exercise."[54] Instead, Jefferson provides a litany of behaviors, emotions, and expressions displayed by indigenous peoples complicating the prominent "barbaric" and "savage" framing. Jefferson insists that they exhibit a great display of bravery, a devoted, committed sense of friendship, and affection for their children.[55] These traits are indicative of communal bonds of duty and socialization, beyond strict contractual or consequential positions, that underscored Jacques Derrida's understanding of a politics of friendship. Derrida pointedly rejected a vision of atomized individuals, articulating instead a certain type of fraternal community populated by known and unknown friends associated with social bonds that are oriented toward the future.[56] Anticipating a community of friends to come, Jefferson is drawing out the fundamental basis of communal bonds found in indigenous peoples that stand in opposition to punitive, disciplinary institutions.

Sketching out the code of a warrior ethic, Jefferson identifies specific characteristics that are salient regarding actions of force and conflict. Mainly, an ethos of bravery blankets society as a source of honor, duty, and sacrifice. Undeterred by intense challenges, Jefferson claims that tribal warriors will confront countless enemies, often accepting a fate of death rather than a submission to surrender. When capture is unavoidable, the experience of torture takes on a near-metaphysical encounter, nearly equated but almost strikingly unknown to "religious enthusiasm with us."[57] The action method is unique through an elevation of stratagem over force to prevent personal injury. Jefferson asserts that action *qua* planning—a fundamental emblem of honor within tribal nations—clearly opposes a "civilized" society that teaches force *over* finesse. Accordingly, education is responsible for preparing a mandate of strength, a point which Jefferson carefully challenges, asserting that the technique of the natives may be natural.[58]

As bravery is framed as a mainstay of indigenous societies, Jefferson stresses that friendship, too, is indispensable. The strong sense of camaraderie is vital as he enlists a story of Colonel Byrd and his near-death experience with the Cherokee Nation. Sent to conduct business with the nation, Jefferson recalls how several of the "disorderedly" members of the delegation killed "one or two of that nation."[59] The tribal council decided that Col. Byrd would be put to death in response. Each night, as the fateful event drew near, the tribal chief, Shilòuee, would visit Byrd, conversing with him and allaying his fears of death. On the night of the intended execution, those nation members charged with the task entered the tent to seize Byrd. Before he could be whisked away, Shilòuee threw his body between the men and declared, "This man is my friend: before you get at him, you must kill me."[60] The chief's passion and intense friendship scene moved the men, and they returned to the council to decide. Friendship prevailed as the council capitulated and reversed the penalty of death initially levied upon Byrd.

As Shilòuee revealed indigenous peoples' moral, compassionate side, invoking a delicate touch of sensibility, Jefferson extends this sign of friendship into the very depth of their emotional reservoir. Dispelling a vision of cold, warrior-like brutes, Jefferson speaks to an emotive, rather than strictly analytic or irrational, side of tribal warriors. A tragedy within the nation, particularly the death of children, incites a "weeping" by the warriors.[61] This expressive quality of the warriors is not a sign of cognitive underdevelopment but a reflection of harmony between body and mind. According to Jefferson, indigenous peoples in North America are formed in the same mold as "Homo sapiens Europaeus."[62]

Jefferson suggests that bravery, friendship, and affection demonstrate natural morality from these positions. He advances this point in Query XI, a section dedicated solely to Virginia's linguistic, geographic, and population patterns of indigenous tribes. "Their only controls are their manners," Jefferson praises, "and that moral sense of right and wrong, which, like the sense of tasting and feeling, in every man makes a part of his nature."[63] The claim concerning Jefferson's disdain for promoting force brought forth through education thus comes full circle. Neither attainment of schooling nor utilizing an "artificial reason," as Charles A. Miller avows,[64] is responsible for an ethical code of responsibility. Instead, as indigenous peoples prove, morality is innate, *contra* moral justifications grounded in claims of self-love, reason, or even utility.[65]

It is essential to note precisely where Jefferson's claim of this innate moral sense appears in his *Notes on Virginia*. In Query VI, Jefferson provides his interpretation of natural history to elevate the physical capacities of America. Integral to those claims was the entry of a discussion on indigenous peoples, specifically their testimonies of the monolithic mammoth of the New World and critical societal elements. A conceptual bridging is thus employed in Query VI into Query XI, where his central thesis concerning morality is found. Highlighting the importance of the text's structure, Dustin Gish and Daniel Klinghard write, "The structure and methodology of the *Notes*, in other words, show Jefferson's concerted effort to overthrow authoritative claims of religion and of science that obscure and distort nature, thereby impeding inquiry into nature and its laws as a foundation for republican government."[66] The interplay between the physical terrain of the continent and the innate moral code of indigenous peoples is not coincidental. Instead, these two categories are consubstantial, helping to reveal his thinking on the interplay between space and politics. Both the fertile vastness of the land and an ethic of responsibility for others found in indigenous tribes render America a suitable model for developing a system of self-government.

To this point, I have explored Jefferson's belief in an innate moral rendering of members of communal societies. It is now necessary to unpack how power maneuvers within indigenous communities, particularly in the role of the figurehead.

The first central claim that is necessary to illuminate is Jefferson's descriptive account of the oratory skills of tribal chiefs. Here, Jefferson's presentation of the oratory capabilities of leaders is bold, importantly functioning as "the culmination of his description of Indians as objects of natural, historical interest."[67] Moreover, it offers a perspective that elevates the intellectual talents of indigenous societies above those of grand orators of antiquity. "I may challenge," Jefferson asserts, "the whole orations of Demosthenes and Cicero, and of any more eminent orator, if Europe has furnished any more eminent, to produce a single passage, superior to the speech of Logan, a Mingo chief, to Lord Dunmore [. . .]."[68] Jefferson proceeds to tell the story of Logan and the actions that inspired such an impressive show of oration after members of his family were murdered by settlers under the command of Captain Michael Cresap, near the Ohio River. To retaliate, three tribes joined together (Shawanese, Mingoes, and Delawares) to combat a band of Virginian militia fighters. In battle, the indigenous tribes were defeated, "sued for peace," and forced into accepting the terms of a treaty.[69] Logan abstained from attending the treaty proceedings, instead dispatching a message to Lord Dunmore, the Governor of Virginia. The distinguished chief proclaimed,

> I appeal to any say, white man to if ever he entered Logan's cabin hungry, and he gave him not meat: if ever he came cold and naked, and he clothed him not. During the last long and bloody war, Logan remained idle in his cabin,

advocating for peace. Such was my love for the whites, that my countrymen pointed as they passed, and said, "Logan is the friend of white men." I had even thought to have lived with you, but for the injuries of one man. Colonel Cresap, the last spring, in cold blood, and unprovoked, murdered all the relations of Logan, not even sparing my women and children. There runs not a drop of my blood in the veins of any living creature. This called on me for revenge. I have sought it: have killed many: I have fully glutted my vengeance: for my country I rejoice at the beams of peace. But do not harbour a thought that mine is the joy of fear. Logan never felt fear. He will not turn on his heel to save his life. Who is there to mourn for Logan—Not one.[70]

The requiem that Logan bestows is indeed sobering. For Jefferson, it show-cases—not just in actions but also in words—a strong sense of bravery within tribal councils. But, more importantly, Logan's solemn and grief-stricken words point to an innate moral sense of indigenous peoples, bringing to life an account of loss, pain, and remembrance. Its ending, too, is haunting, if not flat-out prophetic, of a certain sagacity of mourning, rhetorically ask-ing, not only who, if any, will provide a lamentation for Logan but also who will grieve the loss of a family, of an entire people eradicated in the name of progress?

While Jefferson's first claim of oratory excellence demonstrates an inti-mate connection between the leader and the ethos of the society, the second premise rests on the leader's mediation skills. Support for this claim is found in the *Appendix* of Jefferson's *Notes on Virginia*. While much of Jefferson's analysis of indigenous societies were generated from his observations and interactions, he also incorporated the opinions of valued colleagues. Printed in the *Appendix* are the remarks of Charles Thomson, perennial secretary of the Continental Congress, and his engagements with numerous indigenous tribes and nations throughout the continent.[71] According to Jefferson, these encounters warranted "too much merit not to be communicated."[72]

In Thomson's view, the chiefs of indigenous societies can typically be generalized as older men who have demonstrated significant prudence and skill in councils.[73] However, Thomson states that leadership does not rest along hereditary lines, as "strangers" have been selected to leadership posi-tions based on their fortitude and aptitude.[74] Once selected—often procured by either election or rotation—the chiefs play a vital role in society, engag-ing with various perspectives and gathering insights on pressing concerns. A council house is present within the community, where communal leaders and wise elders assemble to discuss important matters. This is a separate setting from the central council meeting locale of the tribe, which retains a symbolic value by representing a non-binding site of expertise, devoid of an authorita-tive command. Crucially, chiefs lack executive or even prerogative powers within the community. Instead, the chief serves as a physical and spiritual vessel to channel the opinions of the members into a collective voice. "Their governmeut [sic] seems to rest wholly on persuasion," Thomson thinks, adding, "they endeavour, by mutual concessions, to obtain unanimity."[75] Therefore, deliberation occurs between warrior-representatives and tribal counselors within a council setting through a type of power that is crucially non-physical yet underscored by a strong influence of generational tradition and respect. Here, dialogue between various actors is central, with the chief retaining only an advisory and mediatory function.

Bernard W. Sheehan confirms this point in his work, *Seeds of Extinction*, citing the Moravian missionary John Heckewelder,[76] "no magistrates, but advisors, to whom the people, nevertheless, pay a willing and implicit obedience, in which age confers rank, wisdom gives power, and moral goodness secures a title to universal respect."[77] So, what is to be made of Thomson, and to a lesser degree, Heckewelder's views in light of Jefferson's assertions in Queries VI and XI? Centrally, Jefferson speaks to an innate capacity for self-governance directly tied to a moral sense that, on the one hand, sees humans as active and social and, on the other hand, as guided by an ethic of responsibility for others. A social aspect, namely this commitment to self-government, is central to Jefferson's political philosophy. As Helen Ingram and Mary Wallace have argued, it is concurrent with a power to "define and reshape society."[78] Therefore, the transformative capacity of a society exposes the unique placement that the tribal chief plays in Jefferson's account. While the source of power—legitimate in form—rests in a communal orientation, its direction requires a particular level of expertise to help refine its commands. Functionally, this stands apart from Rousseau's Legislator by ushering in a leadership figure that only offers but does not institute collective decisions. The tribal chief holds a symbolic value: a figure that serves as a conciliator to ensure internal peace and harmony in a dialogical fashion, rather than an antagonistic or paternal relationship.

The restrained executive authority of the chief—a point that the French anthropologist Pierre Clastres further explorcs[79]—reveals how power is possessed and controlled within indigenous societies. It is suggestive of reliance on public opinion to internally govern a community that, in turn, shapes behaviors and customs while maintaining social exclusion and banishment as forms of punishment. The limited scope of influence by the chiefs coupled with a horizontal axis of communal power and the efficacy of moral public opinion, rather than a top-down flow of authority, thus functions as a checking mechanism within the societies.

In Query VI, Jefferson suggests that a central principle of indigenous societies centers on a prohibition of compulsion. While there is an unfettered, expansive sense of freedom within the members of the societies, Jefferson points out that there is a careful checking mechanism that influences rather than commands action.[80] Acting out of duty, Jefferson believes that persuasion, manners, and customs operate as a means to limit both encroachments on freedom and radical individualism.[81] This point is vital to prevent a reduction of Jefferson's thought to the logical conclusion of excessive individualism found in early nineteenth-century anarchist thought, particularly in the work of Proudhon, as well as the atomistic, individual reading of society that underscores liberal ideology. Instead, Jefferson sees indigenous societies as a type of society that renders positive law superfluous by an innate moral and social sense that confers a natural duty upon all members of the community, as they possess "no natural right in opposition to [. . .] social duties"[82] since "man was destined for society."[83] Jefferson clarifies this point in a letter to Francis W. Gilmer on June 7, 1816. Critiquing Hobbes's claim that justice comes from convention, Jefferson writes, "Man was created for social intercourse [. . .] then man must have been created with a sense of justice." Refuting Hobbes, Jefferson turns to indigenous societies as an example to demonstrate that they have "not yet submitted to the authority of positive laws, or of any acknoleged [sic] magistrate." As a result, indigenous peoples experience a sense of freedom, where one is "perfectly free to follow his own inclinations," but refrains from violating the rights of others to avoid the "disesteem of his society, or, as we say, by public opinion."[84]

This exclusion of forms of excessive compulsion is reaffirmed in Query XI. "Having never submitted themselves to any laws," Jefferson attests, their societies are restricted by refusing "any coercive power."[85] Again, Jefferson hammers the point that manners, not law, govern indigenous communities in a harmonious and tranquil fashion, evident in the rarity of crimes and culture of dialogue rather than vitriolic contestation.[86] The absence of positive law within indigenous societies throws Jefferson's very necessity of government into question. In a probing passage that signals a tepid hesitation toward governmental power and will resurface in a letter to Madison in 1787, Jefferson ponders the true extent of laws for a society. Jefferson is caught at an impasse between the striking absence and rejection of regulation seen in indigenous communities and the excessive application of law found in the "civilized Europeans." Jefferson's inquiry is haunting and potentially heretical to the entire system of Enlightenment political thinking when he asks which society "submits man to the greatest evil"?[87] His reply is ripe with symbolic imaginary in a move that reintegrates his philosophical claims onto his naturalistic, biological articulations of Query VI. Considerations of societal arrangement, thereby, incite a return to the scene of the physical terrain of America. He writes, "the sheep are happier of themselves, than under the care of the wolves."[88] In a sweeping, devastating line of text, Jefferson obliterates the civilized-barbarian binary, casting doubt on the necessity of government *qua* positive law.

It is easy to cast Jefferson's telling of indigenous societies in an anarchist light. However, his depiction of these societies is incompatible with such a position. Instead, Jefferson is clear that there is a level of regulation, a built-in mechanism of control that, over time, becomes naturalized. The lack of compulsion, and importantly for our sake, the refusal to incorporate seats of authority that wield authoritative decrees, function nearly instinctually as a unified social system sustained precisely because of the moral obligations of the community and the inherent force of public opinion.[89] For these reasons, Jefferson saw the customs and behaviors of indigenous societies controlled by a less-coercive form of power—argument over positive law—as more in accord with the innate rights that are "impressed on the sense of every man."[90] The absence of artificial class distinctions, such as possessions or entitlements, was rendered obsolete, enabling a type of freedom intrinsically bound to a moral plane. The result was, to Jefferson, a balancing of freedom and obligation, a fraternal interplay that relied on the forceful sway of public opinion for the people to be the genuine source of power. Challenging the idea that "great societies" cannot exist without governments, Jefferson stakes his claim that the indigenous populations of North America retain the fundamental principle that a *division* is necessary. He claims, commenting on how they maintain their harmonious condition, "The savages, therefore, break them into small ones."[91] Not only must titular positions of authority and expertise be recallable while possessing a symbolic value, but the very root of power must be accessible by all members. Division, in this sense, then takes on a sociological aspect, forming social units that always situate power on an identifiable, accessible axis. To transfer the authorship of collective decisions away from such a point violates the authority's creative and communal orientation.

Jefferson's evaluation of indigenous societies offers an alternate setting for political power and localized decision-making mechanisms—beyond governmental form—to take root. It has significantly produced a new way of thinking about power. Primarily, it points to how power can be collective, not by looking *backward* in a non-progressive lineation, but *behind* the monolithic model of the market man. It is necessary to discuss how this conception of power functions concerning forms of societal arrangement. To do so, I must now leave behind the groundwork delineated in his *Notes on Virginia* and turn to a careful assortment of personal letters.

SOCIETAL FORMS, HAPPINESS, AND PROPERTY

Jefferson opens his January 16, 1787, letter to Virginia statesman, Edward Carrington, locating himself in a tumultuous France. With the bankrupt French government facing a mounting crisis, King Louis XVI convened a unique gathering of prominent French nobility. This meeting, the Assembly of Notables, marks an important note in Jefferson's letter as he mentions his good friend, Marquis de Lafayette's, inclusion in the gathering. While France was dealing with its predicament, Jefferson refers to the growing unrest in Massachusetts, commonly referred to as Shays' Rebellion. As these two nations confront internal discord and division, Jefferson reaffirms that the people are the ultimate arbitrators of checking governmental power, retaining that primary function, even in error.

To ensure that the people remain adequately informed and, in turn, well-trained to prevent excessive encroachments on power at the government's hands, Jefferson notes that public opinion is the basis of government, advising for its constant maturation. Affirming his preference for societies influenced by opinion over positive law as well as the possibility of societies without government, he avows,

> I am convinced that those societies (as the Indians) that live without government enjoy an infinitely greater degree of happiness in their general mass than those who live under European governments. Among the former, public opinion is in the place of law and restrains morals as powerfully as laws ever did. Among the latter, under pretence of governing they have divided their nations into two classes, wolves and sheep. I do not exaggerate. This is a true picture of Europe.[92]

Again, the passage restates now-familiar themes of Jefferson's thought (opinion *over* law, custom *over* coercion, harmony *over* artificial division) as discussed in his *Notes on Virginia*. What is significant here is how a society lacking centralized government can still *produce happiness* for its members.[93] This claim cannot be understated, particularly in consideration of its placement concerning the larger corpus of the letter. After discussing the internal turmoil of two "Enlightened" nations, in the form of the early American republic and the French regime, Jefferson offers a flat-out radical alternative configuration of society: a replication of the small, communal associations of the indigenous peoples in the New World.

The passage also marks a return of the vivid, animalistic imagery in Query XI of his *Notes on Virginia*. Turning the Indian-as-beastlike[94] rhetoric on its head, Jefferson, again, casts agents of excessive governmental power as wolves. Unlike his earlier claim, Jefferson clarifies who these menacing wolves are. In a horrifying image, he claims that the wolves are, in fact, the rich. Jefferson suggests that the rich do not simply prey on but devour the poor, unlike any other animal in nature. He concludes in a melancholy fashion, cautioning Carrington about the genuine possibility that "you and I, and Congress, and Assemblies, judges and governors shall *all become wolves*"[95] if they become too distant and unresponsive to the desires of the people.

The letter to Carrington signals a refinement of Jefferson's perspective on indigenous societies found in his *Notes on Virginia*. While his earlier writing suggests a fundamental level of domestic tranquility among the indigenous population, his January 1787 letter to Carrington far exceeds that claim by presenting societies without a centralized government as a vehicle for public happiness and morality.[96] Its opposite, in this case, is a society defined by a cannibalistic mentality, a fractured association that situates the rich and poor in antagonistic terms.

Nearly two weeks after his letter to Carrington, Jefferson expands the twofold societal classification to James Madison. His January 30 letter opens in an exemplary fashion, hopeful that the "late troubles in the Eastern states" will not result in a firm belief that a government by force is the only viable path for its establishment.[97] Jefferson, of course, like the Carrington letter, is making direct reference to the events surrounding Shays' Rebellion. However, in this letter, Jefferson details, in several stirring passages, his general perspective on rebellions and how such actions render a regenerative quality to a body politic. Specifically, Jefferson provides a political typology, classifying various forms of societies. He details three conditions, writing,

> 1. Without government, as among our Indians. 2. Under governments wherein the will of every one has a just influence, as is the case in England in a slight degree, and in our states in a great one. 3. Under governments of force: as is the case in all other monarchies and in most of the other republics. To have an idea of the curse of existence under these last, they must be seen. It is a government of wolves over sheep.[98]

Not surprisingly, Jefferson rejects governments by force, likening them, once again, to animalistic imagery that is prominent throughout his writings. In conjunction with his January 16 letter to Carrington, force extends beyond a physical, coercive realm as it applies directly to economic class stratification. A government of wolves over sheep is thus a body politic fraught with internal class division, a dichotomized society along the lines of financial status.

As found in England and the early American republic, the second form is presented as the most feasible and pragmatic route. While Jefferson admits that liberty and happiness are found in this form, he hesitates against a full-out endorsement, suggesting that it only enjoys a "*degree*" of those fundamental principles. Moreover, " evils" hinder the second form, namely, "the principal of which is the turbulence to which it is subject."[99] However, Jefferson is clear that this form is undoubtedly preferable compared to a government by force. His reasoning, "*Malo periculosam, libertatem quam quietam servitutem,*"[100] is commonly translated as, "I prefer dangerous freedom over peaceful slavery." While not perfect, the second form, at the very least, affords a *possibility of freedom* compared to a condition of slavery found in the third form, even under the guise of a benevolent leader.

To Jefferson, the first form of societal arrangement is seen in indigenous societies without centralized government troubles his thought. "It is a problem, not clear in my mind," Jefferson raises, "that the 1st. condition is not the best."[101] The very idea of a society without a government and positive law haunts Jefferson's thinking. In a short, nearly dismissive way, almost characterized by a tone of avoidance, Jefferson offers the underlying problem with such a configuration: "I believe it to be inconsistent with any great degree of population."[102]

Nevertheless, Jefferson's conclusion is incomplete and logically reversed by applying his thought on the issue of size. In his *Notes on Virginia*, Jefferson resolves this very tension, offering strictly how indigenous societies handle the problem of size: by breaking them into smaller units.[103] This premise should not be cast off as idyllic or utopian. For it finds a practical application, identified by Jefferson in his modeling of indigenous societies, which then becomes mapped upon his speculative vision for America in the ward system. The communal spirit found in indigenous communities coupled with a network of decentralization to institute a politics of all is not exogenous to Jefferson's thought; instead, it is the lifeblood of the small, fraternal units of the wards. Peter S. Onuf has remarked that the idea of division—a central principle of Jefferson's theorization of the ward republics—calls "into question the very possibility of government itself."[104] Rather than reading such a claim in a potentially negative or even terminal light as Onuf does, much can be acquired by envisioning the wards as capable of a fraternal interrogation of the very necessity of a governmental form concerning Jefferson's political typology. The upshot of this alternative line of thought enables a richer and more radical dimension of his thinking to be released, one that challenges not only a reification of state power but more fundamentally facilitates "a therapeutic corrective to unwise or unjust national policies."[105]

More explicit articulation of Jefferson's belief in a society without government, and its accompanying condition of happiness, would not come for nearly three decades following his January 1787 letter to Madison. This time Jefferson would draw an even starker contrast between indigenous societies and the second form of his political typology, found here in the case of England. Written to his former personal secretary and close friend, William Short, on January 15, 1816, Jefferson is firmly entrenched in the retirement phase of his life. Although no longer a public servant, Jefferson's letters from this period offer a sharp critique of the increasing sway of the federal government, the defense branches, and the financial sector. Critical of the excessive level of spending by the War and Navy Departments, Jefferson mourns the loss of former Secretary of the Treasury Albert Gallatin to retirement and his ability to thwart the *faux frais*, or "incidental expenses," of those departments.[106] Additionally, he levies a vehement attack on the banking establishment, referring to them as a "mob of banks" responsible for a growing level of "permanent public debt," which, accordingly, is "inevitably fatal" to the people.[107]

Jefferson continues criticizing how impactful high levels of taxation can be on a population. Rebuking governments that leave their citizens with barely anything to exist on following tax payments, he turns his attention to the deplorable conditions for English workers. He writes, "I am informed by one who speaks from experience that of the 15d or 18d a day received by an English laborer, he pays 10d or 12d to government, the remaining 5d or 6d barely sufficing to keep body & soul together."[108] Jefferson's scathing critique resumes drawing out an alternative societal arrangement to the excessive levels of exploitation. "Government in this case costs certainly more than it is worth," he candidly asserts, then offering a point of comparison, "the laboring class would be happier as the Indians are, without government."[109] Jefferson's reasoning is swift and consistent with previous claims, concluding, "for I imagine there *can be no comparison* between the happiness of an Indian & an English laborer."[110]

Although cursory, Jefferson's depiction of indigenous societies is compelling. Firstly, Jefferson's claim of an indigenous person *being happier* than an English laborer runs counter to John Locke's telling of the uncultivated wilderness of America. In Chapter V, "On Property," §41, of his *Second Treatise of Government*, Locke compares an indigenous tribal leader in America and an English laborer. He claims, "a king of a large and fruitful territory there [in America], feeds, lodges, and is clad worse than a day-labourer in England."[111] Unlike Locke, Jefferson clarifies on two occasions then, first in his 1787 letter to Carrington and again in his 1816 letter to Short, that indigenous societies experience more happiness than found in the grueling life of an exploited English laborer.

Furthermore, secondly, the closing lines of Jefferson's letter to Short are revealed from a political economy standpoint. Jefferson captures the wretched conditions facing English workers in only a few words. Written nearly three decades *before* Friedrich Engels described the struggles facing Manchester workers in *The Condition of the Working Class in England*, Jefferson recognizes the impact that economic life plays on the well-being of an individual. "What is to become of those destitute millions, *who consume today what they earned yesterday?*"[112] In his introduction, Engels indirectly references Jefferson's analogous solemn diagnosis of workers "to keep body & soul together."[113] Vitally, the letter helps to reveal a side of Jefferson's thought that sees a strict interplay between politics and economics and the need to abolish economic exploitation in the American republic.

The three letters presented (Carrington, Madison, and Short) help to shape the formal structure of Jefferson's political typology. In them, they convey Jefferson's thinking on the various forms of sociability and carefully accentuate his belief that societies without centralized government can produce, but also in opposition to the second and third categories of his typology, generating a greater degree of happiness. Strict monarchies, constitutional-parliamentary monarchies, and even the infant American republic stand outside this categorization as Jefferson hammers the point that indigenous societies are the archetype of such a configuration.

While these three letters acquire a discernibly theoretical depth concerning our investigation of his *Notes on Virginia,* it is important to caution against the development of a settled conceptualization of indigenous societies. This hesitation is fundamental to Jefferson's understanding of theory formulation, particularly regarding abstracting verifiable conclusions concerning indigenous peoples in North America. According to Jefferson, proper theorization always requires more collection of data and more facts that can be added in the appropriate examination of a specific condition. Eschewing theoretical determinism, Jefferson writes, "I wish that the persons who go thither would make very exact descriptions of what they see of that kind, without forming any theories." He continues, "The moment a person forms a theory, his imagination sees in every object only the tracts which favor that theory."[114] Jefferson's own words are apropos here as well.

Jefferson's writing on indigenous societies demonstrates his aversion to coercive forms of political power and his belief that social organizations of this order could attain happiness. From this position, the third characteristic of radical democracy was offered: a moral and sociable view of human nature compels political subjects to collaborate with a powerless figurehead, serving as a conciliator for internal peace and harmony.

It is, however, essential to problematize Jefferson's essentialist reading of indigenous societies. As Elise Marienstras has pointed out, even a Jeffersonian interpretation of nature and the frontier's potential to escape the defects of the Old World is contaminated by an imperialist quality. "The nature of the republic was imperialist from the very beginning,"[115] Marienstras asserts, and Jefferson's presidential policies—tainted with naivety and brutality[116]—were directly responsible for western migration and the accompanying acts of forced assimilation and genocide. In a fascinating, brief letter written in 1824,

Jefferson discusses, in a tone balanced with remorse, the horrors inflicted upon indigenous peoples at the hands of the American republic, writing, "I wish that was the only blot in our moral history, and that no other race had higher charges to bring against us."[117] He is, of course, making direct reference to the violence committed upon indigenous peoples and, as well, the appalling continuation of slavery in the south.

Jefferson's commitment to agrarian society was a central strain of his thinking that initiated agricultural development processes upon indigenous communities. Convinced that their current state of progress was stunted,[118] firmly entrenched in a hunting and gathering phase, an introduction of agriculture would benefit both indigenous peoples and the American republic.[119] In his second inaugural address of 1805, Jefferson stresses such a position. Jefferson promotes an embrace of toiling the soil in an 1806 letter to the "Chiefs of the Osages, Missouris, Kansas, Ottoes, Panis, Ayowas, Sioux, Poutewattamies, Foxes and Sacs" nations. He writes, "My children, you have had opportunities of seeing many things among us, you have seen how by living in peace, cultivating the earth and practicing the useful arts, we, who were once but a few travellers landing on this Island, are now a great people and growing daily greater."[120] He asserts, "You too possess good lands, and abundance of it, by cultivating that and living in peace you may become as we are." The shift to agricultural development was thus twofold to Jefferson and the expanding republic. It carefully ushered in a relinquishing of land, typically by exerting forms of force, while at the same time fostering an economic climate that necessitated "Indians to participate in the commercial market"[121] to subsist.

While Jefferson's analysis of indigenous societies was flat-out incorrect on several fronts (a neoclassical discourse interpretation of their discursive patterns, the defense of American nature over indigenous communities, the failure to see the role that collective memory maintained, and the depiction of subjugated women,[122] to name just a few), his writings on the matter are significant not because of what he got correct but rather how they could be taken up. As Matthew Crow suggests, "part of the fascination Jefferson felt with regards to Native Americans came from a desire to see them as fit material for historical conjecture and political theory."[123] Crow's point is critical because it enables Jefferson's claims to be used and situated within a political context. The malleability of Jefferson's thought does not necessarily produce either a revisionist or an apologist account; relatively, by drawing out his views on power and, subsequently, how power can be shared collectively, a more democratic reading germinates.

NOTES

1. Jon Meacham, *Thomas Jefferson: The Art of Power* (New York: Random House, 2012), xxiii.

2. By this claim, I am directly referencing the expansionist tone of Jefferson's writings on two occasions in letters written to George Rogers Clark (1780) and Benjamin Chambers (1805). A third letter written to James Madison in 1809 also imports a similar theme, albeit shifts the phrase to an empire *for* liberty. See the following letters: TJ to George Rogers Clark, December 25, 1780, in Boyd, *PTJ*, 4: 233–38; TJ to Benjamin Chambers, December 28, 1805, *FO,* National Archives, http://founders.archives.gov/documents/Jefferson/99-01-02-2910; TJ to James Madison, April 27, 1809, in Looney, *PTJ*, Retirement Series, 1: 168–70.

3. See Robert J. Miller, *Native America, Discovered and Conquered: Thomas Jefferson, Lewis & Clark, and Manifest Destiny* (Westport, CT: Praeger Publishers, 2006), 94–98.

4. For an excellent example of this work, see Jennifer Pitts, "Political Theory of Empire and Imperialism," *Annual Review of Political Science* 13 (2010): 211–35. Also, see Singh Mehta, *Liberalism and Empire: A Study in Nineteenth-Century British Liberal Thought* (Chicago: The University of Chicago Press, 1999).

5. Robert A. Williams, Jr., "Thomas Jefferson: Indigenous American Storyteller," in *Thomas Jefferson and the Changing West: From Conquest to Conservation*, ed. James P. Ronda (Albuquerque: University of New Mexico Press, 1997), 45.

6. Williams, Jr., "Thomas Jefferson: Indigenous American Storyteller," 45.

7. TJ, *The Writings of Thomas Jefferson*, vol. 1: 1760–1775, ed. Paul Leicester Ford (New York: G. P. Putnam's Sons, 1892), 85.

8. François Barbé-Marbois, "Marbois' Queries Concerning Virginia," November 30, 1780, in Boyd, *PTJ*, 4: 166–67.

9. To approach Jefferson's thought, an entry into his epistolary canon is necessary to draw out the central tenets of his writings. Surprisingly, Jefferson published very little by way of completed manuscripts. In addition to his *Notes*, his only other "major" publication was in 1801, when he took up the task of writing a handbook on senatorial behavior and practices. See TJ, *A Manual of Parliamentary Practice* (Philadelphia: Parrish, Dunning & Mears, 1853).

10. TJ, *The Writings of Thomas Jefferson*, vol. 1, 85.

11. Ibid., 86.

12. Lee Alan Dugatkin, *Mr. Jefferson and the Giant Moose: Natural History in Early America* (Chicago: The University of Chicago Press, 2009), 22.

13. Buffon writes, "In America, Nature . . . [has] adopted upon a smaller scale." Georges Louis Marie Leclerc Buffon, *Histoire Naturelle, Générale et Particulière*, vol. IX (Paris: Imprimerie Royale, Plassan, 1749–1804), 72. Also, see J. S. Barr, *Barr's Buffon*, vol. VII (London: J. S. Barr, 1792), 15.

14. TJ, *Notes*, 44. Emphasis added.

15. Dugatkin, *Mr. Jefferson and the Giant Moose*, 22.

16. TJ, *Notes on Virginia*, 45.

17. Buffon's claim was not necessarily new to eighteenth-century French or Western political thought. The idea of a colder climate impacting development can be found in BK VII of Aristotle's *Politics*.

18. Dugatkin, *Mr. Jefferson and the Giant Moose*, 23.

19. Buffon, *Histoire Naturelle*, vol. IX, 104.

20. Ibid., 110.

21. Ibid.

22. Buffon, *Histoire Naturelle*, Vol. XV, 455.

23. TJ, *Notes*, 47. Also, see Lee Alan Dugatkin, "Thomas Jefferson Versus Count Buffon: The Theory of New World Degeneracy," *The Chautauqua Journal* 1, article 17 (2016): 11.

24. William Howard Adams, *The Paris Years of Thomas Jefferson* (New Haven, CT: Yale University Press, 1997), 121.

25. TJ, *Notes*, 23–34.

26. Ibid., 35–39.

27. Ibid., 39.

28. Here, I draw upon but also mark a distinction with Robert Dawidoff's characterization of Virginia in Jefferson's account. While Dawidoff frames the setting as a "kind of *el dorado* and a kind of hell," a duality that I affirm, I suggest an immanent dialectical quality at play in Jefferson's account. An inherent potentiality to transcend the hellish state of affairs brought about through the institution of slavery, the corruptive nature of centralized governmental power, and the corrosive effects of industrialization. See Robert Dawidoff, "Rhetoric of Democracy," in *Thomas Jefferson and the Politics of Nature*, ed. Thomas S. Engeman (Notre Dame, IN: University of Notre Dame Press, 2000), 108.

29. There is a fundamental contradiction between slavery and freedom premised along the lines of race found in Jefferson's depiction of the inferiority of Blacks presented in his *Notes on Virginia*. Here, Jefferson integrates both, in his view, a naturalistic reading of the mind and body of Blacks into the proper institutional design to promote political freedom. See Caroline Levander, *Cradle of Liberty: Race, The Child, and National Belonging From Thomas Jefferson to W. E. B. Du Bois* (Durham, NC: Duke University Press, 2006), 38.

30. Richard B. Bernstein, *Thomas Jefferson: The Revolution of Ideas* (Oxford, UK: Oxford University Press, 2004), 79.

31. Charles A. Miller argues that Jefferson's blend of environmentalism and human nature sought to place America on the same level against claims of inferiority to the Old World. According to Miller, Jefferson does not simply reverse the thesis of New World degeneracy by elevating America above the Old World but rather attempts to fix the status of "equality" among the two hemispheres. See Charles A. Miller, *Jefferson and Nature: An Interpretation* (Baltimore, MD: The Johns Hopkins University Press, 1988), 61–62.

32. Jacques Roger, *Buffon: A Life in Natural History*, ed. L. Pearce Williams, trans. Sarah Lucille Bonnefoi (Ithaca, NY: Cornell University Press, 1997), 420.

33. TJ, *Notes*, 39–41, 52.

34. Ibid., 41.

35. For a meaningful discussion on the presence of the Great Chain of Being in Jefferson's *Notes on Virginia*, see Donald Jackson, *Thomas Jefferson & the Stony Mountains: Exploring the West from Monticello* (Norman: University of Oklahoma Press, 1993), 29–30. For Jefferson's belief in non-extinction, see Robert L. Kelly and Mary M. Prascinuas, "Did the Ancestors of Native Americans Cause Animal Extinctions in Late-Pleistocene North America?" in *Native Americans and the Environment: Perspectives on the Ecological Indian*, eds. Michael Eugene Harkin and David Rich Lewis (Lincoln: University of Nebraska Press, 2007), 95–97.

36. Ibid., 44.

37. See Keith Thomson, *A Passion for Nature: Thomas Jefferson and Natural History*, Monticello Monograph Series (Chapel Hill: The University of North Carolina Press, 2008), 65–66.

38. See Gaye Wilson, "Jefferson, Buffon, and the Mighty American Moose," *Monticello Newsletter* 13, no. 1 (Spring 2002).

39. David G. Post, *In Search of Jefferson's Moose: Notes on the State of Cyberspace* (Oxford, UK: Oxford University Press, 2009), 66.

40. See Dugatkin, *Mr. Jefferson and the Giant Moose*, 81–100.

41. TJ to Buffon, October 1, 1787, in Boyd, *PTJ*, 12: 194–95.

42. Thomson, *A Passion for Nature*, 70.

43. TJ to John Sullivan, October 5, 1787, in Boyd, *PTJ*, 12: 208–9.

44. Daniel Webster, "Notes on Mr. Jefferson's Conversation 1824 at Monticello, 1825," *The Papers of Daniel Webster, Correspondence*, volume 1, 1798–1824, eds. Charles M. Wiltse and Harold D. Moser (Hanover, NH: Dartmouth College/University Press of New England, 1974), 377.

45. See Jackson, *Thomas Jefferson & the Stony Mountains*, 29–30. Also see Roderick Frazier Nash, *The Rights of Nature: A History of Environmental Ethics* (Madison: The University of Wisconsin Press, 1989), 113.

46. Miller, *Jefferson and Nature*, 65.

47. See E. C. Spary, *Utopia's Garden: French Natural History from Old Regime to Revolution* (Chicago: The University of Chicago Press, 2000), 19.

48. Frederick Doveton Nichols and Ralph E. Griswold, *Thomas Jefferson: Landscape Architect* (Charlottesville: The University of Virginia Press, 1978), 126.

49. Robert W. Tucker and David C. Hendrickson, *Empire of Liberty: The Statecraft of Thomas Jefferson* (Oxford, UK: Oxford University Press, 1990), 50.

50. Maurizio Valsania nods to this vital point in Jefferson's naturalistic philosophy grounded in materiality. He writes, "Far from being weak, [. . .] such a native product of the American land was a perfect model for American citizens to follow." See Maurizio Valsania, *Jefferson's Body: A Corporeal Biography* (Charlottesville: The University of Virginia Press, 2017), 78.

51. TJ, *Notes*, 61.

52. Ibid.

53. Ibid.

54. Ibid.

55. Ibid., 61–62.

56. See Jacques Derrida, *The Politics of Friendship*, trans. George Collins (New York: Verso), 2005.

57. Ibid., 62.

58. Ibid., 61. Jefferson states in a perplexed fashion, "or perhaps this *is* nature." Emphasis added. Amos Stoddard, who, in 1805, traveled with a delegation of indigenous peoples to Washington, substantiated this point. Stoddard claims, "They speak from nature, and not from education." Cited in Bernard W. Sheehan, *Seeds of Extinction: Jeffersonian Philanthropy and the American Indian* (Chapel Hill: The University of North Carolina Press, 1972), 108.

59. Ibid., 62. It is important to note that the story of Shilòuee and Byrd appears in a rather lengthy footnote by Jefferson. Although not centrally located within the text, my claim suggests that it is imperative to Jefferson's understanding of an innate moral sense within indigenous peoples.

60. Ibid., 63.

61. Ibid.

62. Ibid., 65. Jefferson uses a Linnaean term for the classification of *Homo sapiens* and the related subspecies.

63. Ibid., 96–97.

64. Miller, *Jefferson and Nature*, 96.

65. See TJ to John Manners, June 12, 1817, in Looney, *PTJ*, Retirement Series, 11: 432–34.

66. Dustin Gish and Daniel Klinghard, "Republican Constitutionalism in Thomas Jefferson's *Notes on the State of Virginia*," *The Journal of Politics* 74, no. 1 (2012), 38.

67. Steven Conn, *History's Shadow: Native Americans and Historical Consciousness in the Nineteenth Century* (Chicago: The University of Chicago Press, 2004), 84.

68. Jefferson, *Notes*, 65.

69. Ibid., 66.

70. Ibid.

71. Jefferson also contacted George Rogers Clark, who provided information on the Cresap affair, and Thomas Hutchins for estimates of tribal populations. Furthermore, Jefferson reached out to Thomas Walker for consultation but to no avail. See Anthony F. C. Wallace, *Jefferson and the Indians: The Tragic Fate of the First Americans* (Cambridge, MA: The Belknap Press of Harvard University Press, 1999), 93–94.

72. Jefferson, *Notes* (Appendix), 208.

73. Ibid., 214.

74. Ibid., 215.

75. Ibid.

76. Jefferson also personally consulted with Heckewelder concerning the events of the Cresap affair and included his insights in the *Appendix* (No. III) of *Notes*. For Heckewelder's discussion, see TJ, *Notes*, 262–67. For a study that showcases how Moravian missionaries, including Heckewelder, saw indigenous languages as highly sophisticated and rich in design, see Sean P. Harvey, *Native Tongues: Colonialism and Race from Encounter to the Reservation* (Cambridge, MA: Harvard University Press, 2015), 82; Gordon M. Sayre, *Les Sauvages Américains: Representations of Native Americans in French and English Colonial Literature* (Chapel Hill: The University of

North Carolina Press, 1997), 202–3. For Jefferson's interest in languages, see Thomas F. Gossett, *Race: The History of an Idea in America* (Oxford, UK: Oxford University Press, 1997), 126.

77. See Sheehan, *Seeds of Extinction*, 110–11.

78. Helen M. Ingram and Mary G. Wallace, "An 'Empire of Liberty': Thomas Jefferson and Governing Natural Resources in the West," in *Thomas Jefferson and the Changing West*, 94.

79. See Pierre Clastres, *Society Against the State: Essays in Political Anthropology*, trans. Robert Hurley and be Stein (New York: Zone Books, 1987). Also see Pierre Clastres, *Archelogy of Violence*, trans. Jeanine Herman (New York: Zone Books, 1994).

80. TJ, *Notes*, 65.

81. See Daniel L. Dreisbach, *Thomas Jefferson and the Wall of Separation Between Church and State* (New York: New York University Press, 2002), 53.

82. TJ to the Danbury Baptist Association, January 1, 1802, in Oberg, *PTJ*, 36: 258.

83. TJ to Peter Carr, with Enclosure, August 10, 1787, in Boyd, *PTJ*, 12: 14–19.

84. See TJ to Francis W. Gilmer, June 7, 1816, in Looney, *PTJ*, Retirement Series, 10:154–56.

85. Jefferson, *Notes*, 96.

86. Ibid., 97.

87. Ibid.

88. Ibid.

89. For Jefferson's understanding of coercive power within specialized seats of authority, mainly found in the Executive Branch, see Jeremy D. Bailey, *Thomas Jefferson and Executive Power* (Cambridge, UK: Cambridge University Press, 2009), 111.

90. See TJ to John Manners, June 12, 1817, in Looney, *PTJ*, Retirement Series, 11: 432–34.

91. Jefferson, *Notes*, 97.

92. TJ to Edward Carrington, January 16, 1787, in Boyd, *PTJ*, 11: 49.

93. This claim becomes more powerful when situated with George Mason's "Virginia Declaration of Rights" (1776). Often cited as a key text that influenced Jefferson's Declaration, Mason opened the document with familiar claims of equality among all men and the possession of natural rights. However, Mason's grandiose language of equality brought about intense debates from his fellow statesmen in late May 1776. Concerned that such language would run counter to a continuation of slavery and, in return, make the institution itself illegitimate, an essential line of text was aided, essentially negating the possibility of freedom for enslaved people and indigenous populations. The phrase, "when they enter into a state of society," crafted by Edmund Pendleton was incorporated into the ratified declaration during the Fifth Virginia Convention in June. Importantly, it presented the ideals of freedom and equality as a two-tier process, first through the departure from a state of nature into society and then a consensual agreement to form a commonwealth. The effects of such a critical shift are enormous, marking society as a bridge into a political community, then, and only then, capable of producing happiness and fulfilling the ideals

of a democratic polity. Jefferson's claims here, then, run counter to such a position, rejecting a double-stage transition into a political community and problematizing the very notion that natural rights, equality, and, importantly, happiness is unique to settled forms of government. For the revision process surrounding Mason's "Declaration," see Jeff Broadwater, *George Mason: Forgotten Founder* (Chapel Hill: The University of North Carolina Press, 2006), 84–85.

94. As Valsania points out, Jefferson's view on indigenous peoples could not entirely escape this image. For Jefferson, according to Valsania, "American Indians were essentially childlike, primitive, bestial, naive," and, crucially, dangerous, and violent. See Valsania, *Jefferson's Body*, 140.

95. TJ to Edward Carrington, January 16, 1787, in Boyd, 49. Emphasis added.

96. See Isaac Briggs, "A Cordial Reunion in 1820," in *Visitors to Monticello*, ed. Merrill D. Peterson (Charlottesville: The University of Virginia Press, 1989), 91.

97. TJ to James Madison, January 30, 1787, in Boyd, *PTJ*, 11: 92.

98. Ibid., 92–93.

99. Ibid., 93.

100. Ibid. Translation provided by the Robert H. Smith International Center for Jefferson Studies, Monticello, VA.

101. Ibid.

102. Ibid.

103. Jefferson, *Notes*, 97.

104. Peter S. Onuf, "Missouri and the 'Empire for Liberty,'" in *Thomas Jefferson and the Changing West,* 120.

105. Gary Hart, *Restoration of the Republic: The Jeffersonian Ideal in 21st Century America* (Oxford, UK: Oxford University Press, 2002), 220.

106. TJ to William Short, January 15, 1816, in Looney, *PTJ*, Retirement Series, 9: 358.

107. Ibid.

108. Ibid.

109. Ibid.

110. Ibid. Emphasis added.

111. John Locke, *Second Treatise of Government*, ed. C. B. Macpherson (Indianapolis, IN: Hackett Publishing Co., 1980), 25–26.

112. Friedrich Engels, *The Condition of the Working Class in England in 1844*, trans. Florence Kelley Wishchnewetzsky (New York: Cosimo Classics, 2008), 17.

113. TJ to William Short, January 15, 1816, in Looney, *PTJ*, Retirement Series, 9: 358.

114. TJ to Charles Thomson, September 20, 1787, in Boyd, *PTJ*, 12: 159–61.

115. Elise Marienstras, "The Common Man's Indian: The Image of the Indian as a Promoter of National Identity in the Early National Era," in *Native Americans and the Early Republic*, eds. Frederick E. Hoxie, Ronald Hoffman and Peter J. Albert (Charlottesville: The University Press of Virginia, 1999), 272.

116. For just one example of the explicit brutality, see TJ to George Rogers Clark, January 1, 1779, in Boyd, *PTJ*, 3: 258–59. In the original draft of this letter, Jefferson wrote, "I think the most important object which can be proposed with such a force

is the extermination of the hostile tribes of Indians who live between the Ohio and Illinois who have harassed us with external hostilities [. . .]." This text was deleted in the final version sent to Clark.

117. TJ to Lydia Howard Huntley Sigourney, July 18, 1824. St. Paul's School in Concord, NH owns this letter. Photostatic copy examined at the Albert and Shirley Small Special Collections Library, University of Virginia, Charlottesville, VA.

118. See TJ to Osages Chiefs, January 4, 1806. Photostatic copy examined at the Albert and Shirley Small Special Collections Library, University of Virginia, Charlottesville, VA. See also, *TJP* at the Library of Congress, series 1: General Correspondence, 1651–1827, microfilm reel: 035, images 1–4.

119. Fergus M. Bordewich, *Killing the White Man's Indian: Reinventing Native Americans at the End of the Twentieth Century* (New York: Anchor Books, 1996), 38.

120. TJ to Chiefs of Indian Tribes, April 11, 1806. This letter is privately owned. Examined at the Albert and Shirley Small Special Collections Library, University of Virginia, Charlottesville, VA.

121. Daniel H. Usner, Jr., "Iroquois Livelihood and Jeffersonian Agrarianism: Reaching behind the Models and Metaphors," in *Native Americans and the Early Republic*, 213.

122. In his *Notes*, commenting on women in indigenous societies, Jefferson writes, "The women are submitted to unjust drudgery. This I believe is the case with every barbarous people" (63).

123. Matthew Ellsworth Crow, "In the Course of Human Events: Jefferson, Text, and the Potentialities of Law," doctoral dissertation (Los Angeles: University of California, Los Angeles, 2011), 210.

Chapter 4

Eruptive Democracy

Challenging the Federal Republic

New England townships and their localized expression of political activity embodied in a meeting structure represent a bastion of democratic practices in eighteenth-century America. As a locale oriented to the "prudential affairs"[1] of the town, the organizational design of the typical township maintained a strong force of political legitimacy and autonomy. The character of the towns embodied a spirit of civic culture that shaped nearly all aspects of communal life, exhibiting a commitment to dialogue, civic engagement, and fraternity. Central to the arrangement of the towns was an emphasis on self-government and sovereignty enacted and upheld by community members, one not entirely dependent on extra sociolegal forces.

Although the New England corridor towns were connected—particularly regarding economic relations[2]—to the dictates of the Crown pre-Revolution and then the federal republic post-ratification, town hall meetings continued to exist as essential sites for local politics. The scope of a community's influence, deliberated over and procured through the town hall meeting, was far-reaching: the administration of local elections, the institutional governance of the town, and the frequent creation of temporary committees in times of need.[3]

These factors undoubtedly influenced Jefferson's admiration for the New England town hall setting. High levels of civic participation found within town hall meetings through a *face-to-face* relationship, rather than a proxy or representative exchange, run concurrently with a politics of all that strives for action and dialogue over passivity and apathy. However, Jefferson's esteem for the town hall locale runs much deeper than a penetrating layer of civic engagement that encases its entire structure.

In Jefferson's view, the New England town hall reveals a democratic expression that holds a unique reservoir of political potential that, when set into motion, reveals itself as a political force capable of destabilizing the entire configuration of a centralized federal republic. This rests at the heart of Jefferson's understanding of radical democracy.

An evaluation of Jefferson's understanding of the New England town hall meeting locale helps to elucidate a central element of his political thinking, particularly the transformative capabilities of a political community to expose, rather than conceal, the inherent divisions of its composition. For Jefferson, the townships of New England exhibited an ability to potentially overturn the union as an essential check on federal power during the tumultuous events that culminated in the 1807 Embargo Act. The political action proceeded along the lines of division that affirmed the plurality and socialness while simultaneously opening new spaces for ongoing dialogue and participation. In this manner, Jefferson sees the town hall setting as a particular site of politics that asserts its unique markers of identification and self-foundation in opposition to a demand for servitude over self-determination. From these spaces of democratic energy, the fourth characteristic is drawn: an active momentum to subvert the logic of the state as a point of rupture against the unsociability and uniformity contained through a political life defined by the state.

To proceed and present Jefferson's evaluation of the New England town hall meeting, it is necessary to evaluate how New England generally and the town hall meeting explicitly have been treated in American political thought. What is central to this register of thought is a casting of Jefferson as a strict southern regional thinker and political advocate. However, such a reading is severely exaggerated and misguided. Instead, Jefferson's perspective toward New England has defined his admiration for the region and his desire for replication and transplantation of the township pattern to his home state of Virginia, where he held "little firsthand experience with democracy."[4] Jefferson's writing on New England, particularly concerning the events of the Embargo Act of 1807, suggests that the township configuration marked a strong impression on his political thinking. The influence of the democratic culture of New England animates Jefferson's politics of all, offering an understanding of politics generated along the lines of division, contestation, and dialogue. Through Jefferson's lens, the democratic potential of the New England town hall meeting demonstrates momentum against the directives of a centralized governmental body to convert a space of conflict into a community of fraternity and sociability.

SURVEYING POLITICAL SPACE

In 1831, Alexis de Tocqueville arrived in the American republic. Enamored with the equality of conditions blanketing the American experiment of self-government, the young French aristocratic lawyer provided a break from the antiquated Aristotelian classification of regimes that always pointed toward a more idealized form. Instead, Tocqueville set his sights on, as Pierre Manent has suggested, the "authority of the present moment."[5] By subverting the political science of antiquity, Tocqueville, deeply entrenched in Montesquieu's liberal worldview, sought to develop a new political science, one capable of solidifying human nature as both particular and historical. In so doing, Tocqueville's account led to a crystallization of human nature that could then be linked up with a generalized understanding of the *état social* (social state).[6] This *état social,* or as Montesquieu proposed, the "general spirit of the nation,"[7] was not seen simply in terms of the endogenous conditions of liberalism, but the logic and totality of the democratic *état social.* For Tocqueville, the American republic and democracy were not the same; rather, America existed as the crucial stage for unveiling the tendencies and contingencies of the inevitable democratic revolution.

Tocqueville's account is undoubtedly innovative as his political *qua* sociological analysis reveals the dangers of an encroaching democratic despotism. The superabundant and restive force of democracy facilitates not simply the obliteration of the individual through a brutalizing, sweeping tyrannical power, but rather a hindrance and conformity of the people in a herd-like manner.[8] The tendency that pushes a democratic people closer to the plane of an "innumerable crowd of like and equal men [. . .] withdrawn and apart"[9] is brought about from the impulse particular to the democratic *état social*: the drive toward centralization. "In democratic societies, centralization will always be greater as the sovereign is less aristocratic," Tocqueville suggests, "that is the rule."[10] Herein lies the Tocquevillian paradox: democracy is characterized by the unprecedented equalization of conditions and the total concentration and amassment of political power in the image of the One, the unencumbered centralized state.

Tocqueville's forecast of the evisceration of the democratic individual certainly casts an ominous shadow over the advantages of the democratic experiment. However, his description of the autonomous and powerful realm of the New England township system represents an alternate space within the centralized state for engagement in localized public affairs. According to Tocqueville, "political life was born in the very bosom of the townships," continuously existing as "independent bodies" while remaining embedded within the nexus of the logic of the centralized state. While still linked to the body of the state, Tocqueville clearly suggests that the "force of free peoples resides" within the localized setting, acting, at times, as a force against the state's encroachments. Acquiescence on the part of the township to the demands of the state occurs only when the township itself deems the social issue to fall outside the scope of its sovereignty.

When this conditionality of submission is linked up with Tocqueville's depiction of the type of political existence inherent within the township, a dynamic dimension of political resistance emerges. Decisively, Tocqueville specifies that the townships impress upon "society," a force that is one "continual" with the ability to agitate. The aim of the inhabitant of the New England township is thus infused with this relentless spirit and, in turn, sustained by the ongoing engagement within the public sphere while being fixed on the governing of society. It is crucial to flag that Tocqueville uses the term "society" rather than "state" in his understanding of the powerful tendency of the township. Suppose we push this careful, nuanced difference in terminology to its limit. In that case, Tocqueville's township then takes on a decisively political figure, signaling an ongoing contestation against the excessive political state in pursuit of a separation between the realm of the political and the constitutionally defined political state. From this perspective, a path beyond the despotic democratic state would not transpire along the contours of Montesquieu's "general spirit of the nation" or purification of Aristotle's regime arrangement, but through and within the actions and experiences of the generalized democratic *état social*. This suggests that the township's specific "continual" and agitating spirit exists within the democratic tendency to equalize conditions. There is indeed a self-reductive quality in this interpretation. Tocqueville's account suggests neither the dissolution of the political state *in toto* nor the collapse of the autonomous realms of political engagement exhibited by the town hall system into the despotic democratic state. Instead, Tocqueville's analysis offers a caesura between the state's formalism and the township's self-instituting powers that draws a path toward a social existence against, yet still within the democratic *état social* that takes on a determinative political force.

The insights, and the real upshot, of Tocqueville's account, are the political possibilities that the township system represents within the context of the more extensive work displayed throughout *Democracy in America*. Placed alongside the landscape of his prophetic prophecy of the inevitable, impending democratic revolution, Tocqueville's discussions on the New England township system have remained a fruitful point of inquiry by accentuating a "restricted sphere"[11] alternatively, demarcated space is antithetical to the foundation of the centralized state. Suppose we approach Tocqueville's account of the township system in this matter. In that case, it is not surprising to see how and why he has remained the quintessential thinker on the advantages of localized self-government. Our turn to Jefferson's understanding of the New England town hall system takes flight from this point. By linking up the affinities between the two thinkers, Jefferson's affirmative writings on the political capabilities of the New England town hall system function as an important site of resistance against the excessive centralization of the state.

What Tocqueville was keen to observe was, in essence, already embedded within Jefferson's account nearly four decades prior. The unsettling and disruptive force of the localized site was for Jefferson equipped with the ability to overrule the union.

CASTING JEFFERSON AS AN ANTI-NEW ENGLANDER

Much has been made of Jefferson's depiction of New England, explicitly deemed an area of scorn and condemnation by him due to the industry-driven, former cradle of aristocratic decadence, underscored by a strong ethos of Puritanism, possibly even devout monarchism at heart.[12] For sure, Jefferson blasted the undemocratic nature of the Massachusetts Constitution for its reliance on property qualifications for citizenship[13] and the fiery spirit of religiosity thwarted an impartial, rational, and scientific examination of political issues from materializing.[14] Cultural and economic issues between the staunch Virginian and the prestige of the northeastern mentality, marvelously illustrated by the aristocratic bent of the Adams family, certainly lend a hand in exacerbating the trope between Jefferson's southern, agrarian worldview in constant battle with the urban, commercial heavy setting of the northeast.

Jefferson, indeed, was critical of the region, especially concerning Northeastern urban centers. However, his distaste for these condensed spaces of city life—areas ripe for crime, corruption, and disease due to rapid industrialization and overcrowding—were greatly influenced by his view of European cities.[15] Nevertheless, significantly, Jefferson's dislike for cities, informed by his European journeys between 1784 and 1789, would dissipate in his later years for reasons concerning economic survival. Morton and Lucia White detail a modification of Jefferson's loyal agrarian standpoint with a tepid reception of urbanization, "His mind had been changed, [. . .] by his concern for national survival. He disliked its manufactures and its banks, but the international situation ultimately forced him to regard the city as an indispensable element of American life."[16] While the shift from Jefferson's anti-urban commentary found widely in his *Notes on the State of Virginia* to his gentle embrace of cities—in conjunction with accompanying processes of industrialization—expressed in private letters to Benjamin Austin and William H. Crawford in 1816 has been documented in scholarship, his casting as a Virginian, agrarian figure has remained resolute.[17] This exhausted narrative centered on an all-around general antagonism against all things originating from the north has thus certainly taken root in scholarship's understanding of Jefferson's fabricated political and regional rival.

Significantly, work by Gary Wills, particularly his study *"Negro President": Jefferson and the Slave Power*, casts Jefferson in a shrewdly Machiavellian light.[18] Wills argues that Jefferson was desirous of establishing a southern hegemony, seeing the possible addition of slave states to the American republic as an effective tactic to destabilize northern merchants' efficacy and political weight and, primarily, the Federalists. Wills also takes Jefferson's involvement and advocacy for the Embargo Act of 1807 as a direct attack on the vitality and prosperity of the northern economy. As engaging as Wills' account appears, his central thesis of Jefferson as a vociferous southern nationalist is undone by examining the details concerning the events that precipitated and the subsequent outcome of the Embargo Act. In an almost redaction fashion, Wills dismisses the southern-driven motives of the embargo, relenting that Jefferson instituted the effects of such a blockade to protect New Englanders from British intrusions. The economic impact of the embargo was, as Wills undeniably admits, ruinous for the southern markets of wheat and cotton, as well as, chiefly, tobacco.[19]

In addition to Wills, Peter S. Onuf sketches out a larger, more robust picture of Jefferson's nationalistic sensibilities informed by a southern milieu. Integral to Onuf's account put forth in *Jefferson's Empire: The Language of American Nationhood* is Jefferson's holding of a fundamental hostility against New England and the mercantilism of the region.[20] Whereas Wills casts Jefferson as a calculating southern strategist, Onuf paints him as a downright passionate opponent of the northeast, desirous of its ultimate destruction.[21] Onuf suggests that Jefferson became alarmed that the Embargo Act and the events surrounding the War of 1812 would spur separationist support in the northeast. Onuf reads Jefferson as being deeply fearful that British loyalists in the region undermined the nation's unity. To Onuf, Jefferson, while firmly secluded in Monticello away from the machinery of governmental affairs, came to believe that only the total obliteration of the northeast through military interventions would save the republic from relapsing back to the British Empire. Drawing from a letter to William Short in November 1814, Onuf uses Jefferson's projection of an imaginary war between a Virginia-led militia force and Massachusetts as the lynchpin in his assessment that Jefferson deemed the expulsion of New England as necessary for the salvation of the union.[22] "The rupture of the union would bring its real enemies out into the open," Onuf asserts, meaning, principally, British loyalists and Federalists.[23] According to Onuf, Jefferson's fantastical war would lead to the safeguarding of the union by "destroying New England."[24]

While the work of both Wills and Onuf illuminate an essential dimension to Jefferson's thought, one that, at times, rings through with notes of northern animus, particularly concerning his negative depiction of Northern cities and the region's industrialization sector, neither account fully considers his more praiseworthy writings on the area. The approach taken by Wills, Onuf, and others[25] has directed its lines of inquiry on Jefferson's responses to the events, such as the Embargo Act, War of 1812, and the Missouri crisis,[26] in the context of policy recommendations. Suppose we adhere to this strict reading of Jefferson against New England. In that case, we can conclude that his worldview and, in turn, his understanding of civic engagement only operated within a firmly entrenched southern nationalistic framework. However, such an understanding is to negate the complementary side of his vision—that is, a political space that accentuates the differences held between individuals played out in politics—which is, as Arthur Scherr argues, sympathetic to New England in the attempt "to foster a harmonious Union."[27] Suppose we are to step back from the dominant interpretation of the Jefferson-New England relationship. This detour brings to the surface his views on the transformative powers inherent within spaces of local politics. In that case, a fruitful dimension emerges, one that affirms the political and physical space of the New England town hall meeting as a scene that sets its sights on the creation of the new, the making of a new order rendered only possible through the "in-between space"[28] of individuals and their exercises in collective power.

NATURE, SPACE, AND DIVISION

Jefferson's first visit to New England occurred in May 1784. He planned to explore better the region's industries, particularly fishery and commerce, to acquire a comprehensive understanding of the national economy. Writing to his friend Edmund Pendleton amid his travels, Jefferson outlines his goal for the northern journey, "I mean to go thro' the Eastern states in hopes of deriving some knolege [sic] of them from actual inspection and enquiry which may enable me to discharge my duty to them somewhat the better."[29] Appointed by Congress to serve as the primary liaison between European nations and the United States regarding trade negotiations,[30] Jefferson's letter to Pendleton expresses openness to the region and a general sense of intrigue and thirst for exploring the New England corridor.

Following his travels, Jefferson maintained an overall appreciation and respect for the eastern states, seen by his denunciation of Marquis de Chastellux's regional opinions expressed in his work, *Travels in North-America in the Years 1780–81–82*. As a former general in the French Expeditionary Force under the command of Rochambeau during the American Revolution, Chastellux cast a negative light over Virginia—mainly in part due to its climate—resulting in an underwhelming work ethic and vast pockets of poverty.[31] In a well-balanced rebuttal letter written to Chastellux on September 2, 1785, Jefferson confirms the impact of the climate on his home state yet paints the citizens of Virginia in a lively, compelling, and candid fashion. While Jefferson's affirmation of Virginia is not surprising, what is striking is his depiction of the inhabitants of New England. In table form, Jefferson compares the characteristics between Virginians and New Englanders, suggesting that the former are "indolent," "unsteady," and "fiery," whereas the latter are "laborious," "persevering," and "cool."[32]

In the summer of 1791, Jefferson once again returned to New England, this time with James Madison by his side. Exploring the sites of Shays' Rebellion and ecological attractions, Jefferson's travel journal and personal correspondences detail an intense exuberance for his discovery of the northeastern terrain.[33] As a continuation of the methodology employed in his *Notes on the State of Virginia*,[34] Jefferson's expeditionary writings carefully integrate elements of nature, such as the curvature of a river or the rolling topography of a mountain range, within a political landscape.[35] For Jefferson, nature is not set aside from politics, operating in a realm outside of its purview;[36] instead, nature is a necessary feature of politics, formed by the dynamic, physical forces of the political, while contained within the historical development of nature and a body politic. In this sense, Jefferson's classification and dissection of the Hessian fly,[37] mapping of Lake George,[38] and vocabulary cataloging of the Unquachog Indians,[39] undertaken on his northern voyage with Madison offers insight into his understanding of political development. For example, Jefferson's investigation of the Hessian fly included thorough documentation of its "habits, life, and depredations" to better understand its growing destructive impact on wheat crops.[40] By examining nature—both in physical and animal forms—Jefferson believes that each element of a specific setting, either positively or negatively, affects the prospects for human emancipation.[41] Therefore, Jefferson's ecological investigations are not separate from his political worldview; instead, they provide a spatial and temporal dimension to the possibility of democracy *within* the boundaries of the American republic.[42]

Jefferson's overall fondness toward New England displayed in his writings during the 1784 and 1791 trips show a vital context to his regional thinking. However, the real thrust of his affirmative praise for New England comes through, not in broad regional stokes, but rather in the details of his appraisal of New England town hall meetings. Approaching flat-out veneration, Jefferson views the localized, participatory, and inclusive structure of town hall meetings as the paradigmatic vehicle for enacting the vital principle of self-government, namely an ability for every citizen to engage in the administration of public affairs personally. To Jefferson, this "vital principle"—one crucially present in New England, according to him—is necessary for the preservation of self-government.[43]

This affirmation by Jefferson for the town hall setting is not, however, limited to the geographical region of New England. The design of Jefferson's ward republics finds its political genealogy from the town hall meetings. Jefferson's vision of a system of wards, first within Virginia and then increased throughout the republic, is striking, an attempt to transplant the energy, force, and dynamic momentum demarcated within the localized northern setting back to Virginia.[44] This attempt for replication is apparent in Jefferson's writings on several occasions.

Writing to John Adams on October 28, 1813, Jefferson distinguishes between a decisive division within a society of the pseudo-aristoi, a classification that is only generated through the arbitrary bestowment of titles and status, and the Americana *homo novus,* in the form of a natural aristocracy,[45] procured through the cultivation of virtue and talents underscored by a "sense of public duty."[46] An inoculation, or as Jefferson suggests, a "separation . . . of the wheat from the chaff" of the pseudo-aristoi is necessary to prevent government corruption.[47] To accomplish such a demanding task, Jefferson resorts to the act of division to dilute, if not flat-out undermine, the influence of an undeserving and corruptive artificial aristocratic class. Referencing his 1776 draft of "A Bill for the More General Diffusion of Knowledge" deliberated within the Virginia state assembly, a piece of legislation that advocated for the shattering of counties into smaller townships and structured around free local schools,[48] Jefferson informs Adams that the underpinnings of the bill were influenced by "*your* townships."[49] Jefferson's proposed path *qua* division for disseminating public education and the undoing of the pseudo-aristoi also contains an important political dimension to the scheme. As the wards would be defined by the self-government of popular control and engagement, Jefferson believed that active, localized citizenries, such as in the case of the New England town hall meetings, possess an ability to mobilize and alter the trajectory of the federal republic. Linking the theoretical possibilities of the wards to the actualities of the town hall venue, Jefferson praises this transformative capacity, asserting, "a general call of ward–meetings by their Wardens on the same day thro' the state would at any time produce the genuine sense of the people on any required point, and would enable the state to act in mass, as your people have so often done, and with so much effect, by their town–meetings."[50]

In a letter to John Taylor, dated May 28, 1816, Jefferson again praises the political structure of New England, this time in direct response to the problems of republican government. Fully aware of how an expansion of political space coupled with a retraction of accessible time for citizenry engagement leads to a diminution of political freedom, Jefferson provides a concise understanding of what constitutes a republic.[51] For Jefferson, all governments contain elements of republicanism, namely a political community formed by the sociability of citizens. However, an actualization of political freedom and equality impinges upon the degree to which the conditions of popular election and control are materialized within the composition of the republic.

The possibility of such a political community is tentative and contingent on the "very narrow limits of space and population."[52] Jefferson clarifies the dubious case for a robust, expansive republican government that maintains individual liberty and popular democratic control, suggesting that the scope of self-government must be kept small and local. Challenging the idea of a vast, commercial republic, Jefferson offers his vision of the ideal size and composition of a political community, arguing, "I doubt if it would be practicable beyond the extent of a New England township."[53]

Just two months following his letter to Taylor, Jefferson took up the troubling issue of space for a republic, suggesting that it "would be impracticable beyond the limits of a city, or small township."[54] In the same letter to Samuel Kercheval, Jefferson locates the *modus operandi* for active political engagement that characterizes the scene of localized politics. Rebuffing the idea that a constitution perfectly encapsulates the will of a nation, Jefferson offers an alternate setting for the maintenance of the American republic: "in the spirit of our people."[55] Jefferson's location of republicanism within the spirit of a people, rather than in constitutional form, is revealing as it points to precisely where he situates such an essential element to the republic. Jefferson claims that the federal judicial branch maintains an unruly and intractable power within the republic in opposition to popular control. The powers endowed within the court system, such as the ability to appoint juries and their irremovable status, cast them as a despotic force *independent* from public control. While Jefferson is not necessarily challenging the importance of an independent judiciary, one free from the sway of political pressure, his genuine concern rests along with an intrusive scope of the judiciary branch into public affairs that should be confined to the people as well as the absence of proper methods for recall of court officials. Attacking the omnipotent nature of the judiciary, Jefferson offers, "justices of the inferior courts are self-chosen, are for life, and perpetuate their own body in succession forever so that a faction once possessing itself of the bench of a county can never be broken up, but hold their county in chains, forever indissoluble."[56] Jefferson's mistrust of a federal judiciary in general, extending even to the Supreme Court, significantly underscored his presidential decisions—in collaboration with the more radical members of his party—to circumvent, if not flat-out destroy, the powers of the federal court system.[57] Jefferson's deeply held suspicion of concentrated federal seats of judicial authority was consistent with his larger view offered in the late-1790s that the federal government had been taken over by "monarchical and aristocratical" despotic forces.[58] His concerns are further defined and strongly emanates throughout his letter to Kercheval, offering instead an alternative judicial design that vests more power at state and local levels. He continues with a probing, yet rhetorical question, aiming to untangle the principles of republicanism with a federal judiciary, asking, "where then is our republicanism to be found?"[59] The answer is clear to him. Since the Constitution exists as a legitimizing force that insulates the despotic tendencies of the judiciary, ultimately leading to an erosion of republican principles of self-government, only the people serve as the necessary—and legitimate—depositories of a spirit of republicanism.

Jefferson is aware that his desire for judges' public appointment and removability is already in practice in one New England state, Connecticut. Elected every six months and subject to public recourse, Jefferson views this experiment in public control over the judiciary at the state level in favorable terms. He attests, "in one state of the Union at least it has been long tried and with the most satisfactory success."[60] However, Jefferson insists that if the popular election of judges is to be deemed unfavorable, then federal appointments should be relegated to the executive branch alone, rather than violating the separation of powers between the executive and legislative branches. Jefferson writes, "by leaving nomination in its proper place among executive functions, the principle of the distribution of power is preserved, and responsibility weighs with its heaviest force on a single head."[61] However, in matters concerning a state court system, from this point, emulating praise of the direct control of state judges found in New England, Jefferson quickly transitions into a discussion of his ward system. Adopting the practices seen in Connecticut at the local level, and importantly, the spirit of republicanism embodied not in constitutional form. Still, through commensurate sociability of the people, Jefferson posits, "The justices thus chosen by every ward, would constitute the county court, would do it's judiciary business, direct roads and bridges, levy county and poor-rates, and administer all the matters of common interest to the whole county."[62] He continues, "these Wards, called townships, in New England, are the vital principle of their governments, and have proved themselves the *wisest invention* ever devised by the wit of man for the perfect exercise of self-government, and for it's preservation."[63]

Jefferson's expression of the central role of a small, localized public space for preserving republican principles is firm. By redirecting a path of civic identity and action away from the contours of constituted authority, Jefferson's appraisal of the New England town hall meetings and the region, more generally, points to the very question of the political. Identifying the spirit of republicanism *qua* the people elevates a priority of the political *over* a deduction of myriad forms of civic action confined to a restrictive space restricted by the Constitution. The design of the wards or even the New England townships offers a multitude of pathways for citizens to engage in the tasks of full citizenship.

Throughout the winter of 1823 and the summer months of 1824 and 1826, Jefferson engaged in a series of correspondences with Maryland merchant and businessman Littleton Dennis Teackle.[64] Seeking out guidance for creating a

public education system that would focus on the principles of political economy, Teackle was directed by the Maryland House of Delegates to contact
Jefferson and acquire his insights into the matter. Although their letters are
primarily concerned with introducing education reform legislation, Jefferson
offers Teackle his most prized and valuable advice. Written in short, episodic
form, due to his deteriorating health, Jefferson proposes a bold idea to bring
about radical change: "the subdivision of counties into districts, called townships to the North and wards here is one of the wisest, smartest basis of a
republican government which has ever occurred to the wit of man."[65]

Jefferson's point here is not off-topic for Teackle's predicament. Instead,
it reveals Jefferson's belief in the value of public education. For Jefferson,
individuals and political communities require accessible space for intellectual
and civic maturation. However, not entirely detached from the overall federal
republic, this separate realm is firmly rooted in a local setting. Jefferson's
prescription to Teackle enables us to confront the main thrust of his view
of the New England town hall setting and its relation to politics. Rather
than obfuscate the inherent divisions of society via a federal configuration,
Jefferson envisions a local community as capable of exposing intra-society,
principally through education and deliberation over public affairs, lines of
exclusion predicated upon title, rank, and birth.

As we saw in his October 1813 letter to John Adams, the notion of division
strongly resonated in Jefferson's thought, particularly concerning the issue
of the aristocracy. A few years later, in a letter to Wilson Cary Nicholas on
April 2, 1816, Jefferson returned to the idea of division. In the letter, Jefferson
stresses a relationship between public education and politics. The relation
between accessible public schools and partitioning public space for political
engagement is vital, emphasizing the importance of education, training, and
dialogue freed from philosophical and economic coercion. Moreover, the
letter further reveals a crucial evolution in Jefferson's thinking that sees how
division can play beyond signifiers of class and status. For Jefferson, division
can now be used to remedy political deficiencies. Expressing his admiration
for division, he writes,

> My partiality for that division is not founded in views of education solely, but
> infinitely more as the means of a better administration of our government and
> the eternal preservation of it's republican principles. the example of this most
> admirable of all human contrivances in government is to be seen in our Eastern
> states; and it's powerful effect in the order and economy of their internal affairs,
> and the *momentum* it gives them as a nation, is the single circumstance which
> distinguishes them so remarkably from every other national association.[66]

Jefferson's language here is direct. Division acquires a vital dimension enabling safeguarding of public space for politics. Once again, Jefferson links the assurance of public space within the townships of New England, frequently referred to as "eastern states" in his writings.

Nearly seven years after this revealing letter, Jefferson communicated with William Cabell Rives, a representative in the Virginia House of Delegates for Albemarle County, concerning an ongoing effort for a statewide reform of primary schools. Seeking guidance, Jefferson continues to profess the need for division. He affirms,

> I think you will find the Massachusets [sic] plan the most simple and most easily accomodated [sic] to our circumstances. indeed it differs from the bill I originally gave mr Cabell on this subject no further than local circumstances required, and particularly in the substitution of specific for pecuniary contributions. you will find in that bill some provisions which you may think proper to introduce into the new system to be proposed. it is laid on the same basis as that of Massachusets [sic], a division into what they call Townships, but I would call by the more orthodox name of Wards. this will be the entering wedge of incalculable good.[67]

Considering the two passages addressed to Wilson and Rives, a division is a *sine qua non* to self-government. Merrill D. Peterson carefully identifies this crucial training infusion for public affairs within the New England education scheme. Peterson writes,

> The principle of public education was not new: common schools had existed in New England for generations. The principal difficulty of Jefferson's plan was the attempt to introduce a system borrowed from the close-knit environment of New England into the spread-out rural environment of New England. But the plan broke sharply with the essentially religious ideal of New England education, *substituting for it the citizen-republicanism of the new nation.*[68]

For Jefferson, the educational and political design used throughout New England served as a crucial model for emulation, coupled with careful modifications, to train a new generation of American citizens. Up to this point, four issues of division central to Jefferson's thought have been identified: i) physical space; ii) educational boundaries; iii) the Americana *homo novus* in a battle against the pseudo-aristoi; and finally, iv) institutions concerning public affairs. These division areas reveal an opening to Jefferson's understanding of politics rooted in a local scene.

Jefferson's understanding of New England town hall meetings takes on a transformative dimension, one that is generated and sustained by an active momentum and training of citizens in a local setting. The nature of the town hall, as understood by Jefferson, denotes a gap between the constituted power structure of the federal republic and the potential for an expression of constituent power by the people. To speak of a gap in this manner is thus to signify a distancing between the *people of the local* and the *fixed seats of the authority of the federal republic*. For Jefferson, then, the townships of New England represent an attempt to diminish the chasm between the people and the federal republic. Moreover, in Jefferson's view, the local politics of the New England townships maintain a potential to obliterate the gap between the local and national through the arrival of a force that could profoundly thwart the direction of the entire nation.

CHALLENGING THE EMBARGO

The most revealing aspect of Jefferson's thinking on the New England town hall setting is directly related to the issue of the Embargo Act of 1807. During his second presidential term, Jefferson was confronted with the problem of escalating hostilities against American merchants and cargo vessels by British and French forces. Embroiled in the Napoleonic Wars, these two nations opposed Jefferson's policy of neutrality, frequently ransacking and confiscating American cargo and seamen.

Following the Chesapeake Affair,[69] a deliberate attack against U.S. sovereignty by the British warship *Leopard*, Jefferson recommended an economical solution in an embargo to avert a full-scale war.[70] Passed by Congress on December 21, 1807, the prohibition significantly tested Jefferson's reflexive approach to political office, as New Englanders strongly detested it due to its adverse economic impacts. While public sentiment throughout the nation praised the war-thwarting effect of the embargo, many throughout New England clamored for, at the very least, modifications to assuage its stringent restrictions, if not a flat-out repeal of the embargo. Growing outrage continued throughout 1807 and 1808, prompting Congress and Jefferson to act.[71] Noble Cunningham Jr. details the uproar emerging from New England, writing,

> Soon after Congress assembled in November 1808, petitions seeking the embargo's repeal poured into the legislature. The most extensive petitioning effort came from Essex, County, Massachusetts, which sent petitions from sixteen towns. The petitions were in printed form with the name of each town written and each petition accompanied by from two to fifteen pages of signatures. The eighty-six pages of signatures appended to the sixteen petitions contained 4,101 names.[72]

In response, the House Foreign Affairs Committee was tasked with re-examining the embargo and crafting alternative paths of recourse, recommending to Jefferson that only Britain and France remain included in the embargo, ostensibly reopening trade routes to South American markets.[73] Unable to resist mounting pressure expressed by petition writing campaigns and public rallies,[74] Jefferson acquiesced and heeded Congress's recommendation, signing into law the Non-Intercourse Act on March 1, 1809, three days before ending his tenure in the White House.[75]

The resistance *against* the embargo speaks to the collective endeavors of New Englanders to form a sectional oppositional force.[76] The citizens' local, direct, and ongoing practices within the town hall setting unleashed a pulsating fervor that exploded upon the national scene. The town hall meeting emerged as "a contested form of political action" that saw an infinitude of individuals merge into a singular political voice strong enough to tilt the federal government toward capitulation.[77]

The idea of division functioned within Jefferson's thought can be extended here within the realm of public affairs, unleashing a momentum that took on a decisively political function. From this momentum-as-method, the New England townships resisted Jefferson's presidential policies, publicly appearing between the poles of the people and the federal republic. In his April 2, 1816, letter to Wilson Cary Nicholas, Jefferson affirms the eastern states' dynamic momentum energy about his call for division across governmental institutions. However, situating this understanding of momentum in dialogue with Jefferson's view of the sectional resistance in opposition to the embargo, an important radical democratic dimension is released.

In correspondence with Joseph C. Cabell, Jefferson asks, "How powerfully did we feel the energy of this organisation in the case of the Embargo?"[78] His response points directly to a specter of democratic action,

> I felt the foundations of the government shaken under my feet by the New England townships. there was not an individual in their states whose body was not thrown, with all it's momentum, into action, and altho' the whole of the other states were known to be in favor of the measure, yet the organisation of this little selfish minority enabled it to *overrule the Union.*[79]

The political practices of New England townships created a fissure in the organizational pattern of the federal republic through eruptive and oppositional pressure. The ability of localized democratic energies to thwart a continuation of the embargo represents a process that forced the federal government into de-escalation. At the same time, it suggests that small political units possess the potential to transcend a policy paradigm of federal governance, taking on an entirely more democratic dimension, one that destabilizes the very pillars of federal power. The communal structure of New England townships speaks to the ability of individuals to erect a sovereign political community outside of the organs of the federal republic, functioning critically as a critique of executive power.[80] Exemplar, in its ability to temporarily suspend a configuration of federal power embodied in constituted form, the energies of the townships, fortified within the parameters of a localized scene of democratic practices, established its very own kind of society on its terms. This signifier of democratic power was consummated through intimate and communal sociability that opposed a social existence of conformity devoid of political inclusivity.

Jefferson closes his letter to Cabell by alluding to his theorization of the ward system. Making mention of Cato's infamous proclamation of *Carthago delenda est*, Jefferson, too, advances his political maxim of division, "divide the counties into wards."[81] Importantly, then, what does Jefferson's letter to Cabell signify? Jefferson's appraisal of New England town hall meetings confirms his belief in a local scene as the optimal setting for politics. Further, Jefferson's letter to Cabell is revealing twofold: firstly, it points to how politics maintains a creative power, an ability to splinter the totality of centralized control, enabling an appearance of the people on a national stage; and secondly, democratic training, dialogue, and action produces incessant energy that bonds individuals into a collective identity, sustained through ongoing interactions with others.[82] These two central features further suggest that Jefferson envisions *local spaces* as the optimal setting for a playing-out of democratic politics and exercising civic duties.

In this aspect, the townships of New England maintain a valuable element in the Jeffersonian imagination. As the wish of the network of New England townships was to force the repeal of the Embargo Act, the citizens of these dissenting enclaves hoped that their own political and economic interests would alter the trajectory of the Jefferson Administration. However, to Jefferson, their actions represented something much more profound: a democratic expression of the people to win a space of its own through deliberation and action.

The democratic energies of the New England town hall meetings point to a condition of political life that is *always defined by struggle*, rather than the mere exercise of naturalized rights of contestation that occur periodically following exhaustion of legally permitted means of recourse. Jefferson's theory of radical democracy sees ongoing political challenges as the norm rather than the exception.

To recapitulate, the fourth characteristic of radical democracy offered is an active momentum to subvert the logic of the state as a point of rupture against the unsociability and uniformity contained through a political life defined by the state.

Democratic action directed against a singular figure of centralized authority is central to Jefferson's thought showing how political action is necessary for winning and constantly re-winning physical space for the practical realization of politics. Politics is the relentless quest for a home, an area that the political can call its own, a struggle caught between a departure in the wilderness and the promissory attainment of a homeland. A centralized governmental authority that operates outside self-government, coupled with self-sovereignty, tends to invoke such a departure. Jefferson's politics of all is thereby a project that attempts to continue an unfinished narrative of the people's struggles against the amassment of political power into a final, fixed image.

NOTES

1. See Massachusetts, *Acts and Resolves of Massachusetts*, vol. 1, 1692–93 (Boston: Wright & Potter Printers, 1869), Ch. 28.

2. For the impact that economic concerns played on the Puritan migration to America and within New England towns, see Barry Levy, *Town Born: The Political Economy of New England from Its Founding to Revolution* (Philadelphia: University of Pennsylvania Press, 2009), 17–50.

3. For the democratic and highly political nature, particularly in the town hall meetings, see Edward M. Cook, Jr., *The Fathers of the Towns: Leadership and Community Structure in Eighteenth-Century New England* (Baltimore, MD: The Johns Hopkins Press, 1976), 191.

4. Frank M. Bryan, *Real Democracy: The New England Town Meeting and How It Works* (Chicago: The University of Chicago Press, 2004), 26, fn 3.

5. Pierre Manent, *The City of Man*, M. LePain trans. (Princeton, NJ: Princeton University Press, 1998), 15.

6. Alexis de Tocqueville, *Democracy in America*, Harvey C. Mansfield and Delba Winthrop eds. and trans. (Chicago: The University of Chicago Press, 2000), 46.

7. Charles-Louis de Secondat, Baron de Montesquieu, *The Spirit of the Laws*, Thomas Nugent trans. (Kitchener, ON: Batoche Books, 2001), 332. Like Tocqueville's methodology, Montesquieu links up the laws, customs, and religious sentiments of a particular "people" to arrive at a generalized understanding of their intrinsic lifeworld and facets of government.

8. Tocqueville, *Democracy in America*, Vol. 1: Part 2, Ch. 6, 234; Vol. 2: Part 4, Ch. 5, 657; Ch. 6, 661–65.

9. Tocqueville, *Democracy in America*, Vol. 2: Part 4, Ch. 6, 663.

10. Tocqueville, *Democracy in America*, Vol. 2: Part 4, Ch. 4, 650.

11. Tocqueville, *Democracy in America*, Vol. 1: Part 1, Ch. 5, 65.

12. Dirk Jan Struik, *Yankee Science in the Making: Science and Engineering in New England from Colonial Times to the Civil War* (New York: Dover Publications, Inc., 1991), 71.

13. Written primarily by John Adams in 1779–1780 and ratified in 1780, the Massachusetts Constitution set stringent property qualifications for political office and voting. Moreover, it established the Congregational Church as the official church of the commonwealth. For Jefferson's view on the countless problems of state constitutions, see TJ to John Hambden Pleasants, April 19, 1824, *TJP* at the Library of Congress, Series 1: General Correspondence, 1651–1827, microfilm reel: 054, images 1–3.

14. See Joseph Haroutinian, *Piety vs. Moralism: The Passing of the New England Theology* (New York: Henry Holt, 1932); Perry Miller, "The New England Consciousness," in *The Responsibility of Mind in a Civilization of Machines*, eds. Jon Crowell and Stanford J. Searl, Jr. (Amherst: University of Massachusetts Press, 1979); Sumner Chilton Powell, *Puritan Village: The Formation of a New England Town* (New York: Anchor Books, 1965).

15. For Jefferson's critique of Northern urban spaces as rampant with crime, disease, and corruption, see TJ, *Notes*, 173; TJ to Uriah Forrest, with Enclosure, December 31, 1787, in Boyd, *PTJ*, 12: 475–79; TJ to Jean Baptiste Say, February 1, 1804, in McClure, *PTJ*, 42: 380–81; TJ to the Trustees of the Lottery for East Tennessee College, May 6, 1810, in Looney, *PTJ*, Retirement Series, 2: 365–66.

16. Morton White and Lucia White, *The Intellectual Versus the City* (Toronto: Mentor Books, 1964), 30–31.

17. For example, see Richard Hofstadter, "Parrington and the Jeffersonian Tradition," *Journal of History of Ideas* 2 (1941): 391–400; Reinhold Niebuhr, *The Irony of American History* (Chicago: The University of Chicago Press, 2008), 30–32. For Jefferson's views on the necessity for American urban spaces of industrialization, see TJ to Benjamin Austin, January 9, 1816, in Looney, *PTJ*, Retirement Series, 9: 333–37; TJ to William H. Crawford, June 20, 1816, in Looney, *PTJ*, Retirement Series, 10: 173–76.

18. Gary Wills, *"Negro President": Jefferson and the Slave Power* (Boston: Mariner Books, 2005).

19. For accounts of the disastrous effect that the Embargo Act had on southern states, see Burton Spivak, *Jefferson's English Crisis: Commerce, Embargo and the Republican Revolution* (Charlottesville: The University Press of Virginia, 1979); Louis Martin Sears, *Jefferson and the Embargo* (Durham, NC: Duke University Press, 1927); Henry Adams, *History of the United States of America During the Administrations of Thomas Jefferson and James Madison*, vol. 4 (New York: Antiquarian Press, 1962), 281–83.

20. Peter S. Onuf, *Jefferson's Empire: The Language of American Nationhood* (Charlottesville: The University of Virginia Press, 2000), 121–37.

21. Onuf also makes this point in "Missouri and the 'Empire for Liberty,'" in *Thomas Jefferson and the Changing West: From Conquest to Conservation*, ed. James P. Ronda (Albuquerque: University of New Mexico Press, 1997), 123.

22. Onuf, *Jefferson's Empire*, 125. For Jefferson's original letter, see TJ to William Short, November 28, 1814, in Looney, *PTJ*, Retirement Series, 8: 107–11.

23. Onuf, *Jefferson's Empire*, 125.

24. Onuf, *Jefferson's Empire*, 121–22. Onuf produces this claim by utilizing a letter from TJ to James Martin on September 20, 1813.

25. See Robert E. Shalhope, "Thomas Jefferson's Republicanism and Antebellum Southern Thought," *The Journal of Southern History* 42, no. 4 (Nov. 1976): 529–56.

26. See Kevin R. C. Gutzman, *Thomas Jefferson—Revolutionary: A Radical's Struggle to Remake America* (New York: St. Martin's Press, 2017), 76–81. Also see Robert Pierce Forbes, *The Missouri Compromise and Its Aftermath: Slavery and the Meaning of America* (Chapel Hill: University of North Carolina Press, 2007); Alan Taylor, *The Internal Enemy: Slavery and War in Virginia, 1772–1832* (New York: W. W. Norton, 2013). For Jefferson's view, see TJ to Albert Gallatin, December 26, 1820, *TJP* at the Library of Congress, Series 1: General Correspondence, 1651–1827, microfilm reel: 052, images 1–4.

27. Arthur Scherr, "Thomas Jefferson's Nationalist Vision of New England and the War of 1812," *The Historian* 69, no. 1 (2007): 5. Also, see Arthur Scherr *Thomas Jefferson's Image of New England: Nationalism Versus Sectionalism in the Young Republic* (Jefferson, NC: McFarland & Company, Inc., Publishers, 2016), 9–22.

28. Hannah Arendt, *On Revolution* (New York: Penguin Books, 1990), 175.

29. TJ to Edmund Pendleton, May 25, 1784, in Boyd, *PTJ*, 7: 292–93.

30. Max Beloff, *Thomas Jefferson and American Democracy* (Middlesex, UK: Penguin Books, 1972), 72, 78–81.

31. François-Jean de Chastellux, *Travels in North-America in the Years 1780–81–82*, trans. George Grieve (New York: White, Gallaher, & White, 1827). See Part II: "Journal of a Tour in Upper Virginia, in the Apalachian Mountains, and to the Natural Bridge," Ch. V, 287, 291–99.

32. TJ to Chastellux, with Enclosure, September 2, 1785, in Boyd, *PTJ*, 8: 467–70.

33. For a general sketch of Jefferson's scientific and leisure activities, see "Jefferson's Journal of the Tour," May 21–June 10, 1791, in Boyd, *PTJ*, 20: 453–56. For more detailed accounts, see TJ to George Washington, June 5, 1791, *The Papers of George Washington*, Presidential Series, vol. 8, March 22, 1791 – September 22, 1791, ed. Mark A. Mastromarino (Charlottesville: The University Press of Virginia, 1999), 229–31; TJ to Thomas Mann Randolph, Jr., June 5, 1791, in Boyd, *PTJ*, 20: 464–66; "Jefferson's Table of Distances and Rating of Inns," May 17–June 19, 1791, in Boyd, *PTJ*, 20: 471–73.

34. TJ, *Notes*. See Queries II, IV, VI, and VII for Jefferson's ecological investigations and analysis. Jefferson then links up the formation of rivers, mountains, vegetative and mineral deposits, as well as the regional climate of Virginia as a constituting force in the development of towns, governmental forms, constitutional creation, and laws. These political creations are thoroughly examined in Queries XII, XIII, and XIV.

35. See Adrienne Koch, *Jefferson and Madison: The Great Collaboration* (New York: Oxford University Press, 1950), 114–16; Stanley Elkins and Eric McKitrick, *The Age of Federalism* (New York: Oxford University Press, 1993), 240–42.

36. Catherine A. Holland examines this central tenet of Jefferson's political-ecological thinking. See "Notes on the State of America: Jeffersonian Democracy and the Production of a National Past," *Political Theory* 29, no. 2 (April 2001): 195.

37. "II. Jefferson's Notes on the Hessian Fly," May 24–June 18, 1791, in Boyd, *PTJ*, 20: 456–62.

38. "V. TJ to Martha Jefferson Randolph," 31 May 1791, in Boyd, *PTJ*, 20: 463–64.

39. "VIII. Jefferson's Vocabulary of the Unquachog Indians," June 14, 1791, in Boyd, *PTJ*, 20: 467–70.

40. Donald Jackson, *Thomas Jefferson & the Stony Mountains: Exploring the West from Monticello* (Norman: University of Oklahoma Press, 1993), 70.

41. See Myra Jehlen, *American Incarnation: The Individual, the Nation, and the Continent* (Cambridge, MA: Harvard University Press, 1986), 57–59; Christopher Looby, "The Constitution of Nature: Taxonomy As Politics in Jefferson, Peale, and Bartram," *Early American Literature* 22 (1987): 252–73.

42. Holland, "Notes on the State of America,"194–95.

43. TJ, "Proposals to Revise the Virginia Constitution: I. Thomas Jefferson to 'Henry Tompkinson' (Samuel Kercheval)," July 12, 1816, in Looney, *PTJ*, Retirement Series, 10: 222–28.

44. John Ferling, *Setting the World Ablaze: Washington, Adams, Jefferson, and the American Revolution* (New York: Oxford University Press, 2000), 165.

45. Erik H. Erikson, *Dimensions of a New Identity: The 1973 Jefferson Lectures in the Humanities* (New York: W. W. Norton & Company, 1974), 32.

46. J. M. Opal, *Beyond the Farm: National Ambitions in Rural New England* (Philadelphia: University of Pennsylvania Press, 2008), 7.

47. TJ to John Adams, October 28, 1813, in Looney, *PTJ*, Retirement Series, 6: 562–68.

48. For a detailed schedule of proposals contained within the bill, see TJ to Joseph Priestley, January 27, 1800, in Oberg, *PTJ*, 31: 339–41.

49. TJ to John Adams, October 28, 1813, in Looney, 562–68. Emphasis added.

50. Ibid.

51. See Major L. Wilson, *Space, Time and Freedom: The Quest for Nationality and the Irrepressible Conflict, 1815–1861* (Westport, CT: Greenwood Press, 1974), 11.

52. TJ to John Taylor, May 28, 1816, in Looney, *PTJ*, Retirement Series, 10: 86–90.

53. Ibid.

54. TJ, "Proposals to Revise the Virginia Constitution," in Looney, 222–28.

55. Ibid.

56. Ibid.

57. See Richard E. Ellis, *The Jeffersonian Crisis: Courts and Politics in the Young Republic* (New York: Oxford University Press, 1971), 234–42.

58. TJ to Philip Mazzei, April 24, 1796, in Oberg, *PTJ*, 29: 73–88.

59. TJ, "Proposals to Revise the Virginia Constitution," in Looney, 222–28.

60. Ibid.

61. Ibid.

62. Ibid.

63. Ibid. Emphasis added.

64. See TJ to Littleton Dennis Teackle, June 22, 1824, *FO,* National Archives, http://founders.archives.gov/documents/Jefferson/98-01-02-4345. Also see TJ to Littleton Dennis Teackle, March 31, 1826, *FO,* National Archives,

http://founders.archives.gov/documents/Jefferson/98-01-02-6002.

65. TJ to Littleton Dennis Teackle, February 14, 1823, *FO,* National Archives, http://founders.archives.gov/documents/Jefferson/98-01-02-3325. In the letter, the word "smartest" appears as "S[. . .]mest." This is most likely due to Jefferson's poor health in writing.

66. TJ to Wilson Cary Nicholas, April 2, 1816, in Looney, *PTJ,* Retirement Series, 9: 623–29. Emphasis added.

67. TJ to William Cabell Rives, January 13, 1823, *TJP* at the Library of Congress, Series 1: General Correspondence, 1651–1827, microfilm reel: 053, image 1.

68. Merrill D. Peterson, *Thomas Jefferson & the New Nation: A Biography* (London: Oxford University Press, 1970), 151. Emphasis added.

69. For a detailed account of the internal discussions of the Jefferson Administration following the Chesapeake Affair, see Dumas Malone, *Jefferson and His Time: Jefferson the President, First Term, 1801–1805* (Boston: Little, Brown and Company, 1970), 562.

70. Sears, *Jefferson and the Embargo*, 48.

71. Spivak, *Jefferson's English Crisis*, 180.

72. Noble Cunningham Jr., *The Process of Government under Jefferson* (Princeton, NJ: Princeton University Press, 1978), 312.

73. Reginald C. Stuart, *The Half-Way Pacifist: Thomas Jefferson's View of War* (Toronto: University of Toronto Press, 1978), 48.

74. James Duncan Phillips, "Jefferson's 'Wicked Tyrannical Embargo,'" *The New England Quarterly* 18, no. 4 (Dec. 1945): 470–71. For the various forms of resistance and efforts to end the embargo by New Englanders, see Thorp Lanier Wolford, "Democratic-Republican Reaction in Massachusetts to the Embargo of 1807," *The New England Quarterly* 15, no. 1 (March 1942): 35–61.

75. Stuart, *The Half-Way Pacifist*, 48.

76. Joseph A. Conforti, *Imagining New England: Explorations of Regional Identity from the Pilgrims to the Mid-Twentieth Century* (Chapel Hill: The University of North Carolina Press, 2001), 120–21.

77. To conceptualize the post-revolutionary crowd and its democratic potential, rather than strictly sociological, see Jason Frank, *Constituent Moments: Enacting the People in Postrevolutionary America* (Durham, NC: Duke University Press, 2010), 82.

78. TJ to Joseph C. Cabell, February 2, 1816, in Looney, *PTJ*, Retirement Series, 9:435–39.

79. TJ to Joseph C. Cabell, February 2, 1816, in Looney, 435–39. Emphasis added.

80. See Bradley D. Hays, "A Place for Interposition: What John Taylor of Caroline and the Embargo Crisis Have to Offer Regarding Resistance to the Bush Constitution," *Maryland Law Review* 67, no. 1 (2007): 202.

81. TJ to Joseph C. Cabell, February 2, 1816, in Looney, 439.

82. See Joseph Francis Zimmerman, *The New England Town Meeting: Democracy in Action* (Westport, CT: Praeger Publishers, 1999), 3.

Chapter 5

Divide the Counties into Wards

A Politics of All

Jefferson's vision of the ward system holds many promises to articulate active democratic politics. Configured as a network of small units, in the form of mini republics, the ongoing political action of its members serves as a safeguard against excessive encroachments by centralized seats of distant governmental authority. Jefferson envisions holistic output from constant engagement within these spaces, namely a physical site that functions as a crucial training ground for localized education and principally the space par excellence for citizens to engage, practice, and learn the art of politics sustained by a politics of all.

In turn, the ward system preserves and reignites the revolutionary spirit of 1776. It also, and more importantly, as Hannah Arendt briefly identified, resolves the theoretical and practical deficiencies of democratic-republicanism, namely the problems of political time-space and the unrelenting quest for empire through an intensification of politics and an enlargement of active participators.[1]

This woefully neglected side of Jefferson's thought helps explain his attempt to reconfigure the classical regime modeling of governmental form away from rule by One/Few/Many. Interestingly, the ward system maintains a significant economic dimension that stresses a pastoral vision of American society rather than a commercial view. Reliance upon a rural, agricultural economic structure affords all members with the necessary political and financial skills to actively engage in the task of self-government through the prevention of an entry into external forms of authority, specifically wage labor.

Jefferson's ideal political design, one that envisions a multitude of local republics, stands in sharp contrast to the Madison-Hamilton paradigm of patrician government. Unlike Jefferson, Madison and Hamilton sought to resolve the inherent flaws of republican regimes through a proliferation of economic activity that would effectively render the citizenry passive.

This vision of an extended commercial republic populated by disinterested, antipolitical subjects produce an antidemocratic form of government. The result, much like Jefferson's plan, operates beyond the conventional modeling of One/Few/Many. However, Madison and Hamilton's scheme eschews the democratic potential of Jefferson's politics, offering instead a system of American governance that places power in the hands of One (centralized national government), decision-making authority in the hands of Few (patrician representatives), and activity, in the form of economics, by the Many. These two distinct visions of American political life offer rich commentary on governmental structures and a historical lens for appraising prior regimes.

A thorough examination of the ward system helps to tease out the fifth characteristic of Jefferson's theory of radical democracy. This characteristic suggests the creation of horizontal networks of political communities that maintain autonomy while simultaneously challenging seats of authority operating outside the instituting community's direct purview.

Moreover, the wards strive to answer the critical problem facing the American republic: the supplanting of active, ongoing processes of political participation and deliberation by citizens for an ensnarement of constituted power that eschews the revolutionary fever of 1776.[2] For Jefferson, the wards aim to thwart an enclosed constituted authority that underscores the Constitution and an unresponsive federal government by subverting the direction of top-down political control back into a local setting predicated upon the active and full participation of all members. By uncovering this uniquely radical principle of a politics of all articulated in the scene of ward republics, the possibility for a democratic revival is offered, one that must transcend the limits of patrician politics to institute a "true democracy" in America effectively.[3]

THE DILEMMA OF THE REPUBLICAN REGIME: POLITICAL TIME-SPACE AND EMPIRE

For Jefferson, the ward system is nothing short of reconstitution of public space for the engagement of all members. Primarily, it sought to resolve two main problems that, according to Jefferson, had plagued republics throughout history. Firstly, the promise of accessible space for the actualization of effective freedom for *a new type of political citizenship* that reflectively prescribes its laws in concert with others while remaining, at least temporarily, free from the material constraints of existence. Furthermore, secondly, the infectious tendency to redraw the boundaries of a body politic through expansion to erect an empire.

Throughout history, the dynamics of republican governing bodies—a lineage spanning from the ancient Greek *polis* to the Roman Republic to the Italian city-states of the Renaissance—carefully accentuates the inherent and often contradictory tension between this promise of political time-space haunting energy and movement toward empire. From these two strenuous poles, a crucial dimension comes to light that captures the main thrust of classical republican theory. This defines a republican body politic as a regime of self-reflectiveness and perpetual scrutiny populated by the people striving to erect self-government *on their terms*. An understanding of this regime thus signifies a particular constitutional form of government and a theory of freedom articulated by the axioms of non-domination and self-institution. It is helpful to interrogate the historical and theoretical deficiencies of classical republican theory as the problems of a *democratic-republican* body politic that takes the *political* to signify the lucid activities of all aimed directly at the institutions of society *in relation to* an understanding of *politics* as an inherently democratic experience enacted through an explicit questioning of the established institutions of society.

Jefferson's theorization of the ward system—a network of civic republics—confronts the issues of political time-space and empire through a framework that inverts the pitfalls that had afflicted republics of antiquity and the Renaissance. By envisioning a common stage for all to engage in public affairs *while at the same time* localizing and redirecting the energetic drive for empire away from imperialistic endeavors, Jefferson reimagines the limitations and possibilities of a republican government. Before turning attention to how Jefferson accomplished such a demanding task, let us first more fully examine the crucial ailments of prior republics.

First, classical republican theory maintains a rich history that imports a commitment to direct and active political engagement as the ideal political participation. However, the feasibility of such a time- and energy-consuming endeavor became untenable due to the stringent labor requirements to fulfill material necessities and population growth. Neither Algernon Sidney nor Jean-Jacques Rousseau's idealized political communities can be seen here as the archetypes for this regime form directly confronted with the issue of political time-space.[4] Any territorial or population growth would undermine the availability (and necessity) for all members to participate in the ongoing process of law creation. The enlargement of the body politic in terms of both territory and population ultimately results in a diminution of *available time* for all citizens to engage politically due to the material necessities of life. The duality of the republican political actor, and in Rousseau's account, one that is conceived as both subject and citizen, becomes untenable and decisively degenerates away from citizenship and toward mere obedience with the inevitable growth of the body politic; a development that is permanently impregnated with the finality of decay and destruction.[5] In turn, the health of a small republican regime impinged upon a fixed boundary and homogenous citizenry linked with a surplus of free time available outside of the confines of the labor process.

Second, as an avid reader of classical antiquity, Jefferson was aware of the troubling expansionist instincts of republican bodies, especially in the transformation of the Roman Republic. Citing English historian Edward Gibbon's *The History of the Decline and Fall of the Roman Empire* in a list of recommended books in October 1809,[6] Jefferson saw a drive to empire predicated along imperialistic grounds as prohibitive to popular sovereignty and individual and societal enlightenment. Writing to Thomas Leiper on June 12, 1815, concerning the tyrannical and defective qualities of Napoleon Bonaparte, Jefferson likens the current depraved state of the European continent to the Roman Empire, stressing, "the establishment, in our day, of another Roman empire, spreading vassalage and depravity over the face of the globe, is not, I hope, within the purposes of heaven."[7] Again, in a letter to John Adams in December 1819, Jefferson suggests that the Roman people were "incapable of exercising a wholesome control" due to the decline of political involvement and the lack of ideas concerning self-government.[8]

Although Gibbon's account appears to have been Jefferson's most important link to the history of Rome, scholarship has crucially missed the influence that Machiavellian thought has played on the subject. In his private library at Monticello, slotted between Xenophon and Voltaire, Jefferson carefully placed volumes four and five of *Opere di Niccolò Macchiavelli, coll aggiunta della inedite*.[9] This work, printed in 1768, featured Machiavelli's fundamental texts, *The Prince* and *Discourses on Livy*. In his journal, dated April 26, 1784, Jefferson briefly summarizes an exchange with the prominent Dutch bookselling firm of Boinod & Gaillard, affirming the acquisition of the text.[10]

This is important not simply because it showcases the depth of Jefferson's historical interests but precisely because there are strong parallels between Rome's downfall and the design of the American republic envisioned by James Madison and Alexander Hamilton. According to Machiavelli, an insatiable ambition plagued the Roman Empire: "Whenever men cease fighting through breasts that whatever high-rank men climb to, never does ambition abandon them."[11] We shall see shortly that both Madison and Hamilton are fully aware of the dynamics of ambition. However, their prescriptions were not an inoculation from its energetic movement but rather a redirection into economic endeavors to pursue an American Empire. As the "city was never again free,"[12] due to its incessant move toward empire, Machiavelli—and, fascinatingly, Montesquieu's *Considerations on the Causes of the Greatness of the Romans and their Decline*[13]—greatly ascribe the expansionist ethos via economic and military pursuits of the republic-turned-empire as a powerful catalyst for the corrosion and ultimate demise of the republic. For Jefferson, Madison, and Hamilton embrace, and transplantation of ambition into an orbit of a vast, depoliticized commercial society will be met with great reluctance and trepidation to avoid the dangers that afflicted the Roman Republic.

THE MADISON-HAMILTON REMEDY TO THE PROBLEMS OF REPUBLICAN SELF-GOVERNMENT

The complications surrounding the dilemma of time-space and the drive for empire were of central concern to the American Framers. James Madison and Alexander Hamilton elaborate and offer a complex transformation of these potentially terminal problems ameliorated by scientific and technical progress detailed throughout *The Federalist Papers*. For Madison and Hamilton alike, the fate of historical political regimes could be avoided by "applying enlightenment science to the task of building a new polity."[14] For America to become an enlightened, free society, a scientific approach to creating a constitution was warranted. If done correctly, the constitution would establish institutions from a scientific standpoint while embedding them within a type of society that permits institutional adaptation, permutation, and change across generations. The possibility for modifications was thus built into the design of the constitution through the insertion of Article V, detailing the amendment process. Their first task, however, was concerned with the issue and potential activity of the people.

Madison's diagnosis of an active citizenry within a democratic society was unsympathetic. He viewed no direct benefit to the extension of political participation to resolve the essential elements of human nature. In *Federalist No. 10*, Madison rejected the prospects of a highly participatory political community, writing, "a pure democracy, by which I mean a society consisting of a small number of citizens, who assemble and administer the government in person, can admit of no cure for the mischiefs of factions."[15] Echoing similar sentiments, Hamilton describes ancient democracies, such as the Greek *polis* and the early Roman Republic, as "petty republics," viewing them with "horror and disgust."[16] For Madison and Hamilton, then, the complications inherent within pure democracies and republican governments necessitated a new method to destabilize the political energy of the Many while simultaneously rechanneling it into other contours of civil society. They would turn to the past to avoid replication to engineer a new political edifice for the American republic, which maintained a static vision of human nature yet a dynamic, progressive vision of society.

To construct a system capable of producing stability and liberty and the ability for modification, Madison and Hamilton sought to devise the

American republic not simply around the shortcomings of prior regimes observed throughout history but rather with human nature.[17] Therefore, examining their understanding of power, individual desires, and group dynamics are necessary to show how the American system was designed to direct central human tendencies while establishing a governmental framework responsive to science, technology, and economic changes.

In *Federalist No. 48*, Madison provides his view of power, contending that institutional mechanisms are necessary to check both men and government precisely because *power always wants to expand*.[18] This power-checking requirement is further linked to an argument advanced in *Federalist No. 51*. Madison suggests that a "necessary partition of power" must be established between governmental departments in this entry.[19] Establishing the American republic as a constitutional government,[20] Madison believed that a division of power, checks and balances, an independent judiciary, and a representative legislature could crucially manage power. This containment of power runs to Madison's bleak view of human nature and, as an offspring, the vital necessity for government: "If men were angels, no government would be necessary."[21] Madison's assertion and his negative view of humankind suggest an inherent difficulty in framing a government that would be administered by "men over men." To achieve this trying task, Madison contends that a double layer of security is needed in which government must be able to control the governed, and the mechanism of government itself too must be checked. Hamilton, too, advances a low view of humankind, accentuating passions' role on an individual. In a vital speech on June 22, 1787, during the Constitutional Convention, Hamilton invokes language strongly influenced by the Scottish philosopher David Hume asking, "Take mankind as they are, and what are they governed by?" His retort is nothing short of pure Humean thought: "passions."[22]

Highly influenced by Hobbesian and Lockean thought,[23] Madison saw individuals as essentially selfish and constantly pursuing power. Madison evokes Machiavellian overtones, suggesting that individuals have a deep-seated interest in ambition and an insatiable thirst to hold high political office.[24] Constructing his argument from these first principles, Madison, much like Hamilton, embraces the writings of Hume to illuminate further his solution to the ills that had plagued republican principalities throughout history, namely an interplay between the boundaries of political space and an impulse toward empire. In "'That Politics May Be Reduced to a Science': David Hume, James Madison, and the Tenth Federalist," Douglass Adair carefully traces Madison's adaptation of Hume's ideas for *Federalist No. 10*. Adair also points out that Madison's June 6 and 26, 1787 speeches at the Federal Convention were strongly presented with Humean inflections.[25] Following David Hume closely, Madison contends that individuals are motivated by passions and private interests, frequently adverse to the "rights of other citizens" or the community's common good. According to Madison, the notion of passions refers to individuals motivated by religious sentiments, whereas the pursuit of interests indicates economic connotations, chiefly attainment of private property.[26] As individuals differ in their passions or interests, Madison is fearful that several citizens could unite, comprising a faction.

To address a threatening emergence of factions, Madison asserts two methods for "curing the mischiefs of faction: the one, by removing its causes; the other, by controlling its effects."[27] Since the latent causes of factions are ontological, both methods categorically fail to remedy the origin and occurrence of factions. The enactment of the first method necessitates the destruction of liberty. In contrast, the second approach is equally impractical. It is predicated upon the annihilation of the "diversity in the faculties of men," which is the locus from where private property rights originate.[28] Since the causes of factions cannot be removed, Madison adopts the position that controlling the influence of factions is the only viable relief.

To control the effects of a faction containing a minority of support, Madison relies on the republican principle of majority rule to squash dissenting objectors. However, Madison's concern is the presence of a majority faction that could impose upon a minority. To deal with the occurrence of a majority faction, Madison offers three remedies to counteract the faction. First, Madison relies on the classical republican tradition of constitutionalism, which leads to a separation of power, effectively breaking up concentrations of power by making it more difficult for a majority faction to achieve what they seek. Second, the role of representatives is crucial. Specifically, Madison articulates an acutely patrician form of political representation depicted by a trustee relationship. For Madison, representatives do not emerge from the lower classes but rather exemplar civic virtue models through their sense of justice, patriotism, and the public good. Third, and finally, Madison sought to dilute the potency of factions through his proclamation of "extend the sphere."[29]

Madison's containment of factions through an enlargement of the republic—a broadening that does not trigger an increase in political time-space—rests upon his desire for a highly commercial state. In "extending the sphere," a stimulation of commerce will occur, spurring the creation of multiple interests, thereby leaving citizens deeply consumed by their economic interests.[30] As a result, political matters will be left to the well-respected, virtuous elites to *"Divide et impera"* (divide and conquer) political capital.[31] His solution, then, is premised on economic conditions with a fundamental view that citizens will be left with little time and energy to engage in self-government and democratic action.[32] Madison's plan is nothing short of extraordinary constitutional engineering.

On the one hand, Madison is cautious not to deny political access through an erasure of the political, thus establishing a narrow entry for the people into the political process as *Federalist No. 37* confirms that all power be *directly* derived from the people.[33] However, on the other hand, Madison carefully devises an intricate system that redirects the citizenry's energy and encloses political power into the hands of elites.[34] Madison's offering of a classical republican interpretation of liberty found in *Federalist No. 37*—crucially underscored by an affinity with anti-Federalist positions—becomes reversed in *Federalist No. 39* with his claim that the American republican government may derive "all its powers directly or *indirectly* from the great body of the people."[35] What Madison's enlightened, modern, and commercial republic leads to is a retraction of the political through an enclosure of political space by redirecting the flow of decision-making power into institutional departments at the hands of elected officials *while at the same time* directing the citizenry into a flourishing, time-consuming market.[36]

Hamilton also saw an expansion of size as beneficial, writing in *Federalist No. 9*, "I mean the enlargement of the orbit within which such systems are to resolve."[37] From this position, then, Hamilton posits that a large, diverse, heterogeneous, and plural society, reminiscent of Montesquieu's notion of intermediary bodies, will ultimately lead to an enlargement of the territorial bounds of the republic resulting in a reduction of the efficacy of factions and proper channeling of passions.[38] Here, Hamilton's view of the human psyche returns with its most substantial sway, shaping his political and economic vision. Since an inherent division between the Few and the Many underscores society,[39] Hamilton believes that a fundamental chasm must be exposed rather than concealed. Political power should be placed into the hands of the Few and the Many, with each body maintaining a vital check within their respected governmental department.[40] Naturally, the House was suitable as the depository for the Many, while the Few, endowed with privilege and virtue, would maintain a voice of opposition in the Senate. Hamilton's remedy for dealing with the unrelenting influence of passions operates within a purely political context. The real genius of his vision rests upon economic prescriptions.

With political power properly stabilized, or more bluntly put, destabilized, an energetic federal government—capable of instituting public credit and debt management through a national bank, sufficient military funding, and engagement with international trade, as Christian Parenti remarks[41]—was essential as *the* institutional mechanism to foster the development and proliferation of a commercial republic.[42] For Hamilton, consolidation of political power into a singular body via the federal government effectively created a redrawing of the legitimate boundaries for economic expansion, bringing with it, undoubtedly, the complete protection and enforcement powers of a comprehensive system that stood as a "permanent barrier" against the people.[43]

Just as Madison offered a redirection of factional interests, Hamilton, too, plunges the passions of individuals and, taking Madison's argument one step further, resettles the federal government into the depths of commercial pursuits. Empire is thus the *raison d'être* for Hamilton's American republic. For both Hamilton and Madison, the *civic republic* of the ancients and the Italian city-states of the Renaissance required an aptly modern transformation into a *commercial republic.*

As an embryo of a fledgling empire,[44] Hamilton's vision of the American state—a project that runs congruently with Madison's political thinking—demonstrates a theoretical attempt to rectify key problematic elements of republican self-government. For both Hamilton and Madison, important institutional mechanisms were necessary to thwart the wild, eruptive ethos of popular sovereignty found in ancient modes of government.[45] Understood as modern scientific inventions, these self-correcting institutional checks,[46] namely, creating a federal system defined by political representation and a division of power across departments offered a promise of surpassing and rectifying the deficiencies plaguing past regimes. Ultimately, Hamilton and Madison advocated for an enlargement of the republic to achieve enlightenment; however, this increase was advanced through economic justifications, effectively stifling the private interests and passions of the citizenry concerning political issues. What remains is an apparent retraction of political time-space—a shrinkage of available resources for active political engagement—in favor of acceleration and proliferation of economic interests propelled by expansionist energy at both the individual and state levels.

APPROACHING THE WARDS: PROPERTY, ECOLOGY, AND PASTORALISM

The Madison-Hamilton paradigm sought to establish the American republic on a direct path toward empire and expansion through the intercession of science, commerce, finance, and self-interest. Central to this vision of a large commercial republic is a particular conception of citizenship that disentangles economic pursuits from political concerns through prioritizing the former. The image of a citizen under the Madison-Hamilton specter is decisively an American iteration of *homo economicus.*

However, this vision directly opposes Jefferson's portrait of the ward republics and citizenship. Instead, Jefferson presents a radical and unorthodox worldview that sees beauty, sublimity, moderation, and the perfectibility of humankind, drawn along the backdrop of the pastoral landscape of the ward republics, as the optimal design to achieve public and private happiness.[47]

For Jefferson, political and economic space, coupled with available time for political engagement, are requisites for citizens to experience freedom—and then, in turn, pursue happiness—understood as a distinctively American version of *zoon politikon*. Compellingly, the development of the Jeffersonian citizen is accompanied by the internationalization of social responsibilities, an essential point drawn from classical thought and ethics, effectively rendering Madison's scheme obsolete.[48] To see how Jefferson uses the ward system to resolve the problems of time-space and empire, exploring his understanding of property and agriculture is essential, for it creates the *conditions* for citizens to achieve political freedom and equality.

For Jefferson, no natural right to property exists, and, as a result, only nature, not man, is the actual creator of value.[49] Since individuals lack natural property rights, these rights are established and enforced via positive law.[50] In a letter to James Madison on September 6, 1789, Jefferson extends his discussion on property, further outlining his unorthodox vision of the relationship between humankind and the earth. Jefferson offers his most unique and radical proposition to prove primogeniture and hereditary claims to property. He categorically asserts, "I set out on this ground, which I suppose to be self-evident, '*that the earth belongs in usufruct to the living*': that the dead have neither powers nor rights over it."[51] From this sweeping claim, Jefferson takes direct aim at both hereditary and aristocratic claims of prior generational supremacy, affirming the right of the *present generation*—freed from long-standing markers of rank, status, and wealth—to recreate the governing institutions for all in the present moment.

This attack on the aristocracy is only adumbrated in his letter to Madison. A fuller articulation of his critique resonates in a missive to John Adams nearly twenty-four years later. Writing to Adams on the benefits of science, understood as an "attainable and useful"[52] field of study, Jefferson marks a distinction between *natural* and *artificial* manifestations of the aristocracy. For Jefferson, virtue and talents—not pedigree or hereditary titles—are the most authentic reflection of a natural aristocracy, the "most precious gift of society."[53] Conversely, Jefferson sees artificial aristocracy predicated on wealth and birth as a "mischievous ingredient in government and provision should be made to *prevent* its ascendency."[54]

Jefferson's condemnation of artificial aristocracy runs directly to his understanding of property and, as a corollary, its instrumental value in achieving happiness. Since the earth is utilized in usufruct and belongs only to the living generation devoid of prior generational claims, no perpetual agreement can be permitted, whether in land entitlements or political constitutions. Instead, Jefferson advocated for releasing debts, civil laws, property rights derived from positive law, and political constitutions for each subsequent generation to exercise individual and generational rights. In short, prior laws, customs, and traditions do not bind *the people of the present* with "every constitution then, and every law, naturally expiring at the end of 19 years."[55] Jefferson's repudiation of the past and his future-oriented vision oppose the intensely pragmatic and respectful reverence held for traditions and institutions held by his fellow American patriots, such as Hamilton, John Adams, and John Marshall.[56]

Jefferson turned to the earth as the appropriate locus for individual development with individuals, each ensuing society unencumbered from the stringency of social, economic, and political hierarchies. Unequivocal in his advocacy for the cultivation of the earth via agricultural endeavors, Jefferson sees farming as the *human activity par excellence*. The striking sub-header for Query VII of his *Notes on the State of Virginia* provides valuable insights into his penchant for farming. Opening the query, Jefferson poses a question, "A notice of all that can increase the progress of human knowledge?"[57] What follows is telling, *contra* intellectual and philosophical proposals, as Jefferson offers a rigorous analysis of the contributing factors, such as suitable temperatures, levels of rainfall, and geographical locations, necessary for the flourishing of agriculture instead. Therefore, human knowledge and progress are symbiotically tied to individuals turning their talents, skills, and energy to enrich the earth. In Query XXII, Jefferson is steadfast in his promotion of agricultural development over-involvement in foreign commerce and financial sectors, postulating, "turn all our citizens to the cultivation of the earth; and, I repeat it, cultivators of the earth are the most *virtuous* and *independent* citizens."[58] Again, he echoes similar sentiments for the virtuous farmer in a August 23, 1785 letter to John Jay. Assaying the prospects of other laborious activities, he contends,

> Cultivators of the earth are the most valuable citizens. They are the most vigorous, the most independent, the most virtuous, and they are tied to their country and wedded to it's [sic] liberty and interest by the most lasting bands. As long as therefore as they can find emploiment [sic] in this line, I would not convert them into mariners, artisans, or anything else.[59]

Considering Jefferson's depiction of aristocracy, those who toil on the land can be seen as members of a natural aristocracy, advancing humankind toward complete emancipation. C. B. Macpherson picks up this latter element of Jefferson's claim, particularly the belief that farmers are *independent* citizens.[60] Macpherson importantly identifies that for Jefferson, an individual's possession of property ensured a life freed from oppressive, exploitative wage labor, *but it also* provided the necessary physical, intellectual, and emotional space for full development. In a letter to Samuel Kercheval, dated July 12, 1816, Jefferson renounces the European laborer's oppressive, dehumanizing working conditions precisely because it does not afford the worker any time to "think."[61] Jefferson writes, "as the people of England are, our people, like them, must come to labor 16. hours in the 24. give the earnings of 15. of these to the government for their debts and daily expences; and the 16th being insufficient to afford us bread, we must live, as they now do, on oatmeal & potatoes."[62] To escape a fate of exploitative labor and excessive taxation, Jefferson turns his sights on the soil. Not only is there more "time" for the Jeffersonian farmer to exercise his capacities, but as Jefferson details in his September 6, 1785 letter to Geismar, there is more "freedom, more ease and less misery" in the rural setting of Monticello compared to the dense urban spaces of Europe.

Further, Cornelius Castoriadis, consistent with Macpherson's appraisal, identifies Jefferson's emphasis on the proper conditions necessary for autonomy, linking his agricultural view directly to his political scheme. Castoriadis writes, "And when one knows of Jefferson's attitude in opposition to the development of large-scale industry (therefore, of a proletariat) in the United States of his time, one can comprehend that behind this attitude lay the idea that democracy had to be based on the small agrarian property."[63] In this sense, Jefferson views an independent farmer as perfectly suited to actively engage in a self-development project due to *sufficient time* and *physical space* affixed to a rural, bucolic landscape. Jefferson's agricultural aesthetic view here, which stresses a corresponding impact between individuals and oppressive working conditions, runs *contra* to the Madison-Hamilton conception of the market man. As those thinkers posited man as self-interested, rational, and economically minded, Jefferson—drawing from classical thought, as our previous section exposed—offers a conceptualization of man that is fundamentally antithetical to the market man model. Instead, Jefferson stresses, "nature hath implanted in our breasts a love of others, a sense of duty to them, a moral instinct."[64] For Jefferson, the heart, an "honest heart" specifically, is the primary blessing of man, not the rational mind.[65] Daniel J. Boorstin observes this innate feeling of duty and fraternity found in Jefferson's vision of man, explaining in *The Lost World of Thomas Jefferson*, "this sense of creaturehood that finally gave the Jeffersonian their sense of community and prevented an emphasis on 'rights' from becoming anarchy."[66]

Importantly, Jefferson expresses worry about ecological degradation and its effect on individual development relating to a "species of happiness."[67] Repudiating ecological destruction as a byproduct of progress enacted by the industrious world, Jefferson opposes any economic system that would destroy the environment. In a note reminiscent of Montesquieu's ecological concern voiced in Book XIV of *The Spirit of Laws*, Jefferson comments on climate and environmental conditions' effects on a body politic.[68] In Query XX of *Notes on the State of Virginia*, Jefferson favors the cultivation of wheat over tobacco precisely because of the extreme impact that tobacco farming has on the land. In a personal note titled, "Scheme for a System of Agricultural Societies," dated March 1811, Jefferson provides a litany of recommendations for the proper treatment of farmlands. Notably, Jefferson mentions a rotation of crops according to soil and climate; a principle of cultivation for wheat; a recognition of effective instruments to "correct the slovenly and unproductive practices too generally prevalent"; the utilization of "manures, plaster, green-dressings, fallows, and other means of ameliorating the soil"; and the creation of a report outlining practical husbandry techniques and practices.[69] Understood in inter-reliant terms, Jefferson views the cultivation and flourishing of the earth as a reflection of the development and progression of humankind. By toiling the soil, Jefferson believes an individual becomes inoculated from the excessive realms of economic and political coercion while at the same time properly engaging and developing their intellectual, physical, and moral faculties. Jefferson, therefore, advocates for both the proper cultivation of the earth *and* society writ large.

Jefferson's ecological concerns also extend to the agricultural system useful for development and sustainability. While Jefferson has frequently been cast as a steadfast advocate of agrarianism, a strict reading of this classification would vitally ignore his fears of ecological ruin *and* his embrace of appropriate scientific and technological advances.[70] Although highly political in orientation, Leo Marx views Jefferson's ecological position beyond the confines of agrarianism, picking up a *pastoral* vision promulgated in his writings. Marx contends, "To call Jefferson an agrarian is to imply that his argument rests, at bottom, upon a commitment to an agricultural economy."[71] Marx continues, clarifying the central distinction, positing that "Although the true agrarians of his day, the physiocrats, had demonstrated the superior efficiency of large-scale agriculture, Jefferson continues to advocate the small, family-sized farm."[72] Marx's analysis strikes a vital chord by carefully accentuating Jefferson's rejection of economic factors as the determining criterion for a societal organization. In Query XIX of *Notes on the State of Virginia*, Jefferson argues against the recommendations of European economists for a full-scale transition from agriculture to manufacturing. Strongly dismissing the prospects of manufacturing and reasoning that it results in a high level of dependency, Jefferson maintains, "Manufacture must therefore be resorted to, of necessity, not of choice, to support the surplus of their people."[73] Michael Hardt explores Jefferson's preference for agriculture over manufacturing precisely because it enables individuals to access productive property freely.[74] "His antagonism to manufacturing," Hardt contends, "follows directly from the fact that he cannot imagine how its productive property can be divided equally and all given equal access to it."[75] Hardt's illustration of Jefferson's economic concerns is essential for they help to draw attention to the inter-related nature between economic equality and political freedom.[76]

Rather than viewing Jefferson, then, as squarely an agrarian thinker, it is more fitting to consider him, as Richard K. Matthews contends in his work *The Radical Politics of Thomas Jefferson*, as a proponent of scientific farming. Arguing in line with Marx's analysis, Matthews contends, "Jefferson seeks a pastoral ideal, a form of scientific farming in which the farmer can take advantage of all the arts of agriculture."[77] Matthews concludes, succinctly summarizing Jefferson's thinking, "Quite simply, he wants all the benefits of science, technology, and agriculture without any of the costs of industrialization."[78] Significantly, Matthews's account stresses Jefferson's promotion of integration between science and pastoralism, an element that ties directly to his refutation of a society governed by an artificial aristocracy. In a letter to John Adams on October 28, 1813, Jefferson fashions his previous ideas on virtue via farming and the dissolution of artificial aristocracy in a discussion on the progression of science. He forecasts that "an insurrection has consequently begun, of science, talents, and courage against rank and birth, which have fallen into contempt. [. . .] and rank, and birth, and tinsel-aristocracy will finally shrink into insignificance."[79] Therefore, Jefferson's promotion of a pastoral society is not indicative of a *prior* sociohistorical epoch but a scientific advancement that acquires the benefits of agrarianism while nullifying the brutalizing effects of modernization and industrialization. For Jefferson, then, pastoralism is not a reactionary process. Instead, it is a future-oriented economic structure sustained by the labors and ingenuity of the present generation to revolutionize production modes, thus enabling individuals more time away from the labor process and greater availability for personal and political energies.[80]

Jefferson's centrality of property and pastoralism has far-reaching implications for his understanding of politics.[81] With his writings on property, ecological concerns, and pastoralism in place, it is appropriate to utilize this backdrop to examine *how* and *in what ways* his ward system fits into his democratic project. In a manner analogous to his vision of pastoralism, Jefferson's ward republics serve as the optimal scene for politics to play out in pursuit of freedom, progress, and happiness.

JEFFERSON'S WARD REPUBLICS: A SPACE FOR A POLITICS OF ALL

The treatment of Jefferson's ward system has been puzzlingly either cursory or absent.[82] Often dismissed and reduced to pure idealism that emerged in the later years of his life, the importance of direct political action by all members of the wards is, thus, woefully missing. However, to cast Jefferson's ward system off as a byproduct that manifested only at the end of his long political career is to dilute the germ of an idea that evolved throughout his thinking for over four decades. Jefferson's vision of a highly participatory political community did not suddenly percolate as a response to administrative and policy shortcomings during his presidency, as Suzanne W. Morse suggests, but rather it first appeared in his writings before ascending to the presidency.[83]

As Dumas Malone observes, Jefferson's 1776 constitutional draft for the Commonwealth of Virginia advocates transmitting knowledge to its citizenry through localized school districts. Further, Malone notes that Jefferson's horizontal scheme of education based at the community level titled "Bill for the More General Diffusion of Knowledge" was dismissed by the Assembly in 1776 and then again in 1779.[84] Malone is correct in emphasizing the destabilizing effect that such a policy platform would have enacted on the dominant social hierarchies of colonial Virginia. However, he fails to trace Jefferson's desire to divide public space as a central method for organizing a political community. Jefferson indicates this earlier impulse in a letter to Joseph Priestly on January 27, 1800, a full year before entering the Executive Branch. He writes,

> About 20. years ago, I drew a bill for our legislature which proposed to lay off every county into hundreds or townships of 5 or 6. miles square, in the center of each of which was to be a free English school; the whole state was further laid off into 10. districts in each of which was to be a college for teaching the languages, geography, surveying and other useful things of that grade; and then a single University for the sciences.[85]

While the letter certainly underscores the importance of education to Jefferson, it also reveals a reimagining of the boundaries of republics, both in substance and size. For Jefferson, the ward system enables enlargement of the overall size of the American republic while at the same time ensuring that all citizens have both the time and space to engage in local politics. Therefore, Jefferson's resolution of the deficiencies of republican politics is a rejection of the Madison-Hamilton scheme through an extension of the republic coupled with an intensification of politics at the local level.

An emphasis on resuscitation and rehabilitation of the political in Jefferson's theorization of ward republics was first noticed in Hannah Arendt's *On Revolution*. In *Nature's Man: Thomas Jefferson's Philosophical Anthropology*, Maurizio Valsania affirms Arendt's casting of Jefferson, suggesting that the concept of the wards is "downright Aristotelian" in orientation.[86] Although hesitant to stress a communitarian side of the wards, Valsania does, however, suggest that, according to Jefferson, the state lacks a legitimate right to its territory. Moreover, Valsania argues that Jefferson's philosophy is centered on a dynamic vision of a democratic society that sees all members freed from the state's scope of authority, empowered instead to engage in the task of self-government in the present moment.[87] Further, Peter S. Onuf argues that Jefferson's theorization of localized democratic politics functions as a mechanism to dislodge a multitude of political societies from the very framework of the state. Jefferson sees the sprawling federal government establishing a corrosive bond between local citizens and a centralized government, necessitating action at the explicit scene of politics found in the wards.[88]

Crucially, Jefferson opposed a large, centralized government. For Jefferson, power isolated in codified departments far removed from the people exacerbates the likelihood of political coercion. Jefferson is curt in his American government assessment in his September 6, 1824 letter to William Ludlow, alleging, "we have more machinery of government than is necessary, too many parasites living on the labor of the industrious."[89] Instead of a proliferation of vast governmental departments erected in state capitals and the federal District of Columbia, Jefferson envisions an inverted pyramidal government scheme with power flowing bottom-up. As chapter 4 detailed, Jefferson saw New England town hall meetings exhibiting a certain momentum of action against the parameters of codified contours of institutionalized power. By turning the source and flow of power on its head—thus returning political power to local communities and citizens—Jefferson assuages the political capital of patrician politics by directly connecting active political participation to individual and societal progression.

At the base of Jefferson's pyramidal government structure is the main concentration of political power housed in the ward republics. Drawing from historical examples of local politics, Jefferson believes that by dividing counties into smaller units, citizens will "attend, when called on and act in person"[90] on matters concerning the immediate community. It is fitting, then, that the Jeffersonian farmer is afforded both available time outside of an exploitive work scene to develop his faculties as well as the material opportunity to engage in politics. The significance of available political time-space cannot be understated. Jefferson sees society separated by a fundamental division between the "laboring and the learned."[91] The ward system facilitates the transformation of the laborer into a learned political subject by ensuring access to political time-space through a minimum level of property and an opening of accessible political space. The result is the production of new forms of association between individuals to rule autonomously, rending political representation complete by firmly linking the people to power and destroying the distance between the people and seats of authority. Such an understanding of the transformative capacity of the function of the wards obliterates the double purpose of political representation to *connect* while simultaneously *separating* the people from political control. Instead, the wards purge the *space* between the ruled and rulers.

Strikingly, then, Jefferson's citizen-farmer stands as a direct rejection of Aristotle's understanding of rural democracy outlined in Book IV of the *Politics*. Under Aristotle's classification of democracies, the best and oldest form is agrarian. In this form, citizen farmers are kept busy in the fields while being less envious of the "possessions of others."[92] Since most of their time is committed to working—an activity that provides them with much satisfaction—the active farmers will be less disposed and available to engage politically. Instead, the task of ruling will be relegated to those with a source of leisure time freed from the material necessities of life. Although Aristotle's account of agrarian democracy provides the citizen-farmer with the ability, or the *exousia*, for political engagement, the feasibility of engaging in the task of "ruling and being ruled"[93] is relegated to those in possession of *ousia*: the complete satisfaction of material and time obligations that permit a direct entry into the realm of politics. Aristotle's agrarian democracy is thereby constructed through the isolation of centrifugal political power safeguarded by an economic border that incubates the center of the *polis* from the contamination of citizen-farmers. For Aristotle, the best type of democracy is agrarian because it is generated by exclusions—a de-politicization of rural life coupled with an amassment of political power codified and restricted in the center of the *polis* maintained by a permanent un-retractable exile of the citizen-farmer.

Therefore, Jefferson's ward system represents an inversion of Aristotle's assessment of an agrarian democratic configuration. For Jefferson, the center of the body politic—the site of the ultimate source of political power—is transported to *each* ward through an erasure of boundaries that dichotomizes citizenship and political rights. Rather, Jefferson's ward system is defined not by an absence—a banishment of some in favor of a few—but rather by an active infusion of plurality and difference found across all members of a political community.

Jefferson envisions these small ward republics "five or six miles square" as fully functional complete units.[94] The scope of each ward's responsibilities are vast, including the institution of public education, a commitment to tend to the poor of the ward, maintenance of public roads, creation of protection agencies via local police and militia, and an operational court system.[95] In a letter to Major John Cartwright shortly before his death, Jefferson provides his most detailed account of the structure of each ward. He writes,

> Each ward would thus be a small republic within itself, and every man in the State would thus become an acting member of the common government, transacting in person a great portion of its rights and duties, subordinate indeed, yet

important, and entirely within his competence. The wit of man cannot devise a
more solid basis for free, durable and well-administered republic.[96]

Jefferson believes that individuals will develop their faculties through local
education in a well-administered republic. The importance of localized,
public, and *accessible* education can be traced back to his August 13, 1786
letter to George Wythe. Jefferson lays the framework for education's role in
this letter's later theorization of ward republics. Jefferson argues, "I think
by far the most important bill in our whole code is that for the diffusion of
knowledge among the people. No other sure foundation can be devised for
the preservation of freedom, and happiness."[97] Jefferson's belief in public
education directly impacts an individual's achievement of happiness, both in
private and vitally, in a public display. Collaborators in public happiness thus
inhabit Jefferson's vision of a political society as he offers, "I am convinced
our own happiness requires that we should continue to mix with the world."[98]

Crucial to Jefferson's promotion of local education within the ward republics is the role that it can play in *destroying* prior economic, social, and
political hierarchies. In an October 28, 1813 letter to John Adams, Jefferson
briefly outlines his vision of ward republics and the necessity for a free
school. However, in this letter, Jefferson posits an alternative benefit to the
advancement of public education, one beyond self-development and maturation, arguing, "Worth and genius would thus have been sought out from every
condition of life, and completely prepared by education for *defeating* the
competition of wealth and birth for public trusts."[99]

For Jefferson, the ward system is not simply a method for ensuring conti-
nuity and rendering political decisions in a localized space. Instead, it is an
explicit scene of questioning by citizens over the space between an immediate
source of accessible power and distant consolidated forms carried out through
a politics of all. Jefferson asks, "What has destroyed liberty and the rights
of man in every government which has ever existed under the sun?"[100] His
response is unequivocal and succinct: the amassment and concentration of all
power into a singular body.[101]

Significantly, Jefferson rejects the compression of all forms of power in
the hands of the "one, the few, the well-born or the many."[102] Jefferson's dis-
missal of consolidated power is intensified by his fears of a growing federal
government in early nineteenth-century America.[103] It is from these fears
that a political regime classification of a rule by the Many will not prevent
civic energies from becoming enclosed within a realm of constituted power,
crucially extinguishing the spirit of 1776. Instead, Jefferson believes that citizens must act in concert daily—shaping and sustaining the wards—in direct
opposition to external threats that attempt to usurp power from the people. In

turn, the Many must be broken up to ensure that *all could* and *all would* be counted against forces antagonistic to political freedom.[104]

For Jefferson, the active participator would rather have his heart torn from his body than power placed in the hands of a tyrannical state actor.[105] In a letter to John Tyler on 26 May 1810, Jefferson's politics of all reaches its pinnacle articulation, as he writes, "Could I once see this I should consider it as the dawn of the republic, and say with old Simeon, 'nunc dimmittes Domine.'"[106] The invocation of the *nunc dimmittes*—commonly referred to as the *Canticle of Simeon* found in the Gospel of Luke (2:29), meaning "Lord, now lettest thou thy servant depart in peace, according to thy word"—was of the utmost importance to Jefferson. Jefferson reminds his readers of the pleasure of reciting such a solemn hymn in several personal correspondences.[107] Writing to Andrew Jackson on December 18, 1823, Jefferson exalts the virtues of education, writing, "if I live to see this I shall sing with cheerfulness the song of old Simeon' Nunc dimittes Domine.'"[108] Notably, the *Canticle of Simeon* is a song of preparation and thankfulness for the coming messiah. Crucial to its message is an appeal to a vision of the future filled with joy and peace for *all peoples* of the world. The words spoken by Simeon upon receiving the Christ-Child, later translated into the Latin Vulgate, accentuate the universality of the messianic promise in the words *omnium populorum*, meaning *all peoples*.

This runs directly to the heart of Jefferson's radical democratic project. The salvation and promise of political power are to be endowed in the hands of the wards. For Jefferson, all governments, especially self-government, are an exercise in experimentation. An ongoing process in pursuit of creating a free and equal political society for the living, unencumbered by past generations, traditions, and institutions. Daniel J. Boorstin is skeptical of Jefferson's notion of perpetual renewal, claiming that all institutions would be in a constant state of flux, taken to its logical conclusion. Boorstin believes that Jefferson assuages this outcome by simply wedding the present generation to temporary permanency to its current institutions.[109] However, herein lies the crucial point. Boorstin misreads Jefferson's capturing of the revolutionary spirit within the wards as a cyclical endeavor that can (and should) only commence roughly every nineteen years. To reduce Jefferson's ward system to an embryonic site for future challenges against forms of oppressive government (or traditional and societal hierarchies, for that matter) is to miss the intent of the wards to oppose structures of power that deny a politics of all. To cast the ward system off as a systematic producer of permanent flux is not a pejorative depiction; instead, it stresses Jefferson's ward republics' ontological and sociological dimension, procured through a primacy of politics *over* regime form.

Michael Hardt makes a similar point. According to Hardt, the history of modern European political thought can be understood by two competing visions of sovereignty. The first line, running from Machiavelli to Spinoza, frames sovereignty as secondary, consummated from an association between the rulers and ruled, configuring the people as *primary*. The second vision, articulated by Hobbes and Bodin, and in Hardt's view, the dominantly victorious line of thought, places the people as subordinate to the autonomous realm of sovereignty. In this manner, the people become *secondary* to the primacy of the terrestrial sovereign (typically understood in religious terms). From this position, Hardt argues that Jefferson can be understood within the first line of thought and that resistance functions as the "constituent foundation" of popular sovereignty. Focusing on Jefferson's remarks around the events of Shays' Rebellion and the French Revolution, Hardt concludes that Jefferson unequivocally embraced a perpetual continuation of resistance (even in violent form) against the government as the "primary safeguard of freedom."[110] Linking the primacy of resistance with the possibility of freedom, Hardt writes, "Freedom for Jefferson is the right of the multitude constantly to exert its power over and determine the actions of government."[111]

Jefferson's theorization of ward republics represents a discontinuity in centralized, distant strains of authority, shaking the very foundations of governmental rule with a potential to "overrule the Union."[112] The transformative powers of the ward republics bring with them an emancipatory dimension that permits a reversal from minority status to political subjectivization and citizenship upon an accessible common stage for all. The work of the wards opens a shared space for the announcement of the rights of all through a rejection of heteronomy in favor of a way of life that permits effective participation in all forms of explicit power for public endeavors.[113] In this manner, Jefferson's ward system exists to solve the fundamental problems plaguing a republican body politic.

By expanding the overall size of the republic—an idea brought to fruition by Jefferson's authorization of the Louisiana Purchase—to provide all with economic security in the form of property ownership, coupled with localization of political space for direct participation, the two tensions become resolved. As a result, the activities of citizens within the wards strive to subvert a patrician order predicated along the lines of exclusion and miscounting by dragging division into the light of public inquiry, ensuring that all are heard, all are counted. Jefferson's ward republics are a scene of intimate politics, like the radical design of the Paris Commune: a place that opens new spaces for the daily participation of citizens to learn, engage, and experience freedom.

Jefferson's desire to obliterate the traditional regime model by thinking beyond the static categories of One/Few/Many represents a unique perspective in the register of American political thought. As Arendt notes, Jefferson's wards were devised to break up the Many, enlarging a political community to ensure that all were counted. The political vision that commences is thus a political order that eschews a patrician logic through radical democratization of who *can* and *should* engage in public affairs. It also enables the fifth and final characteristic of his vision of radical democracy to emerge: the creation of horizontal networks of political communities that maintain autonomy while simultaneously challenging seats of authority operating outside the instituting community's direct purview.

Like the thinking of Scottish philosopher David Hume, Jefferson's view of the ward system affirms the position that all power is inherent in the people, not in governmental form.[114] Direct training and action of citizens are central ingredients to Jefferson's understanding of democracy, which was, for him, the only pure form of republicanism.[115] Only by engaging does one learn how to become a collaborator in a political community defined by deliberation, action, and sacrifice. Democratic training thus becomes a constant activity, an experiment that (potentially) transforms individuals from an individualistic worldview to a communal plane. For Jefferson, the paradigm locus for democratic training is a localized setting, for it provides individuals with the opportunity to come face-to-face with all community members and the space for self-expression.

In this light, political freedom indicates an individual's entry among other citizens, always in public view. Political freedom, then, must be understood to be contingent upon the other, not merely in a physical and temporal sense, but as it is only possible through the freedom of another in a coterminous relationship between *libertas* and *civitas*.[116] On the other hand, political equality for Jefferson is intrinsically wedded to political freedom. The economic aspect of the ward system serves to escape an exploitative economic system to ensure self-sufficiency and, conclusively, happiness. Akin to classical republican theory, Jefferson believes that political freedom can be realized only when an individual is freed from the brutality of exploitive labor. It should not be surprising then that his vision calls for an extension and guarantee of property to ensure time and space for political engagement and the appropriate landscape for developing an individual's capabilities. For Jefferson, a system of little republics most properly provides for obligatory elements, providing citizens "direct and *constant* control" of decision-making instruments.[117]

NOTES

1. See Richard K. Matthews, *The Radical Politics of Thomas Jefferson: A Revisionist View* (Lawrence: University Press of Kansas, 1986), 81–89; Michael Hardt,

"Jefferson and Democracy," *American Quarterly* 59, no. 1 (2007): 70–71; Michael Hardt, introduction to *The Declaration of Independence* (London: Verso, 2007), xviii–xxi; Hannah Arendt, *On Revolution* (London: Penguin Press, 1965), 239–55.

2. See Antonio Negri, *Insurgencies: Constituent Power and the Modern State*, trans. Maurizia Eoscagli (Minneapolis: University of Minnesota Press, 1999), 147–53.

3. See TJ to Samuel Kercheval, September 5, 1816, in Looney, *PTJ*, Retirement Series, 10: 367–69.

4. See Algernon Sidney, *Discourses Concerning Government* (London: Printed by J. Darby, 1704), §44. Also, see Jean-Jacques Rousseau, *On the Social Contract*, ed. Roger D. Masters, trans. Judith R. Masters (New York: St. Martin's Press, 1978), Book the Third, Ch. I.

5. The inevitability of decay and the death of the body politic are undeniably central themes in the history of political thought. Plato's regime classification carefully illuminates the cyclical deterioration of political bodies and the corresponding new form. In Montesquieu's epistolary novel, yet significantly political, *Persian Letters*, the subject of decay is embedded within the historiography of the Troglodytes. For Montesquieu, political bodies are always subject to decay; however, this is accelerated when the ancestral past is repressed. Therefore, the essential duty of political citizenship is to preserve and keep the past alive in the present and projected into the future for the body politic. In his *On the Social Contract* and his unfinished *Constitutional Project for Corsica*, Jean-Jacques Rousseau discusses the devolution of the body politic immediately triggered once it is enacted into existence. Moreover, Rousseau cautions that a separation between the political body and the institutional arrangement of political power will most certainly lead to decline and decay. See Charles-Louis de Secondat Montesquieu, *Persian Letters*, trans. C. J. Betts (Baltimore, MD: Penguin Books, 1973), Letters XI–XIV. Also see Rousseau, *On the Social Contract*, Book the Third, Ch. X and Book the Fourth, Ch. VI; Jean-Jacques Rousseau, *Constitutional Project for Corsica*, in *Political Writings*, ed. and trans. Frederick Watkins (Madison: The University of Wisconsin Press, 1986), 279–321.

6. See "Enclosure: Thomas Jefferson's List of Recommended Books," October 4, 1809, in Looney, *PTJ*, Retirement Series, 1: 580–82.

7. TJ to Thomas Leiper, June 12, 1815, in Looney, *PTJ*, Retirement Series, 8: 531–34.

8. TJ to John Adams, December 10, 1819, *TJP* at the Library of Congress, Series 1: General Correspondence, 1651–1827, microfilm reel: 051, images 1–2.

9. See TJ, *Thomas Jefferson's Library: A Catalog with the Entries in His Own Order*, eds. James Gilreath and Douglas L. Wilson (Washington, D.C.: Library of Congress, 1989), Ch. 2, entry 144.

10. TJ to Boinod and Gaillard, April 26, 1784, in Boyd, *PTJ*, 7: 124.

11. Niccolò Machiavelli, *Discourses on Livy* (New York: The Modern Library, 1950), Bk. I, Ch. XXXVII.

12. Machiavelli, *Discourses on Livy*, Bk. III, Ch. XXIV.

13. See Charles-Louis de Secondat Montesquieu, *Considerations on the Causes of the Greatness of the Romans and their Decline*, trans. David Lowenthal (New York: Free Press, 1965), Ch. IX, 91–97.

14. Daniel Klinghard, "Technology, Progress, and American Constitutionalism," in *Rival Visions: How Jefferson and His Contemporaries Defined the Early American Republic*, eds. Dustin Gish and Andrew Bibby (Charlottesville: University of Virginia Press, 2021), 276.

15. James Madison, *The Federalist No. 10*, November 22, 1787, *The Papers of James Madison*, vol. 10, May 27, 1787–March 3, 1788, ed. Robert A. Rutland, Charles F. Hobson, William M. E. Rachal, and Frederika J. Teute (Chicago: The University of Chicago Press, 1977), 263–70.

16. Alexander Hamilton, *The Federalist No. 9*, November 21, 1787, *The Papers of Alexander Hamilton*, vol. 4, *January 1787–May 1788*, ed. Harold C. Syrett (New York: Columbia University Press, 1962), 333–39. Also, see Robert W. T. Martin, "Reforming Republicanism: Alexander Hamilton's Theory of Republican Citizenship and Press Liberty," *Journal of the Early Republic* 25, no. 1 (2005): 21–46.

17. While not as extreme as Jefferson, Jeremy D. Bailey stresses that the common understanding that Madison strongly favored stability over republican liberty is inaccurate. Instead, Bailey suggests that the importance of stability has long been overestimated in Madison's thought to the detriment of his commitment to republican liberty and the creation of a constitution that provides energy, stability, and liberty. See Jeremy D. Bailey, *James Madison and Constitutional Imperfection* (Cambridge, UK: Cambridge University, 2015), 11.

18. See James Madison, *The Federalist No. 48*, February 1, 1788, *The Papers of James Madison*, vol. 10, 456–60.

19. James Madison, *The Federalist No. 51*, February 6, 1788, *The Papers of James Madison*, vol. 10, 476–80.

20. See Hamilton, *The Federalist No. 9*, *The Papers of Alexander Hamilton*, vol. 4, 333–39.

21. Madison, *The Federalist No. 51*, 476–80.

22. Alexander Hamilton, "Constitutional Convention. Remarks on the Ineligibility of Members of the House of Representatives for Other Offices," June 22, 1787, *The Papers of Alexander Hamilton*, vol. 4, 216–17.

23. As a child, it is believed that Madison was familiar with at least one of Hobbes's works. However, in 1782 it is documented that he purchased a copy of *Leviathan* initially owned by William Byrd II of Westover. See James Madison to James Madison, Sr., ca. February 12, 1782, *The Papers of James Madison*, vol. 4, *1 January 1782–31 July 1782*, ed. William T. Hutchinson and William M. E. Rachal (Chicago: The University of Chicago Press, 1965), 64–65. Madison was quite acquainted with the writings of John Locke, particularly *An Essay Concerning Human Understanding*, first published in London in 1690. For Madison, both Locke and Montesquieu helped look at issues of political liberty, although their writing predates a further revelation of Enlightenment thought. This again demonstrates the future-looking ethos that the American Framers believed they uniquely maintained. In "Helvidius" Number 1, August 24, 1793, Madison writes, "Writers, such as Locke and Montesquieu, who have discussed more particularly the principles of liberty and the structure of government, lie under the same disadvantage, of having written before these subjects were illuminated by the events and discussions which distinguish a very recent period." See

Madison, *The Papers of James Madison*, vol. 15, March 24, 1793–April 20, 1795, ed. Thomas A. Mason, Robert A. Rutland, and Jeanne K. Sisson (Charlottesville: The University Press of Virginia, 1985), 66–74. In a August 12, 1793 letter to TJ, Madison admits that he frequently cites Montesquieu, albeit only from memory and typically inaccurately. See Madison, *The Papers of James Madison*, vol. 15, 59–60.

24. Garrett Ward Sheldon, *The Philosophy of James Madison* (Baltimore, MD: The Johns Hopkins University Press, 2001), 55.

25. Douglass Adair, "'That Politics May Be Reduced to a Science': David Hume, James Madison, and the Tenth Federalist," *Huntington Library Quarterly* 20, no. 4, Early American History Number (Aug. 1957): 343–60. Also, see James Madison to TJ, October 24, 1787, *The Papers of James Madison*, vol. 10, 205–20.

26. Drew R. McCoy, *The Last of the Fathers: James Madison and the Republican Legacy* (Cambridge, UK: Cambridge University Press, 1989), 41.

27. Madison, *The Federalist No. 10*, 263–70.

28. Ibid.

29. Ibid.

30. See Stephen L. Elkin, *Reconstructing the Commercial Republic: Constitutional Design after Madison* (Chicago: The University of Chicago Press, 2006), 24.

31. James Madison to TJ, October 24, 1787, *The Papers of James Madison*, vol. 10, 205–20.

32. See Richard K. Matthews, *If Men Were Angels: James Madison and the Heartless Empire of Reason* (Lawrence: University Press of Kansas, 1995), 153.

33. James Madison, *The Federalist No. 37*, January 11, 1788, *The Papers of James Madison*, vol. 10, 359–65.

34. Woody Holton, *Unruly Americans and the Origins of the Constitution* (New York: Hill and Wang, 2007), 10.

35. James Madison, *The Federalist No. 39*, January 16, 1788, *The Papers of James Madison*, vol. 10, 377–82. Emphasis added.

36. For a discussion on how democratic practices become muted when power becomes concentrated within the boundaries of constitutional form, see Sheldon S. Wolin, "Fugitive Democracy," *Constellations* 1, no. 1 (1994): 11–25; Sheldon S. Wolin, "Norm and Form: The Constitutionalizing of Democracy," in *Athenian Political Thought and Reconstruction of American Democracy*, eds. J. Peter Euben, John R. Wallach, and Josiah Ober (Ithaca, NY: Cornell University Press, 1994), 29–58.

37. Hamilton, *The Federalist No. 9*, 333–39.

38. See Harvey Flaumenhaft, *The Effective Republic: Administration and Constitution in the Thought of Alexander Hamilton* (Durham, NC: Duke University Press, 1992), 63.

39. Alexander Hamilton, "Alexander Hamilton's Notes," June 18, 1787, *The Papers of Alexander Hamilton*, vol. 4, 178–87.

40. Darren Staloff, *Hamilton, Adams, Jefferson: The Politics of Enlightenment and the American Founding* (New York: Hill and Wang, 2005), 84.

41. Christian Parenti, *Radical Hamilton: Economic Lessons from a Misunderstood Founder* (London: Verso, 2020), 149–65.

42. For Hamilton's economic plan, see Colleen A. Sheehan, *James Madison and the Spirit of Republican Self-Government* (Cambridge, UK: Cambridge University Press, 2009), 41–45; Michael P. Federici, *The Political Philosophy of Alexander Hamilton* (Baltimore, MD: The Johns Hopkins University Press, 2012), 187–213.

43. See "James Madison's Version," June 18, 1787, *The Papers of Alexander Hamilton*, vol. 4, 187–95. Also, see Colleen A. Sheehan, "Madison versus Hamilton: The Battle over Republicanism and the Role of Public Opinion," in *The Many Faces of Alexander Hamilton: The Life and Legacy of America's Most Elusive Founding Father*, eds. Douglas Ambrose and Robert W. T. Martin (New York: New York University Press, 2006), 175.

44. Alexander Hamilton, "The Defence No. II," July 25, 1795, *The Papers of Alexander Hamilton*, vol. 18, *January 1795–July 1795*, ed. Harold C. Syrett (New York: Columbia University Press, 1973), 493–501.

45. See James Madison, *The Federalist No. 38*, January 12, 1788, *The Papers of James Madison*, vol. 10, 365–72; Also, see Andreas Kalyvas, "Popular Sovereignty, Democracy, and the Constituent Power," *Constellations* 12, no. 2 (2005): 229.

46. See Lance Banning, *The Sacred Fire of Liberty: James Madison and the Founding of the Federal Republic* (Ithaca, NY: Cornell University Press, 1995), 188.

47. In several letters, Jefferson describes Nature in terms of the "beautiful" and "sublime." His political vision thus strives for integration in a naturalistic setting rather than a destructive entry *qua*, conquest and domination. In this way, politics takes on a holistic, aesthetic dimension where citizens use nature as a means of expression, ever cognizant of ecological destruction brought about by human activity.

48. Joseph J. Ellis, *American Sphinx: The Character of Thomas Jefferson* (New York: Alfred A. Knopf, 1997), 101.

49. TJ to Benjamin Austin, January 9, 1816, *The Works of Thomas Jefferson*, vol. 11, ed. Paul Leicester Ford (New York: Knickerbocker Press, 1904), 502–3.

50. TJ to James Madison, September 6, 1789, *The Papers of James Madison*, vol. 12, March 2, 1789–January 20, 1790 and supplement October 24, 1775–January 24, 1789, ed. Charles F. Hobson and Robert A. Rutland (Charlottesville: The University Press of Virginia, 1979), 382–88.

51. TJ to James Madison, September 6, 1789, 382–88. Jefferson's emphasis.

52. See Allan Bloom, *The Closing of the American Mind* (New York: Simon & Schuster, 1987), 349.

53. TJ to John Adams, October 28, 1813, in Looney, *PTJ,* Retirement Series, 6: 562–68.

54. TJ to John Adams, October 28, 1813, in Looney, 562–68. Emphasis added.

55. TJ to James Madison, September 6, 1789, 382–88.

56. Daniel J. Boorstin, *The Lost World of Thomas Jefferson* (Boston: Beacon Press, 1966), 241.

57. TJ, *Notes,* 77.

58. Ibid., 183.

59. TJ to John Jay, August 23, 1785, in Boyd, *PTJ*, 8:426–28.

60. C. B. Macpherson, *Democratic Theory: Essays in Retrieval* (Oxford, UK: Clarendon Press, 1975), 135. Emphasis added.

61. TJ, "Proposals to Revise the Virginia Constitution: I. Thomas Jefferson to 'Henry Tompkinson' (Samuel Kercheval)," July 12, 1816, in Looney, *PTJ*, Retirement Series, 10: 222–28.

62. TJ, "Proposals to Revise the Virginia Constitution," in Looney, 222–28.

63. Cornelius Castoriadis, "The Athenian Democracy: True and False Questions," in *The Rising Tide of Insignificancy (The Big Sleep)*, translated from the French and edited anonymously as a public service (2003), 320–21. http://www.notbored.org/RTI.pdf.

64. TJ to Thomas Law, June 13, 1814, in Looney, *PTJ*, Retirement Series, 7: 412–16.

65. TJ to Peter Carr, August 19, 1785, in Boyd, 406.

66. Boorstin, *The Lost World of Thomas Jefferson*, 245.

67. TJ to Charles Willson Peale, May 5, 1809, in Looney, *PTJ*, Retirement Series, 1: 187.

68. Charles de Secondat Montesquieu, *The Spirit of the Laws*, trans. Thomas Nugent (New York: Hafner Publishing Co., 1949). See Book XIV, "Of laws as relative to the nature of the climate," chapters I, II, XI, XIV, and XV.

69. TJ, "Scheme for a System of Agricultural Societies," March 1811, *The Complete Jefferson* (Freeport, NY: Books for Libraries Press, 1969), 353.

70. For readings of Jefferson and agrarianism, see A. Whitney Griswold, "The Agrarian Democracy of Thomas Jefferson," *American Political Science Review* 40, no. 4 (1946): 657–81; A. W. Foshee, "Jeffersonian Political Economy and the Classical Republican Tradition: Jefferson, Taylor, and the Agrarian Republic," *History of Political Economy* 17, no. 4 (1985): 523–50; Tarla Rai Peterson, "Jefferson's Yeoman Farmer as Frontier Hero a Self-defeating Mythic Structure," *Agriculture and Human Values* 7, no. 1 (1990): 9–19; Lisi Krall, "Thomas Jefferson's Agrarian Vision and the Changing Nature of Property," *Journal of Economic Issues* 36, no. 1 (2002): 131–50.

71. Leo Marx, *The Machine in the Garden: Technology and the Pastoral Ideal in America* (New York: Oxford University Press, 1964), 125.

72. Marx, *The Machine in the Garden*, 126.

73. TJ, *Notes*, 172.

74. Michael Hardt, "Jefferson and Democracy," 56.

75. Ibid., 57.

76. On this point, Barry Shank believes that Hardt places too much emphasis on Jefferson's economic views, particularly concerning access to productive property. Instead, Shank contends that Jefferson's contradictory position on property (and, in turn, slavery) negate Hardt's juxtaposition of it with the concepts of singularity and the common. See Barry Shank, "Jefferson, the Impossible," *American Quarterly* 59, no. 2 (2007): 291–99.

77. Matthews, *The Radical Politics of Thomas Jefferson*, 47.

78. Ibid.

79. TJ to John Adams, October 28, 1813, in Looney, *PTJ*, Retirement Series, 6: 562–68.

80. Jefferson's pastoralism would undergo modification following the War of 1812 when he embraced domestic manufacturing in the United States. However, Jefferson

believed an intensification of a manufacturing sector would be non-exploitative since citizens could withdraw their labor and return to their lands. See TJ to François André Michaux, December 14, 1813, in Looney, *PTJ*, Retirement Series, 7: 52–53; TJ to William Short, November 28, 1814, in Looney, *PTJ*, Retirement Series, 8: 107–11. Also see Joseph Dorfman, "The Economic Philosophy of Thomas Jefferson," *Political Science Quarterly* 55, no. 1 (1940): 98–121.

81. For example, see Dean Caivano, "The Question of Sharing: Thomas Jefferson and the Idea of Communal Property," *Histories*, vol. 1, no. 3 (2021): 85–99.

82. Examples of this can be found in Adrian Kuzminski's work, *Fixing the System: A History of Populism, Ancient and Modern* (New York: Continuum, 2008). Kuzminski traces the political and historical development of populism to mean a "direct right to property is a necessary condition of genuine democracy" (3). Citing both European and American examples of political movements that would represent a populist appeal, the study provides an in-depth examination of localized politics. Importantly, Kuzminski does include an analysis of Jefferson's ward system; however, this coverage does not appear until the appendix. In Kevin R. C. Gutzman's *Thomas Jefferson—Revolutionary*, Jefferson's ward system is explored marginally. In two cases, the ward republics are portrayed as idealist endeavors tied only to hypothetical reforms to the Constitution of the Commonwealth of Virginia. See Kevin R. C. Gutzman, *Thomas Jefferson—Revolutionary: A Radical's Struggle to Remake America* (New York: St. Martin's Press, 2017), 11, 65.

83. Suzanne W. Morse, "Ward Republics: The Wisest Invention for Self-Government," in *Thomas Jefferson and the Education of a Citizen*, ed. James Gilreath (Washington, D.C.: Library of Congress, 1999), 265.

84. Dumas Malone, *Jefferson and His Time: Jefferson the Virginian* (Boston: Little, Brown and Company, 1948), 283. It is important to note that primary schools were eventually created in Virginia. Passed in 1796, these schools' construction and operational costs relied on local funding.

85. TJ to Joseph Priestley, January 27, 1800, in Oberg, *PTJ*, 31: 339–41.

86. Maurizio Valsania, *Nature's Man: Thomas Jefferson's Philosophical Anthropology* (Charlottesville: The University of Virginia Press, 2013), 48.

87. Ibid., 66.

88. TJ to Gideon Granger, August 13, 1800, in Oberg, *PTJ*, 32: 95–97.

89. TJ to William Ludlow, September 6, 1824, *TJP* at the Library of Congress, Series 1: General Correspondence, 1651–1827, microfilm reel: 054, images 1–2.

90. TJ to Samuel Kercheval, in Looney, *PTJ*, Retirement Series, 10: 222–28.

91. TJ to Peter Carr, September 7, 1814, *Thomas Jefferson: Writings*, 1348.

92. Aristotle, *Politics*, trans. T. A. Sinclair (London: Penguin Books, 1981), 368.

93. Ibid., 362.

94. TJ, *Notes*, 153.

95. TJ to Major John Cartwright, June 5, 1824, *The Complete Jefferson*, 295.

96. Ibid.

97. TJ to George Wythe, August 13, 1786, *TJP* at the Library of Congress, Series 1: General Correspondence, 1651–1827, microfilm reel: 006, images 1–4.

98. TJ to Mary Jefferson Eppes, March 3, 1802, in Oberg, *PTJ*, 36: 676–77.

99. TJ to John Adams, October 28, 1813, in Looney, *PTJ,* Retirement Series, 6: 562–68. Emphasis added.

100. TJ to Joseph C. Cabell, February 2, 1816, *Thomas Jefferson: Writings*, 1380.

101. TJ to Joseph C. Cabell, 1380.

102. Ibid., 1381.

103. Ibid., 1380.

104. Arendt, *On Revolution*, 254.

105. TJ to Joseph C. Cabell, 1380.

106. TJ to John Tyler, May 26, 1810, *Thomas Jefferson: Writings*, 1227.

107. See TJ to Lafayette, May 17, 1816, in Looney, *PTJ*, Retirement Series, 10: 62–64; TJ to Spencer Roane, September 6, 1819, *TJP* at the Library of Congress, Series 1: General Correspondence, 1651–1827, microfilm reel: 051, images 1–4; TJ to Joseph C. Cabell, January 31, 1821, *TJP* at the Library of Congress, Series 1: General Correspondence, 1651–1827, microfilm reel: 052, images 1–2; TJ to James Monroe, June 14, 1823, *FO,* National Archives, http://founders.archives.gov/documents/Jefferson/98-01-02-3571.

108. TJ to Andrew Jackson, December 18, 1823, *TJP* at the Library of Congress, Series 1: General Correspondence, 1651–1827, microfilm reel: 054, images 1.

109. Boorstin, *The Lost World of Thomas Jefferson*, 212–13.

110. Hardt, "Jefferson and Democracy," 62.

111. Ibid., 65.

112. TJ to Joseph C. Cabell, February 2, 1816, 1381.

113. See Cornelius Castoriadis, "Power, Politics, Autonomy," in *Philosophy, Politics, Autonomy: Essays in Political Philosophy*, ed. David Ames Curtis (New York: Oxford University Press, 1991), 173.

114. TJ to Major John Cartwright, June 5, 1824, 295.

115. TJ to Isaac H. Tiffany, August 26, 1816, 349.

116. See Chaïm Wirszubski, *Libertas as a Political Idea at Rome* (Oxford, UK: Oxford University Press, 1968).

117. TJ to John Taylor, May 28, 1816, in Looney, *PTJ*, Retirement Series, 10: 86–90.

Conclusion

In a 1943 book review of Saul Padover's *Jefferson* featured in *The American Historical Review*, J. G. de Roulhac Hamilton suggested that it takes "considerable courage" to write anything original about Thomas Jefferson.[1] Nearly two decades later, historian Douglass Adair affirmed the reviewer's perspective, extending it beyond the realm of courage to a place of necessity to better grasp the foundations of Jeffersonian democracy.[2]

In the twenty-first century, the specter of Alexander Hamilton's thought has firmly dominated cultural and academic circles. This fascination has upheld and further mythologized an edifice of state power erected upon capitalistic logic, one capable of further mutating, adapting, and policing the neoliberal order. While the fetishization of Hamilton is deeply problematic, it reveals an impulse by the American people to constantly celebrate the key founders of the American republic. Perhaps, however, another return is warranted, not one that venerates or exonerates the moral character of any of the political architects of the republic, but one that centers the ailing corpus of the American republic on reimagining new avenues for political action. A return to Jefferson's philosophy may be helpful to rehabilitate—not the man—but the republic.

This lurking return will manifest from diverse origins, from attempts to rethink the limitations of Jefferson's thought to efforts to purge American history—and the present—from the horrors of slavery to considerations on how, if possible, to rehabilitate democratic institutions and norms. In many ways, the horizon for Jeffersonian studies is situated between the poles of denunciation and expansion, with public receptions shifting on vicissitudes of culture, history, and politics. Similar to how J. G. de Roulhac Hamilton's name has undergone processes of removal—his name has been scrubbed for upholding and shaping a culture of American white supremacy from an academic building at the University of North Carolina at Chapel Hill—Jefferson's legacy, too, hangs precariously in the balance.

On the one hand, work on Jefferson can virtually be found anywhere across the social and natural sciences, from anthropology to Critical Race Studies to oceanography. These efforts' "original" content impinges upon theoretical and methodological commitments that rely on particularities of Jefferson's thought, drawing from unique vantage points that shine a light on features congruent to such a reading. While this process is sustained through a selection-omission method, it helps to illuminate the vastness of Jefferson's writings both in subject content and in sheer volume, highlighting perhaps the great difficulty of engaging with his thought, namely a scarcity of time and resources coupled with a seemingly endless reservoir of material.

On the other hand, Adair's embrace of the "courage" claim helps to tease out a crucial aspect of research on America's third president, suggestive of exhaustion of analyses. From historical interpretations to biographies to cinematic presentations, Jefferson, the grand champion of American independence, has resonated across the republic's life. Jefferson has firmly saturated the American mind—often in ways that speak or reify a national identity, but also in ways that further legitimatize a lineage of systematic and institutional racism that still infects present-day America.

Lines from Jefferson's thought and life have been thoroughly drawn outward, and their landing points are telling: the social fabric of the United States remains ensnared by his influence, and his legacy looms largely. From a strictly academic standpoint, scholarship is flooded with work on Jefferson, affirming Adair's claim. Jefferson, the great American liberal, the staunch republican, the revolutionary, the statesman, the scientist, and many other renditions have left their impressive mark, imprinted on countless reams of paper, perhaps leaving no space available for new, original readings to germinate.

It is not too far of a stretch to ask, what remains? What remains uncharted within the Jeffersonian imagination? Moreover, and more pointedly, what does this moment within the history of the American republic offer for a "courageous" attempt to procure an original reading of the Sage of Monticello?

There is perhaps not a more polarizing figure in the republic's history than Jefferson. Intellectually, his writings were vast and impressive, employing a sharp legalistic worldview that stressed the sanctity of natural rights, the ability of a people to self-govern, a holistic ecological perspective, and a sociological examination of the sources and origins of power and morality. Politically, Jefferson stands as a pillar of American democracy, resolutely committed to public service, evident in his duties as governor of Virginia, minister to France, secretary of state, vice president, and, of course, president, governing to strengthen states' rights, civil liberties, religious tolerance, and economic prosperity concurrent with Western expansion. Culturally, Jefferson was a titan of the early American intelligentsia. A renaissance man deeply interested in the more refined offerings of life, thoroughly invested in the study of architecture, biology, linguistics, and history. However, it was not all highbrow, high-art decadence for Jefferson. His writings and lifestyle contained an essential element of pragmatism and pastoralism, natural curiosity, and a desire to return to the ground beneath us. Soil, plants, and the plow went hand-in-hand with his telescope, compass, and thermometer.

Strikingly, Jefferson remains the quintessential figure of the early republic: an iconoclast of tyrannical governments favoring a new experiment in societal design and self-government instead, one instituted and constantly reinstituted by free, laboring, self-sufficient individuals—sustained, of course, by a slave economy—constituted on a unique terrain that could escape the dreaded fate of republican time. In this light, to study Jefferson is to witness an ill-fated attempt to construct a new order, a new type of self-government, which offered the ultimate promise of democracy: freedom and equality for all.

This is, however, an incomplete illustration of Jefferson. While the scholarly pursuits of Jefferson are fruitful for these very reasons, they also have the potential to be problematic and deeply troubling. While this concern has undoubtedly always been an aspect of Jeffersonian scholarship—taken up in varying manners—recent years have witnessed a surge in critical voices emerging from *outside* the academy. From journalistic exposés to acts of vandalism to protests, these voices—appearing on the public stage at times in the form of the people and in other instances as a mob—have sought to reconsider Jefferson's legacy, seeking to recapture history for the sake of revision, if not, in some circles, flat-out destruction.

For these dissenting voices, to wrestle with Jefferson requires a confrontation with the issue of slavery and how, for generations now, it has continued to pollute the picturesque soil of the "little mountain" and the veneration that surrounds him. There is, however, a very valid argument to be made that by continuing to study Jefferson, scholars can reaffirm an irredeemable ontological and epistemological violence against the histories of radicalized peoples. Praise and celebration, or even academic analyses, on Jefferson, do have the potential to legitimatize further histories of institutional racism, white supremacy, and patriarchy that are predicated on exclusion and erasure but fetishize an image of settler-colonial power. This objection to studying *anything Jefferson-related* does not significantly fall prey to an *ad hominem* or even straw man position.

Studying Jefferson *is* complicated and problematic. Moreover, these concerns do hold water culturally, politically, and historically, particularly as the nation continues to grapple with racial injustices. Once again, the question of "what remains?" emerges front and center in the theater of public discourse.

Here, a turn to Hannah Arendt's thought, particularly to one of the most important political texts of the twentieth century, her 1963 work *Eichmann in Jerusalem,* is helpful to our present juncture. It is important to stress that Jefferson and Adolf Eichmann are not comparable historical comparisons. However, Arendt's method speaks to how we can assess complicated, troubled, and problematic historical actors. Arendt's primary aim in her coverage for *The New Yorker* of the public trial was to understand cognitively, psychologically, and ethically who Eichmann was and how such a person could have authorized such heinous acts as a primary architect of the Holocaust. Lost in the strong criticism levied against her reporting at the time is perhaps the most crucial aspect of her analysis, a point that informed her overarching politico-philosophical project. Commenting on the objective of her work, she asserts, "Yet I know that in every action that takes place a person is expressed by his action and his speech. Speech is also a form of action. That is one form of venture. The other is we start something. We weave our strand into a network of relations. What comes of it we never know."[3]

For Arendt, this meant thinking, speaking, and acting, as her analysis was meant to spur discussion in the public sphere. While Arendt maintained that Eichmann was guilty and responsible (and thus deserved to die), she believed that his trial served a valuable purpose, principally enabling citizens to hear of his transgressions and collectively decide on his fate.

In this vein and to follow Arendt, it is necessary to reaffirm that *thinking is dangerous. Thinking* about complicated and complex issues may be the most provocative activity available to the human mind. At a time when our public sphere is so profoundly devoid of dangerous thinking and complex questions, a reintroduction of an *unknown Jefferson* strives to initiate a *rethinking* of the foundations of the American republic and the potential for political theorization and, if fitting, resist it, tearing down the regal statues of bronze and marble that reach across the American horizon. The fate of Jefferson remains in the hands of the American polity.

Thus, we must be mindful of Isaiah Berlin's words on how intended consequences can produce new and more nefarious trappings that constrain liberty. Berlin warned that within every project of emancipation, there remains a seed of domination.[4] Such an assertion should be judiciously applied to Jefferson.

There is something quite daring in Jefferson's thoughts. There remain aspects of his thought that are both unorthodox to the American register and potentially heretical to the edifice of a consolidated, people-less republic. Scholarship has certainly not shied away from this position, casting Jefferson across a broad ideological spectrum, deeply woven in revolutionary garb. For Joseph Ellis, aspects of Jefferson's vision correspond to the thought of Lenin and Mao.[5] Ellis is not alone in his distaste for Jefferson's radical flare, evident in Conor Cruise O'Brien's claim that situates his political philosophy in line with troubling figures such as Pol Pot and Timothy McVeigh.[6] Following a similar classification, Michael Hardt insists that Jefferson is a central figure of the revolutionary constellation inhabited by Marx, Bolívar, and Guevara. However, unlike Ellis and O'Brien, Hardt's claim is offered in a complementary shade to urge a rethinking of Jefferson's political philosophy and contemporary democratic potential.[7] While these accounts provoke a sense of tremendous radicalism, Jefferson's thought has also resonated in opposite directions. Pondering how Jefferson's belief has endured, legal scholar David Mayer believes that one specific twentieth-century political philosopher came closest to fulfilling his political vision. For Mayer, that thinker was Ayn Rand.[8]

So, what are we to make of such a diverse treatment of Jefferson? Indeed, elements of "dangerous" thinking exist within Jefferson's thought. On the one hand, something that can be abstracted in acts of mass revolutionary action and, on the other hand, in a vision of a society premised along the lines of Objectivist philosophy and a purely unfettered capitalistic system.

However, these assessments are short-sided and incomplete. Neither Pol Pot nor Rand is a complimentary companion to the Jeffersonian galaxy. Nevertheless, the juxtaposition is telling because it shows how the American polity has never really come to terms with Jefferson's political project. As Reinhold Niebuhr attests, it has never indeed achieved his vision of political and economic equality for all.[9] However, it has never entirely escaped the great struggle between character and ideal under challenging ways.

Commentaries on Jefferson's philosophy have undoubtedly demonstrated these provocative attributes. Yet, these presentations have all-too-often relief on distortion, or even theoretical monogyny, to construct a narrow view of his philosophy. The real upshot to exploring Jefferson's political writings emerges from a voyage along the contours of theoretical originality immanent in content and in a particular arrangement of writings that moves beyond entrenched ideological foundational points. Such an approach offers a fresh perspective to both American studies broadly and democratic theory specifically by assessing *his* historical reading of the efforts of the people to win back the realm of the political. In this way, any hope for a new radical reading of Jefferson to ameliorate the ailments of the decaying republic is dashed away. Instead, it is in the ways that the struggles of sociopolitical agents throughout history, those seeking to gain political status, have shaped his vision for a more accessible, equitable, and democratic American republic that promising inroads are available.

Jefferson's thought alone is the not answer to overcome the perils of the present moment. His faith in the people and his trust in individuals to self-govern speaks to the importance of locating moments of democratic eruption when assessing shared histories or theorizing from the present, or even thinking, talking, or performing politics.

The answer to "what remains?" thus reveals itself as an announcement of affirmation: plenty remains left for exploration, for it can assist inquiries into our collective understanding and histories of democratic action. Further, it can illuminate the contradictory nature of the American republic from foundation to present and prompt, perhaps, more questions than answers. Critically, rethinking Jefferson's political project can renew and remind us that the question of autonomy is not an unanswerable inquiry but a meaningful pursuit that requires members of a political community to become and actively participate as *thinkers* of an autonomous collective.

A theorization of Jefferson's political philosophy—one animated by a politics of all—is an attempt to think *outside* of the Jeffersonian paradigm, which is defined by the contradictions of the sociopolitical realities of the early republic, and the inversion of Enlightenment emancipatory dialectics. An exploration into how Jefferson assessed and understood political challenges by the people *against* centralized seats of power, rather than a strict intra-interpretation focused on the contours of his thought, opens a heterodox passageway inviting us to rethink the origins of the early republic as well as offering a theory of political action predicated along the lines of constant, fleeting, and eruptive moments of contestation against conventional forms of political rule. In so doing, five characteristics of a theory of radical democracy emerged. To enumerate:

1. An impulse to create a public space accessible through the supplementation of available time, sustained by perpetual questioning and refusal to enclose the political within the realm of a centralized framework.
2. A rejection of codified, entrenched laws that place authorship outside of self-government favors the constant renewal of guiding principles determined by the community itself.
3. A moral and sociable view of human nature compels political subjects to collaborate with a powerless figurehead, serving as a conciliator for internal peace and harmony.
4. An active momentum to subvert the logic of the state as a point of rupture against the unsociability and uniformity contained through a political life defined by the state.
5. The creation of horizontal networks of political communities that maintain autonomy while simultaneously challenging seats of authority that operate outside the instituting community's direct purview.

These five characteristics point to an alternative conception of democracy, one strikingly beyond the orbit of liberal representative democracy. Envisioning democracy along these lines—as a politico-ethical stance against oppressive power—stresses how democratic values, norms, and culture are first-order principles in contradistinction to formal institutionalized processes that filter and constrain democratic energies. A theory of radical democracy elucidated from Thomas Jefferson's political philosophy impresses upon the political landscape of the present moment a specter that reasserts popular sovereignty, a primary of active politics, and a widening of the realm of citizenship to encircle all.

Jefferson firmly believed in generational autonomy. He was desirous of creating a society that would enable the present generation to escape prior hierarchies and stations of artificial privilege. This sense of openness and downright veneration for the living permeated his thinking on constitutions and progress. Condemning those that hold constitutions with "sanctimonious reverence," Jefferson affirmed the necessity for periodic revision of laws, enabling the living to determine the governing forces of society. "The dead have no rights," Jefferson insists, "They are nothing; and nothing cannot own something." Instead, Jefferson was unequivocal in his stressing of the primacy of the living, stressing, "this corporeal globe, and every thing upon it, belongs to it's [sic] present corporeal inhabitants, during their generation. They alone have a right to direct what is the concern of themselves alone, and to declare the law of that direction."[10]

Jefferson's fondness for societal renewal and generational autonomy was concomitant with his outlook on intellectual and scientific advancement. By freeing present and future generations from the past, Jefferson envisioned a diffusion of light, meaning a proliferation of education for all,[11] to foster the development of advanced modes of inquiry, enabling disclosure of "new truths."[12] For Jefferson, the progression of the human mind and, as a corollary, society writ large necessitates a reflectiveness and malleability to laws and institutions to more appropriately "keep pace" with change. Jefferson believed that political instruments must be recalibrated to capture, transmit, and reflect scientific, economic, and social improvements as societies become more enlightened.[13] Blending materiality and social production components, Jefferson expressed this necessity for political responsiveness and recreation, highlighting an adverse effect of permanently ossified, unadaptable institutions, writing, "we might as well require a man to wear still the coat which fitted him when a boy."[14]

The currently divided, hyper-partisan scene of American politics should take note of Jefferson's commitment to generational autonomy. American political parties have long struggled with energizing the youth vote, turning—in recent election cycles—to a more robust entry into new forms of voter outreach. While a digital entry across various social media platforms coupled with a tighter reliance on celebrity endorsements has resulted in marginal electoral gains for Democrats and Republicans alike, there remains a divisive generational rift on political style and substance. The millennial and Generation Z voters have greatly struggled to locate their voice(s) in the landscape of contemporary American politics, profoundly exacerbated by a firmly entrenched political class that often holds the younger generation in contempt, cast off as woefully inept in civic virtue *and* economic proficiency.

However, branding younger voters as "apathetic" or "disinterested" conceals a pulsating feeling held by many of these generations that their concerns are *unseen* or *unheard* and that they genuinely lack a space—beyond the narrowly digitized, ultra-filtered borders of social media—to *engage* in politics. However, important examples, such as the powerful adolescent voices that resonated in the wake of the tragedy in Parkland, Florida, and recent electoral successes in the House of Representatives by millennial candidates, affirm a vibrant sense of civic responsibility held among younger citizens. Drawing from these influential youthful voices and actions, radical politics must develop innovative strategies from both within formal politics of representation and outside the liberal-democratic state to develop new approaches to direct action and democratic decision-making from an intersectional and intergenerational perspective.

A radical democratic presentation of Jefferson's thought offers valuable entry points and alternative perspectives into significant challenges that face twenty-first-century America. The solution to these problems, and others, does not exist within the Jeffersonian worldview or any prominent figures of the early republic. Instead, surveying Jefferson's thought—a vision constrained by personal contradiction and theoretical limitations of exclusion—brings to the surface the complicated histories of the republic, including prominent narratives and neglected voices, stories, and events banished from the collective memory of a nation. Jefferson, the revolutionary figure, third president of the United States, and slaveholder, "still survives" to summon John Adams' dying words in commemorative, controversial, and mystifying ways. However, his vision of true democracy—defined by a politics of all—remains incomplete, permanently open for the present generation and all those to come to create.

NOTES

1. J. G. de Roulhac Hamilton, *Jefferson* by Saul K. Padover, *The American Historical Review* 48, no. 2 (1943): 356.

2. Douglass Adair, *The Intellectual Origins of Jeffersonian Democracy: Republicanism, the Class Struggle, and the Virtuous Farmer* (New York: Lexington Books, 2000), 1.

3. Hannah Arendt, interview by Güther Gaus, *Zur Person*, ZDF, October 28, 1964.

4. See Isaiah Berlin, "Jewish Slavery and Emancipation," in *The Power of Ideas*, ed. Henry Hardy (Princeton, NJ: Princeton University Press, 2013).

5. Joseph J. Ellis, *American Sphinx: The Character of Thomas Jefferson* (New York: Alfred A. Knopf, 1997), 150–51.

6. Conor Cruise O'Brien, *The Long Affair: Thomas Jefferson and the French Revolution, 1785–1800* (Chicago: The University of Chicago Press, 1996), 150, 313–14.

7. See Michael Hardt, introduction to *The Declaration of Independence* (London: Verso, 2007).

8. See David N. Mayer, "The Forgotten Essentials of Jefferson's Philosophy, *The Atlas Society*, June 23, 2010, https://www.atlassociety.org/post/the-forgotten-essentials-of-jeffersons-philosophy.

9. Reinhold Niebuhr, *The Irony of American History* (Chicago: The University of Chicago Press, 2008), 31.

10. TJ, "Proposals to Revise the Virginia Constitution: I. Thomas Jefferson to 'Henry Tompkinson' (Samuel Kercheval)," July 12, 1816, in Looney, *PTJ*, Retirement Series, 10: 222–28.

11. See TJ to the Trustees of the Lottery for East Tennessee College, May 6, 1810, in Looney, *PTJ*, Retirement Series, 2: 365–66. Also, see TJ to Charles Yancey, January 6, 1816, in Looney, *PTJ*, Retirement Series, 9: 328–31.

12. TJ, "Proposals to Revise the Virginia Constitution," in Looney, *PTJ*, Retirement Series, 10: 222–28.

13. This line of thinking shapes the primary contours of John Dewey's thoughts on democratic education and social transformation. See John Dewey, *Democracy and Education* (New York: The Free Press, 1944), 9.

14. TJ, "Proposals to Revise the Virginia Constitution," in Looney, *PTJ*, Retirement Series, 10: 222–28.

Bibliography

Adair, Douglass. *Fame and the Founding Fathers: Essays of Douglass Adair*. Edited by H. Trevor Colburn. Indianapolis, IN: Liberty Fund, 1998.

———. *The Intellectual Origins of Jeffersonian Democracy: Republicanism, the Class Struggle, and the Virtuous Farmer*. Edited by Mark E. Yellin. New York: Lexington Books, 2000.

———. "'That Politics May Be Reduced to a Science': David Hume, James Madison, and the Tenth Federalist." *Huntington Library Quarterly* 20, no. 4, Early American History Number (1957): 343–60.

Adams, Henry. *History of the United States of America During the Administrations of Thomas Jefferson and James Madison*, vol. 4. New York: Antiquarian Press, 1962.

Adams, William Howard. *The Paris Years of Thomas Jefferson*. New Haven, CT: Yale University Press, 1997.

Arendt, Hannah. "The Concept of History." In *Between Past and Future*. New York: Penguin Books, 2006.

———. *The Human Condition*. Chicago: The University of Chicago Press, 1998.

———. Interview with Güther Gaus. *Zur Person*. ZDF, October 28, 1964.

———. *On Revolution*. New York: Penguin Books, 1990.

———. "On Violence." In *Crises of the Republic*. New York: Harcourt, Brace & Co., 1972.

———. *The Origins of Totalitarianism*. New York: Harcourt, Brace & Co., 1973.

Aristotle. *Politics*. Translated by T. A. Sinclair. London: Penguin Books, 1981.

Badiou, Alain. *Pocket Pantheon*. Translated by David Macey. London: Verso, 2016.

Bailey, Jeremy D. *James Madison and Constitutional Imperfection*. Cambridge, UK: Cambridge University, 2015.

———. *Thomas Jefferson and Executive Power*. Cambridge, UK: Cambridge University Press, 2009.

Bailyn, Bernard. *The Ideological Origins of the American Revolution*. Cambridge, MA: The Belknap Press of Harvard University, 1992.

Bancroft, George. *A History of the United States, From the Discovery of the American Continent*. Boston: Little, Brown and Company, 1834.

———. *History of the Formation of the Constitution of the United States of America*. New York: D. Appleton, 1882.

Banning, Lance. *The Sacred Fire of Liberty: James Madison and the Founding of the Federal Republic*. Ithaca, NY: Cornell University Press, 1995.

Barr, J. S. *Barr's Buffon*, vol. VII. London: J. S. Barr, 1792.

Bean, Michael Knox. *Jefferson's Demons: Portrait of a Restless Mind*. New York: Free Press, 2003.

Beloff, Max. *Thomas Jefferson and American Democracy*. Middlesex, UK: Penguin Books, 1972.

Beer, George L. *The Commercial Policy of England toward the American Colonies*. New York: Columbia College, 1893.

Beitzinger, A. J. *A History of American Political Thought*. Eugene, OR: Resource Publications, 1972.

Berlin, Isaiah. "Jewish Slavery and Emancipation." In *The Power of Ideas*. Edited by Henry Hardy. Princeton, NJ: Princeton University Press, 2013.

Bernstein, Richard B. *Thomas Jefferson: The Revolution of Ideas*. Oxford, UK: Oxford University Press, 2004.

Blackstone, William. *Commentaries on the Laws of England*. Buffalo: William S. Hein & Co., 1992.

Bloom, Allan. *The Closing of the American Mind*. New York: Simon & Schuster, 1987.

Bober, Natalie S. *Thomas Jefferson: Draftsman of a Nation*. Charlottesville: The University of Virginia Press, 2007.

Boorstin, Daniel J. *The Lost World of Thomas Jefferson*. Boston: Beacon Press, 1948.

Bordewich, Fergus M. *Killing the White Man's Indian: Reinventing Native Americans at the End of the Twentieth Century*. New York: Anchor Books, 1996.

Boucher, Jonathan. *Reminiscences of an American Loyalist, 1738–1789*. Boston: Houghton Mifflin, 1925.

Breaugh, Martin, and Dean Caivano, "A Living Critique of Domination: Exemplars of Radical Democracy from Black Lives Matter to #MeToo" *Philosophy and Social Criticism* (May 2022). doi:10.1177/01914537221093726.

Briggs, Isaac. "A Cordial Reunion in 1820." In *Visitors to Monticello*. Edited by Merrill D. Peterson. Charlottesville: The University of Virginia Press, 1989.

Broadwater, Jeff. *George Mason: Forgotten Founder*. Chapel Hill: The University of North Carolina Press, 2006.

Browne, Stephen Howard. "Jefferson's First Declaration of Independence: A Summary View of the Rights of British America Revisited." *Quarterly Journal of Speech* 89, no. 3 (2003): 235–52.

Bryan, Frank M. *Real Democracy: The New England Town Meeting and How It Works*. Chicago: The University of Chicago Press, 2004.

Buffon, Georges Louis Marie Leclerc. *Histoire Naturelle, Générale et Particulière*, vol. IX. Paris: Imprimerie Royale, Plassan, 1749–1804.

Burstein, Andrew, and Nancy Isenberg. *Madison and Jefferson*. New York: Random House, 2010.

Bury, J. B. *The Ancient Greek Historians*. New York: Dover Publications, 1958.

Caivano, Dean. "The Question of Sharing: Thomas Jefferson and the Idea of Communal Property." *Histories* 1, no. 3 (2021): 85–99.

Cartledge, Paul. *Democracy: A Life*. Oxford, UK: Oxford University Press, 2016.

Castoriadis, Cornelius. *The Castoriadis Reader*. Edited by David Ames Curtis. Oxford, UK: Blackwell Publishers, 1997.

———. *Philosophy, Politics, Autonomy: Essays in Political Philosophy*. Edited by David Ames Curtis. New York: Oxford University Press, 1991.

———. *Political and Social Writings, Volume 2*. Edited by David Ames Curtis. Minneapolis, MN: University of Minnesota Press, 1988.

———. "The Athenian Democracy: True and False Questions." In *The Rising Tide of Insignificancy (The Big Sleep)*. Translated from the French and edited anonymously as a public service. (2003). http://www.notbored.org/RTI.pdf.

Chastellux, François-Jean de. *Travels in North-America in the Years 1780–81–82*. Translated by George Grieve. New York: White, Gallaher, & White, 1827.

Chinard, Gilbert. "Polybius and the American Constitution." *Journal of the History of Ideas* 1, no. 1 (1940): 38–58.

———. *Thomas Jefferson: The Apostle of Americanism*. Ann Arbor: The University of Michigan Press, 1957.

Clastres, Pierre. *Archelogy of Violence*. Translated by Jeanine Herman. New York: Zone Books, 1994.

———. *Society Against the State: Essays in Political Anthropology*. Translated by Robert Hurley. New York: Zone Books, 1989.

Cobbett, William, and Thomas Cursor Hansard, eds. "The King's Speech on Opening the Session." In *The Parliamentary History of England: From the Earliest Period to the Year 1803*, vol. XVIII. London: Printed by T. C. Hansard, 1813.

Cogliano, Francis D. *Thomas Jefferson: Reputation and Legacy*. Charlottesville: The University of Virginia Press, 2006.

Colburn, H. Trevor. *The Lamp of Experience: Whig History and the Intellectual Origins of the American Revolution*. Chapel Hill: University of North Carolina Press, 1965.

———. "Thomas Jefferson's Use of the Past." *The William and Mary Quarterly* 15, no. 3 (1958): 56–78.

Conforti, Joseph A. *Imagining New England: Explorations of Regional Identity from the Pilgrims to the Mid-Twentieth Century*. Chapel Hill: The University of North Carolina Press, 2001.

Conn, Steven. *History's Shadow: Native Americans and Historical Consciousness in the Nineteenth Century*. Chicago: The University of Chicago Press, 2004.

Constant, Benjamin. *De la liberté des Anciens ompare à celle des Modernes* in *Oeuvres politiques de Benjamin Constant*. Edited by Charles Loundre. Paris, 1874.

Cook, Jr., Edward M. *The Fathers of the Towns: Leadership and Community Structure in Eighteenth-Century New England*. Baltimore, MD: The Johns Hopkins Press, 1976.

Crawford, Margaret. *Building the Workingman's Paradise: The Design of American Company Towns*. London: Verso, 1995.

Crow, Matthew Ellsworth. "In the Course of Human Events: Jefferson, Text, and the Potentialities of Law." Doctoral dissertation. Los Angeles: University of California, Los Angeles, 2011.

Cunningham, Jr., Noble. *The Process of Government under Jefferson.* Princeton, NJ: Princeton University Press, 1978.

Curtis, Christopher Michael. *Jefferson's Freeholders and the Politics of Ownership in the Old Dominion.* Cambridge, UK: Cambridge University Press, 2012.

Dawidoff, Robert. "Rhetoric of Democracy." In *Thomas Jefferson and the Politics of Nature.* Edited by Thomas S. Engeman. Notre Dame, IN: University of Notre Dame Press, 2000.

Derrida, Jacques. *The Politics of Friendship.* Translated by George Collins. New York: Verso. 2005.

Dewey, John. *Democracy and Education.* New York: The Free Press, 1944.

Dickerson, Oliver Morton. *The Navigation Acts and the American Revolution.* New York: A. S. Barnes, 1963.

Dickinson, John. *The Political Writings of John Dickinson, Esquire, Late President of the State of Delaware, and of the Commonwealth of Pennsylvania,* vol. 2. Archives & Special Collections, Dickinson College, Carlisle, PA. Wilmington, DE: Bonsal and Niles, 1801.

Dorfman, Joseph. "The Economic Philosophy of Thomas Jefferson." *Political Science Quarterly* 55, no. 1 (1940): 98–121.

Dreisbach, Daniel L. *Thomas Jefferson and the Wall of Separation Between Church and State.* New York: New York University Press, 2002.

Dugatkin, Lee Alan. *Mr. Jefferson and the Giant Moose: Natural History in Early America.* Chicago: The University of Chicago Press, 2009.

———. "Thomas Jefferson Versus Count Buffon: The Theory of New World Degeneracy." *The Chautauqua Journal* 1, article 17 (2016): 1–14.

Eicholz, Hans L. *Harmonizing Sentiments: The Declaration of Independence and the Jeffersonian Idea of Self-Government.* New York: Peter Lang Publishing, 2001.

Elkin, Stephen L. *Reconstructing the Commercial Republic: Constitutional Design after Madison.* Chicago: The University of Chicago Press, 2006.

Elkins, Stanley, and Eric McKitrick. *The Age of Federalism.* New York: Oxford University Press, 1993.

Ellis, Joseph J. *American Sphinx: The Character of Thomas Jefferson.* New York: Alfred A. Knopf, 1997.

Ellis, Richard E. *The Jeffersonian Crisis: Courts and Politics in the Young Republic.* New York: Oxford University Press, 1971.

Ellis, William. *A Treatise on Government. Translated from the Greek of Aristotle.* London: Sowerby, 1778.

Engels, Friedrich. *The Condition of the Working Class in England in 1844.* Translated by Florence Kelley Wishchnewetzsky. New York: Cosimo Classics, 2008.

Erikson, Erik H. *Dimensions of a New Identity: The 1973 Jefferson Lectures in the Humanities.* New York: W. W. Norton & Company, 1974.

Euben, J. Peter, Josiah Ober, and John R. Wallach, eds. *Athenian Political Thought and the Reconstruction of American Democracy.* Ithaca, NY: Cornell University Press, 1994.

Federici, Michael P. *The Political Philosophy of Alexander Hamilton.* Baltimore, MD: The Johns Hopkins University Press, 2012.

Ferling, John. *Setting the World Ablaze: Washington, Adams, Jefferson, and the American Revolution.* New York: Oxford University Press, 2000.

Fink, Zera S. *The Classical Republicans: An Essay in the Recovery of a Pattern of Thought in Seventeenth-Century England.* Evanston, IL: Northwestern University Press, 1945.

Flaumenhaft, Harvey. *The Effective Republic: Administration and Constitution in the Thought of Alexander Hamilton.* Durham, NC: Duke University Press, 1992.

Fliegelman, Jay. *Declaring Independence: Jefferson, Natural Language, & the Culture of Performance.* Stanford, CA: Stanford University Press, 1993.

Forbes, Robert Pierce. *The Missouri Compromise and Its Aftermath: Slavery and the Meaning of America.* Chapel Hill: University of North Carolina Press, 2007.

Foshee, A. W. "Jeffersonian Political Economy and the Classical Republican Tradition: Jefferson, Taylor, and the Agrarian Republic." *History of Political Economy* 17, no. 4 (1985): 523–50.

Frank, Jason. *Constituent Moments: Enacting the People in Postrevolutionary America.* Durham, NC: Duke University Press, 2010.

Galloway, Joseph. *The Claim of the American Loyalists, Reviewed and Maintained Upon Incontrovertible Principles of Law and Justice.* Boston: Gregg Press, 1972.

Gerber, Scott Douglas. *To Secure These Rights: The Declaration of Independence and Constitutional Interpretation.* New York: New York University Press, 1995.

Gibson, Lawrence. *The British Empire Before the American Revolution.* New York: Knopf, 1958.

Gish, Dustin, and Andrew Bibby, eds. *Rival Visions: How Jefferson and His Contemporaries Defined the Early American Republic.* Charlottesville: University of Virginia Press, 2021.

Gish, Dustin, and Daniel Klinghard. "Republican Constitutionalism in Thomas Jefferson's *Notes on the State of Virginia.*" *The Journal of Politics* 74, no. 1 (2012): 35–51.

Gossett, Thomas F. *Race: The History of an Idea in America.* Oxford, UK: Oxford University Press, 1997.

Greenlees, Janet. *Female Labour Power: Women Workers' Influence on Business Practices in the British and American Cotton Industries, 1780–1860.* Hampshire, UK: Ashgate Publishing Limited, 2007.

Griswold, A. Whitney. "The Agrarian Democracy of Thomas Jefferson." *American Political Science Review* 40, no. 4 (1946): 657 81.

Gutman, Herbert G. "Work, Culture, and Society in Industrializing America, 1815–1919." *The American Historical Review* 78, no. 3 (June 1973): 531–88.

Gutzman, Kevin R. C. *Thomas Jefferson—Revolutionary: A Radical's Struggle to Remake America.* New York: St. Martin's Press, 2017.

Hamilton, Alexander. *The Papers of Alexander Hamilton.* New York: Columbia University Press, 1973.

Hamilton, J. G. de Roulhac. *Jefferson* by Saul K. Padover. *The American Historical Review* 48, no. 2 (1943): 356–57.

Hardt, Michael. Introduction to *The Declaration of Independence,* vii–xxv. London: Verso, 2007.

———. "Jefferson and Democracy." *American Quarterly* 59, no. 1 (2007): 41–78.

Haroutinian, Joseph. *Piety vs. Moralism: The Passing of the New England Theology.* New York: Henry Holt, 1932.

Hart, Gary. *Restoration of the Republic: The Jeffersonian Ideal in 21st Century America.* Oxford, UK: Oxford University Press, 2002.

Harvey, Sean P. *Native Tongues: Colonialism and Race from Encounter to the Reservation.* Cambridge, MA: Harvard University Press, 2015.

Hayes, Kevin J. *The Road to Monticello: The Life and Mind of Thomas Jefferson.* Oxford, UK: Oxford University Press, 2008.

Hays, Bradley D. "A Place for Interposition: What John Taylor of Caroline and the Embargo Crisis Have to Offer Regarding Resistance to the Bush Constitution." *Maryland Law Review* 67, no. 1 (2007): 200–21.

Heath, Kingston Wm. *The Patina of Place: The Cultural Weathering of a New England Industrial Landscape.* Knoxville: The University of Tennessee Press, 2001.

Hellenbrand, Harold. *The Unfinished Revolution: Education and Politics in the Thought of Thomas Jefferson.* Newark: University of Delaware Press, 1990.

Herodotus. *The History of Herodotus*, vol. 1. Translated by Isaac Littlebury. London: Printed for D. Midwinter, 1737.

Hitchens, Christopher. *Thomas Jefferson.* New York: HarperCollins, 2005.

Hobbes, Thomas. *Leviathan.* Indianapolis, IN: Hackett Publishing, 1994.

Hofstadter, Richard. "Parrington and the Jeffersonian Tradition." *Journal of History of Ideas* 2 (1941): 391–400.

Holland, Catherine A. "Notes on the State of America: Jeffersonian Democracy and the Production of a National Past." *Political Theory* 29, no. 2 (April 2001): 190–216.

Holman, Christopher. *Politics as Radical Creation: Herbert Marcuse and Hannah Arendt on Political Performativity.* Toronto: University of Toronto Press, 2013.

Holt, J. C. *Magna Carta.* Cambridge, UK: Cambridge University Press, 2015.

Holton, Woody. *Unruly Americans and the Origins of the Constitution.* New York: Hill and Wang, 2007.

Horsman, Reginald. *Race and Manifest Destiny: The Origins of American Racial Anglo-Saxonism.* Cambridge, MA: Harvard University Press, 1981.

Hume, David. *Hume's Moral and Political Philosophy.* Edited by Henry D. Aiken. New York: Hafner Publishing Company, 1948.

Ingram, Helen M., and Mary G. Wallace. "An 'Empire of Liberty': Thomas Jefferson and Governing Natural Resources in the West." In *Thomas Jefferson and the Changing West: From Conquest to Conservation.* Edited by James P. Ronda. Albuquerque: University of New Mexico Press, 1997.

Jackson, Donald. *Thomas Jefferson & the Stony Mountains: Exploring the West from Monticello.* Norman: University of Oklahoma Press, 1993.

Jacoby, Felix. *Atthis, The Local Chronicles of Ancient Athens.* Oxford, UK: Clarendon Press, 1949.

Jaeger, Werner. *Paideia: The Ideals of Greek Culture: Volume III: The Conflict of Cultural Ideals in the Age of Plato.* Translated by Gilbert Highet. Oxford, UK: Oxford University Press, 1986.

Jayne, Allen. *Jefferson's Declaration of Independence: Origins, Philosophy, and Theology*. Lexington: The University Press of Kentucky, 1998.

Jefferson, Thomas. *Autobiography of Thomas Jefferson*, 1743–1790. Edited by Paul Leicester Ford. New York: G. P. Putnam's Sons, 1914.

———. To Chiefs of Indian Tribes, April 11, 1806. This letter is privately owned. Examined at the Albert and Shirley Small Special Collections Library, University of Virginia, Charlottesville, VA.

———. *The Complete Jefferson*. Freeport, NY: Books for Libraries Press, 1969.

———. "An Essay Towards Facilitating Instruction in the Anglo-Saxon and Modern Dialects of the English Language for the Use of the University of Virginia." New York: J. F. Trow, Printer, 1851.

———. *Founders Online*. National Archives.

———. To Lydia Howard Huntley Sigourney, July 18, 1824. St. Paul's School in Concord, NH owns this letter. Photostatic copy examined at the Albert and Shirley Small Special Collections Library, University of Virginia, Charlottesville, VA.

———. To George W. Lewis, October 25, 1825. Photostatic copy examined at the Albert and Shirley Small Special Collections Library, University of Virginia, Charlottesville, VA.

———. *A Manual of Parliamentary Practice*. Philadelphia: Parrish, Dunning & Mears, 1853.

———. *Notes on the State of Virginia*. Boston: Lilly & Wait, 1832.

———. To Osages Chiefs, January 4, 1806. Photostatic copy examined at the Albert and Shirley Small Special Collections Library, University of Virginia, Charlottesville, VA.

———. *The Papers of Thomas Jefferson*, vols. 1–45, 1760–1805. Princeton, NJ: Princeton University Press, 2021.

———. *The Papers of Thomas Jefferson*, Retirement Series, vols. 1–18. Princeton, NJ: Princeton University Press, 2021.

———. "A Summary View of the Rights of British America: Set Forth in Some Resolutions Intended for the Inspection of the Present Delegates of the People of Virginia, Now In Convention." American Imprint Collection, Thomas Jefferson Library Collection, Library of Congress, Washington, D.C. Williamsburg, VA: Printed by Clementina Rind, 1774.

———. *Thomas Jefferson's Library: A Catalog with the Entries in His Own Order*. Edited by James Gilreath and Douglas L. Wilson. Washington, D.C.: Library of Congress, 1989.

———. *The Thomas Jefferson Papers* at the Library of Congress, Series 1: General Correspondence, 1651–1827.

———. *Thomas Jefferson: Writings*. Edited by Merrill D. Peterson. New York: Library of America, 1984.

———. *The Works of Thomas Jefferson*, vol. 11. Edited by Paul Leicester Ford. New York: Knickerbocker Press, 1904.

———. *The Writings of Thomas Jefferson*, vol. 1: 1760–1775. Edited by Paul Leicester Ford. New York: G. P. Putnam's Sons, 1892.

Jehlen, Myra. *American Incarnation: The Individual, the Nation, and the Continent*. Cambridge, MA: Harvard University Press, 1986.

Jones, Howard Mumford. *O Strange New World*. New York: Viking Press, 1964.

Kalyvas, Andreas. "Popular Sovereignty, Democracy, and the Constituent Power." *Constellations* 12, no. 2 (2005): 223–44.

———. "The Tyranny of Dictatorship: When the Greek Tyrant Met the Roman Dictator." *Political Theory* 35, no. 4 (2007): 412–42.

Kaminski, John P. *Thomas Jefferson: Philosopher and Politician*. Madison, WI: Parallel Press, 2005.

Katz, Stanley N. "Thomas Jefferson and the Right to Property in Revolutionary America." *The Journal of Law & Economics* 19, no. 3 (1976): 467–88.

Kaufman, Eric P. *The Rise and Fall of Anglo-America*. Cambridge, MA: Harvard University Press, 2004.

Kelly, Robert L., and Mary M. Prascinuas. "Did the Ancestors of Native Americans Cause Animal Extinctions in Late-Pleistocene North America?" In *Native Americans and the Environment: Perspectives on the Ecological Indian*. Edited by Michael Eugene Harkin and David Rich Lewis. Lincoln: University of Nebraska Press, 2007.

Kidd, Thomas. *Thomas Jefferson: A Biography of Spirit and Flesh*. New Haven, CT: Yale University Press, 2022.

Koch, Adrienne. *Jefferson and Madison: The Great Collaboration*. New York: Oxford University Press, 1950.

———. *The Philosophy of Thomas Jefferson*. Chicago: Quadrangle Books, 1964.

Krall, Lisi. "Thomas Jefferson's Agrarian Vision and the Changing Nature of Property." *Journal of Economic Issues* 36, no. 1 (2002): 131–50.

Kuzminski, Adrian. *Fixing the System: A History of Populism, Ancient and Modern*. New York: Continuum, 2008.

Lefort, Claude. *Machiavelli in the Making*. Translated by Michael B. Smith. Evanston, IL: Northwestern University Press, 2012.

Lehmann, Karl. *Thomas Jefferson, American Humanist*. Charlottesville: The University Press of Virginia, 1985.

Levander, Caroline. *Cradle of Liberty: Race, The Child, and National Belonging From Thomas Jefferson to W. E. B. Du Bois*. Durham, NC: Duke University Press, 2006.

Levy, Barry. *Town Born: The Political Economy of New England from Its Founding to Revolution*. Philadelphia: University of Pennsylvania Press, 2009.

Linebaugh, Peter. *The Magna Carta Manifesto: Liberties and Commons for All*. Berkeley: University of California Press, 2008.

Locke, John. *An Essay Concerning Human Understanding; with thoughts on the conduct of the understanding*. London: Printed for Allen & West, 1795.

———. *Second Treatise of Government*. Edited by C. B. Macpherson. Indianapolis, IN: Hackett Publishing Company, 1980.

Looby, Christopher. "The Constitution of Nature: Taxonomy As Politics in Jefferson, Peale, and Bartram." *Early American Literature* 22 (1987): 252–73.

Machiavelli, Niccolò. *Discourses on Livy*. New York: The Modern Library, 1950.

Macpherson, C. B. *Democratic Theory: Essays in Retrieval.* Oxford: Clarendon Press, 1975.

Madison, James. *The Papers of James Madison*, Congressional Series. Charlottesville: The University Press of Virginia, 1985.

Maier, Pauline. *From Resistance to Revolution: Colonial Radicals and the Development of American Opposition to Britain, 1765–1776.* New York: W. W. Norton & Co., 1972.

Maistre, Joseph de. *Considerations on France.* Edited by Richard A. Lebrun. Cambridge, UK: Cambridge University Press, 1994.

———. *Against Rousseau: On the State of Nature and On the Sovereignty of the People.* Translated and edited by Richard A. Lebrun. Montreal: McGill-Queen's University Press, 1996.

Malone, Dumas. *Jefferson and His Time, Vols. I–VI.* Boston: Little, Brown and Company, 1948–1981.

Manent, Pierre. *The City of Man.* Translated by M. LePain. Princeton, NJ: Princeton University Press, 1998.

Mapp, Jr., Alf J. *Thomas Jefferson: America's Paradoxical Patriot.* Lanham, MD: Rowman & Littlefield Publishers, 1987.

Marienstras, Elise. "The Common Man's Indian: The Image of the Indian as a Promoter of National Identity in the Early National Era." In *Native Americans and the Early Republic.* Edited by Frederick E. Hoxie, Ronald Hoffman, and Peter J. Albert. Charlottesville: The University Press of Virginia, 1999.

Martin, Robert W. T. "Reforming Republicanism: Alexander Hamilton's Theory of Republican Citizenship and Press Liberty." *Journal of the Early Republic* 25, no. 1 (2005): 21–46.

Marx, Leo. *The Machine in the Garden: Technology and the Pastoral Ideal in America.* New York: Oxford University Press, 1964.

Massachusetts. *Acts and Resolves of Massachusetts*, vol. 1, 1692–93. Boston: Wright & Potter Printers, 1869.

Matthews, Richard K. *If Men Were Angels: James Madison and the Heartless Empire of Reason.* Lawrence: University Press of Kansas, 1995.

———. *The Radical Politics of Thomas Jefferson: A Revisionist View.* Lawrence: University Press of Kansas, 1986.

Matthews, Richard K., and Elric M. Kline. "Jefferson Un-Locked: The Rousseauan Moment in American Political Thought." In *History, On Proper Principles: Essays in Honor of Forrest McDonald.* Edited by Lenore T. Early and Stephen M. Klugewicz. Wilmington, DE: ISI Books, 2010.

Mayer, David N. "The Forgotten Essentials of Jefferson's Philosophy." *The Atlas Society*, June 23, 2010. https://www.atlassociety.org/post/the-forgotten-essentials-of-jeffersons-philosophy.

McCoy, Drew R. *The Last of the Fathers: James Madison and the Republican Legacy.* Cambridge, UK: Cambridge University Press, 1989.

Meacham, Jon. *Thomas Jefferson: The Art of Power.* New York: Random House, 2012.

Mehta, Uday Singh. *Liberalism and Empire: A Study in Nineteenth-Century British Liberal Thought.* Chicago: The University of Chicago Press, 1999.

Miller, Charles A. *Jefferson and Nature: An Interpretation.* Baltimore, MD: The Johns Hopkins University Press, 1988.

Miller, Perry. "The New England Consciousness." In *The Responsibility of Mind in a Civilization of Machines.* Edited by Jon Crowell and Stanford J. Searl, Jr. Amherst: University of Massachusetts Press, 1979.

Miller, Robert J. *Native America, Discovered and Conquered: Thomas Jefferson, Lewis & Clark, and Manifest Destiny.* Westport, CT: Praeger Publishers, 2006.

Montesquieu, Charles-Louis de Secondat. *Considerations on the Causes of the Greatness of the Romans and their Decline.* Translated by David Lowenthal. New York: Free Press, 1965.

———. *Persian Letters.* Translated by C. J. Betts. Baltimore, MD: Penguin Books, 1973.

———. *The Spirit of the Laws.* Translated by Thomas Nugent. New York: Hafner Publishing Co., 1949.

Morse, Suzanne W. "Ward Republics: The Wisest Invention for Self-Government." In *Thomas Jefferson and the Education of a Citizen.* Edited by James Gilreath. Washington, D.C.: Library of Congress, 1999.

Nagley, Winfield E. *Foundations of Thomas Jefferson's Philosophy.* University of Hawaii: Hawaii Bicentennial Commission, 1976.

Nash, Roderick Frazier. *The Rights of Nature: A History of Environmental Ethics.* Madison: The University of Wisconsin Press, 1989.

Negri, Antonio. *Insurgencies: Constituent Power and the Modern State.* Translated by Maurizia Eoscagli. Minneapolis: University of Minnesota Press, 1999.

Nelson, Eric. *The Greek Tradition in Republican Thought.* Cambridge, UK: Cambridge University Press, 2004.

Nichols, Frederick Doveton, and Ralph E. Griswold. *Thomas Jefferson: Landscape Architect.* Charlottesville: The University of Virginia Press, 1978.

Niebuhr, Reinhold. *The Irony of American History.* Chicago: The University of Chicago Press, 2008.

O'Brien, Conor Cruise. *The Long Affair: Thomas Jefferson and the French Revolution, 1785–1800.* Chicago: The University of Chicago Press, 1996.

Oliver, Peter. *Origin & Progress of the American Rebellion: A Tory View.* Edited by Douglass Adair and John A. Schultz. Stanford, CA: Stanford University Press, 1961.

Onuf, Peter S. *Jefferson's Empire: The Language of American Nationhood.* Charlottesville: The University of Virginia Press, 2000.

———. *Jeffersonian Legacies,* ed. Charlottesville: The University of Virginia Press, 1993.

———. "Missouri and the 'Empire for Liberty.'" In *Thomas Jefferson and the Changing West: From Conquest to Conservation.* Edited by James P. Ronda. Albuquerque: University of New Mexico Press, 1997.

Opal, J. M. *Beyond the Farm: National Ambitions in Rural New England.* Philadelphia: University of Pennsylvania Press, 2008.

Paine, Thomas. *The Rights of Man, Part the Second.* In *The Complete Writings of Thomas Paine,* vol. 1. Edited by Philip S. Foner. New York: Citadel Press, 1945.

Parenti, Christian. *Radical Hamilton: Economic Lessons from a Misunderstood Founder*. London: Verso, 2020.

Pelling, Christopher. *Literary Texts and the Greek Historian*. London: Routledge, 2000.

Peterson, Merrill D. "Jefferson and Commercial Policy, 1783–1793." *The William and Mary Quarterly* 22, no. 4 (1965): 584–610.

———. *Thomas Jefferson & the New Nation: A Biography*. London: Oxford University Press, 1970.

Peterson, Tarla Rai. "Jefferson's Yeoman Farmer as Frontier Hero a Self-defeating Mythic Structure." *Agriculture and Human Values* 7, no. 1 (1990): 9–19.

Phillips, James Duncan. "Jefferson's 'Wicked Tyrannical Embargo.'" *The New England Quarterly* 18, no. 4 (Dec. 1945): 466–78.

Pitts, Jennifer. "Political Theory of Empire and Imperialism." *Annual Review of Political Science* 13 (2010): 211–35.

Pocock, J. G. A. *The Ancient Constitution and the Feudal Law: A Study of English Historical Thought in the Seventeenth Century*. London: Cambridge University Press, 1987.

———. *The Machiavellian Moment: Florentine Political Thought and the Atlantic Republican Tradition*. Princeton, NJ: Princeton University Press, 1975.

———. *Politics, Language and Time: Essays on Political Thought and History*. Chicago: The University of Chicago Press, 1989.

———. "Virtue and Commerce in the Eighteenth Century." *The Journal of Interdisciplinary History* 3, no. 1 (Summer 1972): 119–34.

Post, Charles. *The American Road to Capitalism: Studies in Class-Structure, Economic Development and Political Conflict, 1620–1877*. Leiden: Brill Press, 2011.

Post, David G. *In Search of Jefferson's Moose: Notes on the State of Cyberspace*. Oxford, UK: Oxford University Press, 2009.

Powell, Sumner Chilton. *Puritan Village: The Formation of a New England Town*. New York: Anchor Books, 1965.

Radin, Max. "The Myth of Magna Carta." *Harvard Law Review* 60, no. 7 (1947): 1060–91.

Rakove, Jack N. *Original Meanings: Politics and Ideas in the Making of the Constitution*. New York: Vintage Books, 1997.

Rancière, Jacques. *On the Shores of Politics*. Translated by Liz Heron. London: Verso, 2007.

Richard, Carl J. *Greeks and Romans Bearing Gifts: How the Ancients Inspired the Founding Fathers*. Lanham, MD: Rowman & Littlefield Publishers, 2008.

———. *The Founders and the Classics: Greece, Rome, and the American Enlightenment*. Cambridge, MA: Harvard University Press, 1994.

Risjord, Norman K. *Thomas Jefferson*. Lanham, MD: Rowman & Littlefield Publishers, 1994.

Robertson, Noel. "From Popular Sovereignty to the Sovereignty of Law: Law, Society, and Politics in Fifth-Century Athens by Martin Ostwald" (Review). *Phoenix* 43, no. 4 (Winter 1989): 365–75.

Roger, Jacques. *Buffon: A Life in Natural History*. Edited by L. Pearce Williams. Translated by Sarah Lucille Bonnefoi. Ithaca, NY: Cornell University Press, 1997.

Rogers, Alan. *Empire and Liberty: American Resistance to British Authority, 1755–1763.* Berkeley: University of California Press, 1974.

Rousseau, Jean-Jacques. *The Basic Political Writings.* Translated by Donald A. Cress. Indianapolis, IN: Hackett Publishing Company, 1987.

———. *Constitutional Project for Corsica.* In *Political Writings.* Edited and translated by Frederick Watkins. Madison: The University of Wisconsin Press, 1986.

———. *On the Social Contract.* Edited by Roger D. Masters. Translated by Judith R. Masters. New York: St. Martin's Press, 1978.

Sayre, Gordon M. *Les Sauvages Américains: Representations of Native Americans in French and English Colonial Literature.* Chapel Hill: The University of North Carolina Press, 1997.

Scanlon, Thomas F. *Greek Historiography.* Chichester, UK: Wiley Blackwell, 2015.

Scherr, Arthur. *Thomas Jefferson's Image of New England: Nationalism Versus Sectionalism in the Young Republic.* Jefferson, NC: McFarland & Company Inc. Publishers, 2016.

———. "Thomas Jefferson's Nationalist Vision of New England and the War of 1812." *The Historian* 69, no. 1 (2007): 1–35.

Sears, Louis Martin. *Jefferson and the Embargo.* Durham, NC: Duke University Press, 1927.

Shalhope, Robert E. "Thomas Jefferson's Republicanism and Antebellum Southern Thought." *The Journal of Southern History* 42, no. 4 (Nov 1976): 529–56.

———. "Republicanism and Early American Historiography." *The William and Mary Quarterly* 39, no. 2 (1982): 334–56.

Shank, Barry. "Jefferson, the Impossible." *American Quarterly* 59, no. 2 (2007): 291–99.

Sheehan, Bernard W. *Seeds of Extinction: Jeffersonian Philanthropy and the American Indian.* Chapel Hill: The University of North Carolina Press, 1972.

Sheehan, Colleen A. *James Madison and the Spirit of Republican Self-Government.* Cambridge, UK: Cambridge University Press, 2009.

———. "Madison versus Hamilton: The Battle over Republicanism and the Role of Public Opinion." In *The Many Faces of Alexander Hamilton: The Life and Legacy of America's Most Elusive Founding Father.* Edited by Douglas Ambrose and Robert W.T. Martin. New York: New York University Press, 2006.

Sheldon, Garrett Ward. *The Philosophy of James Madison.* Baltimore, MD: The Johns Hopkins University Press, 2001.

———. *The Political Philosophy of Thomas Jefferson.* Baltimore, MD: The Johns Hopkins University Press, 1991.

Shrimpton, Gordon S. *History and Memory in Ancient Greece.* Montreal: McGill-Queen's University Press, 1997.

Sidney, Algernon. *Discourses Concerning Government.* London: Printed by J. Darby, 1704.

Sloan, Herbert E. *Principle and Interest: Thomas Jefferson and the Problem of Debt.* Charlottesville: The University of Virginia Press, 1995.

Spary, E. C. *Utopia's Garden: French Natural History from Old Regime to Revolution.* Chicago: The University of Chicago Press, 2000.

Spivak, Burton. *Jefferson's English Crisis: Commerce, Embargo and the Republican Revolution*. Charlottesville: The University Press of Virginia, 1979.

Staloff, Darren. *Hamilton, Adams, Jefferson: The Politics of Enlightenment and the American Founding*. New York: Hill and Wang, 2005.

Steele, Brian. *Thomas Jefferson and American Nationhood*. Cambridge, UK: Cambridge University Press, 2012.

Stoner, James R. "Jefferson and the Common Law Tradition." In *Reason and Republicanism: Thomas Jefferson's Legacy of Liberty*. Edited by Gary L. McDowell and Sharon L. Noble. Lanham, MD: Rowman & Littlefield Publishers, 1997.

Strauss, Leo. "What is Political Philosophy?" *Journal of Politics* 19, no. 3 (Aug. 1957).

Struik, Dirk Jan. *Yankee Science in the Making: Science and Engineering in New England from Colonial Times to the Civil War*. New York: Dover Publications, Inc., 1991.

Stuart, Reginald C. *The Half-Way Pacifist: Thomas Jefferson's View of War*. Toronto: University of Toronto Press, 1978.

Taylor, Alan. *The Internal Enemy: Slavery and War in Virginia, 1772–1832*. New York: W. W. Norton, 2013.

Theocharaki, Anna Maria. "The Ancient Circuit Wall Of Athens: Its Changing Course and the Phases of Construction." *Hesperia: The Journal of the American School of Classical Studies at Athens* 80, no. 1 (January–March 2011): 71–156.

Thomson, Keith. *A Passion for Nature: Thomas Jefferson and Natural History*. Monticello Monograph Series. Chapel Hill: The University of North Carolina Press, 2008.

Thucydides. *History of the Peloponnesian War: The Complete Hobbes Translation*. Chicago: The University of Chicago Press, 1989.

Tocqueville, Alexis de. *Democracy in America*. Edited and translated by Harvey C. Mansfield and Delba Winthrop. Chicago: The University of Chicago Press, 2000.

Tucker, Robert W. and David C. Hendrickson. *Empire of Liberty: The Statecraft of Thomas Jefferson*. Oxford: Oxford University Press, 1990.

Usner, Jr., Daniel H. "Iroquois Livelihood and Jeffersonian Agrarianism: Reaching behind the Models and Metaphors." In *Native Americans and the Early Republic*. Edited by Frederick E. Hoxie, Ronald Hoffman, and Peter J. Albert. Charlottesville: The University Press of Virginia, 1999.

Valsania, Maurizio. *Jefferson's Body: A Corporeal Biography*. Charlottesville: The University of Virginia Press, 2017.

———. *Nature's Man: Thomas Jefferson's Philosophical Anthropology*. Charlottesville: The University of Virginia Press, 2013.

Vonnegut, Jr., Kurt. *Breakfast of Champions*. New York: A Delta Book, 1973.

Wallace, Anthony F. C. *Jefferson and the Indians: The Tragic Fate of the First Americans*. Cambridge, MA: The Belknap Press of Harvard University Press, 1999.

Washington, George. *The Papers of George Washington*, Presidential Series, vol. 8, March 22, 1791–22 September 1791. Edited by Mark A. Mastromarino. Charlottesville: The University Press of Virginia, 1999.

Webster, Daniel. *The Papers of Daniel Webster, Correspondence,* volume *1, 1798–1824.* Edited by Charles M. Wiltse and Harold D. Moser. Hanover, NH: Dartmouth College/University Press of New England, 1974.

Weir, Robert G.A. "The Lost Archaic Wall around Athens." *Phoenix* 49, no. 3 (Autumn 1995): 247–58.

White, Morton and Lucia White. *The Intellectual Versus the City.* Toronto: Mentor Books, 1964.

Williams, Jr., Robert A. "Thomas Jefferson: Indigenous American Storyteller." In *Thomas Jefferson and the Changing West: From Conquest to Conservation.* Edited by James P. Ronda. Albuquerque: University of New Mexico Press, 1997.

Wills, Gary. *Inventing America: Jefferson's Declaration of Independence.* New York: Vintage Books, 1979.

———. *"Negro President": Jefferson and the Slave Power.* Boston: Mariner Books, 2005. Wilson, Douglas L. "Jefferson vs. Hume." *The William and Mary Quarterly* 46, no. 1 (1989): 49–70.

Wilson, Gaye. "Jefferson, Buffon, and the Mighty American Moose." *Monticello Newsletter* 13, no. 1 (Spring 2002).

Wilson, Major L. *Space, Time and Freedom: The Quest for Nationality and the Irrepressible Conflict, 1815–1861.* Westport, CT: Greenwood Press, 1974.

Wirszubski, Chaïm. *Libertas as a Political Idea at Rome.* Oxford: Oxford University Press, 1968.

Wolford, Thorp Lanier. "Democratic-Republican Reaction in Massachusetts to the Embargo of 1807." *The New England Quarterly* 15, no. 1 (Mar. 1942): 35–61.

Wolin, Sheldon S. "Fugitive Democracy." *Constellations* 1, no. 1 (1994): 11–25.

———. "Hannah Arendt: Democracy and The Political." *Salmagundi* no. 60 (Spring–Summer 1983): 3–19.

———. "Norm and Form: The Constitutionalizing of Democracy." In *Athenian Political Thought and Reconstruction of American Democracy.* Edited by J. Peter Euben, John R. Wallach, and Josiah Ober. Ithaca, NY: Cornell University Press, 1994.

———. *Politics and Vision.* Princeton, NJ: Princeton University Press, 2004.

———. "Transgression, Equality, and Voice." In *Fugitive Democracy: And Other Essays.* Edited by Nicholas Xenos. Princeton, NJ: Princeton University Press, 2016.

Wood, Ellen Meiksins. *Democracy Against Capitalism: Renewing Historical Materialism.* Cambridge, UK: Cambridge University Press, 1995.

Wood, Gordon S. *The Creation of the American Republic, 1776–1787.* Chapel Hill: University of North Carolina Press, 1998.

Wright, Benjamin Fletcher. *American Interpretations of Natural Law: A Study in the History of Political Thought.* London: Routledge, 2017.

Zimmerman, Joseph Francis. *The New England Town Meeting: Democracy in Action.* Westport, CT: Praeger Publishers, 1999.

Index

About the Author

Dean Caivano was educated at York University in Toronto, Canada, and currently teaches political science and history at Merced College in the Central Valley of California, USA. His research focuses on radical and critical democracy, early American political thought, and emancipatory politics.

www.ingramcontent.com/pod-product-compliance
Lightning Source LLC
Chambersburg PA
CBHW022318280326
41932CB00010B/1143